W9-ABM-473

MOSCOW
1900~1930

MOSCOW
1900~1930

Edited by Serge Fauchereau

Essays by
Serge Fauchereau, André Lischke, Elena Rakitina
Noël Simsolo, Andrzej Turowski, and Stanislas Zadora

MALLARD
PRESS

MALLARD PRESS
An imprint of BDD Promotional Book Company, Inc.
666 Fifth Avenue
New York, N.Y. 10103

Mallard Press and its accompanying design and logo
are trademarks of BDD Promotional Book Company, Inc.

Original French language edition: *Moscou 1900-1930*

Copyright © 1988 by Office du Livre S.A.
Fribourg, Switzerland

English translation: Copyright © 1988 by Office du Livre S.A.
Fribourg, Switzerland

World English language rights reserved
by W.S. Konecky Associates, Inc.

ISBN: 0-794-5737-4

Printed in Hong Kong

Contents

Contributors   7

Introduction   9
Serge Fauchereau

1 Everyday Life   23
Stanislas Zadora

Before the Bolshevik
   Revolution   23
Revolutionary Changes   40
The 1920s   44

**2 The Arts Before the
Revolution, 1900–1917**   47
Serge Fauchereau

The Wanderers   47
Serov, Vrubel and the
   Decorative Arts in Abramtsevo   48
The World of Art and
   the Golden Fleece Movements   54
Ciurlionis, Kandinsky   62
The Collectors Shchukin and
   Morozov   65
Futurism: From Hylaea to the
   Union of Youth   68
Larionov, Neoprimitivism,
   Rayonism   73
Malevich: From Cubo-Futurism
   to Suprematism   78
Tatlin Versus Malevich: The Last
   Glimmers of Futurism   84

**3 The Arts After the
Revolution, 1917–1930**   89
Stanislas Zadora

The Reorganization of Art and
   Education   89
Agitprop, Proletkult   92
Tatlin and Malevich   95
The Applied Arts and the
   Search for New Forms   96
Constructivism, Inkhuk   97
The Elimination of the
   Avant-Garde   103

4 Literature   111
Serge Fauchereau

Realism: From Tolstoi to
   Gorky   111
Symbolism Between
   St. Petersburg and Moscow   115
Futurism   121
Futurist Theories and Works:
   Zaum   124
Acmeism as a Reaction Against
   Futurism   132
Writers in the Revolution   135
Maiakovsky and the Left Front
   of the Arts   138
Old and New Trends   140
Proletarian Literature and
   Social Control   145

5 The Theater   149
Elena Rakitina

Stanislavsky and the
    Moscow Art Theater   149
From the Free Theater to the
    Kamernyi Theater: The
    Power of Aestheticism   155
The Post-Revolutionary
    Theater as an Instrument
    of Propaganda   159
Meierhold and the
    Experimental Theater   165
New Political and
    Ideological Pressures   172

**6 Town Planning and
    Architecture**   179
Andrzej Turowski

Architecture at the End of the
    Nineteenth Century   179
Art Nouveau   180
The Architectural Ideas of the
    Revolution   196
Tatlin's Tower and the
    Avant-Garde   198
Ladovsky and ASNOVA   202
Art Deco   206
Productivism and
    Functionalism   206

From Vesnin to Utopia   209
The Palace of Soviets   214

7 Musical Life   217
André Lischke

Moscow and St. Petersburg   217
Romanticism and Symbolism:
    Rakhmaninov and Skriabin   222
The Private Theaters   223
The Bolshoi Theater   223
Stanislavsky and the Opera   228
The Ballet   228
The Conservatory and
    Musical Instruction   231
Religious Music   231
Popular Music   232
Musical Politics, 1918–1930   233

8 The Cinema   241
Noël Simsolo

Birth of the Moscow Cinema   241
First Russian Films   242
Avant-Garde and
    Popular Cinema   244
The Cinema and the
    Revolution   246
Vertov, Eisenstein, Pudovkin   254
The End of NEP   264

Index   268

Contributors

Serge Fauchereau, author of some fifteen books, has collaborated on several exhibitions at the Musée national d'Art moderne, Centre Georges Pompidou, Paris (*Paris–New York, Paris–Berlin, Paris–Moscou, Les Réalismes*, etc.), at the Palazzo Grassi, Venice (*Futurismo & Futurismi*), and elsewhere. He is the editor of the present volume.

André Lischke, a musicologist specialized in Russian music, has published several works on the subject.

Elena Rakitina is a drama critic who has published extensively on Russian and Soviet theater. She makes her home in Mainz, West Germany.

Noël Simsolo has made several full length and short feature films. A film critic with many books to his name he is a producer with Radio France, France Culture.

Andrzej Turowski is professor of art history at the University of Poznan, Poland, and is currently visiting professor at the University of Clermont-Ferrand. He has written many works on modern art in Central Europe.

Stanislas Zadora has been associated with the Musée national d'Art moderne, Centre Georges Pompidou, Paris, for the past ten years where he has collaborated on the exhibitions *Paris–Moscou* and *Présence polonaise*. He has selected the illustrations for the present volume.

Introduction

Only in the last ten years or so has Moscow come to be recognized as an important center of twentieth-century modernism in the arts and in thought. A few scholars and collectors—one thinks of the Greek George Costakis and the American John E. Bowlt—were already well aware of this; however, it took an exhibition in Paris in 1979, "Paris–Moscou 1900–1930," which ran for nearly six months, to bring this home to the Western public at large and to the international press.

The man behind that great public synthesis of Russian culture was Pontus Hulten, then director of the Musée d'Art Moderne of the Georges Pompidou Center in Paris. It was Hulten's initiative and determination that led to the creation of a small Franco-Soviet working group. Gradually this team assembled an enormous array of the finest and most distinctive works from the various fields of Russian and Soviet art and literature for the exhibition, which was shown first in Paris and in Moscow two years later (1981). Further research has been undertaken subsequently and other shows mounted, exploring the subject in greater depth and refining our knowledge of artists, movements, or areas of study (books, printed fabrics, cubo-futurism).

So it seems only right and proper to me to pause on the threshold of a work such as this to pay tribute to Pontus Hulten, partly because I, along with my colleagues Stanislas Zadora, Jean-Hubert Martin, and others, had the honor to serve as Hulten's assistant, but principally because it was his drive and his enthusiasm that brought about that major cultural event: the exhibition "Paris–Moscou 1900–1930."

Not until the installation of the Russian Orthodox metropolitan in Moscow in 1326 and the end of the Mongol yoke was the principality of Moscow elevated to the status of capital city of Russia. Ivan the Terrible strengthened Muscovite centralism in the sixteenth century, and with the advent of the Romanovs in the following century the commercial power of the city began to grow rapidly. In 1712, however, Moscow lost its position as the country's political capital when Peter the Great chose to rule from St. Petersburg. During the Napoleonic wars a hundred years later, much of Moscow was destroyed. Yet the city was quickly rebuilt, because it had never lost its position as the economic capital of Russia. The process of industrialization that characterized the nineteenth century saw the population of Moscow increase by leaps and bounds. The city's rivalry with St. Petersburg probably reached its peak around the turn of the century. So important a part did Moscow's working population play in the

1   P. Kalendo: **Theater Square, Moscow**, 1922.
At the beginning of the century Theater Square (now Sverdlov Square), one of Moscow's central squares, was the site of the Bolshoi ("Great"), Malyi ("Little"), and Nezlobin theaters and two luxury hotels, the Metropole and the Continental.

9

2 The **Kremlin and Red Square**,
ca. 1910.
Still one of Europe's most popular tour-
ist attractions, Red Square dates from
the late fifteenth century. Its most recent
monument is the Lenin Mausoleum, the
world's most visited tomb.

3 Some of the Kremlin squares were
permanently closed to ordinary mortals.
Others were open to all and accommo-
dated popular gatherings for special occasions such as this St. Petersburg–
Moscow motor race in 1908.

4 **Our Lady of Iberia Gate**.
The Kremlin wall once contained a
number of gates. Many of them were
destroyed in the years 1928-32.

5 Entrance to **St. Basil's Cathedral**
(Church of Basil the Blessed; Red
Square side).
Built on the orders of Ivan the Terrible
after the capture of Kazan (1553-60),
St. Basil's Cathedral stands out among
Moscow churches by virtue of its dis-
tinctive style. It has come to be re-
garded as the showpiece of Russian
national architecture.

11

6 **The Kremlin** seen from the Moscow (Moskva) River.
The Moskva and the Iauza are the principal river arteries of the city.

strikes and riots that shook the country in 1905 and 1917 that, once the revolution had triumphed, the new leaders decided to give Moscow back its official position as the nation's capital. The new capital's continuing industrialization, coupled with Soviet centralism, finally established Moscow's supremacy as Russia's first city.

Moscow's history and culture make it a capital apart: Moscow is not Paris or London, Mexico City, or Tokyo and, as we shall have occasion more than once to remark, neither is it St. Petersburg/

12

Petrograd/Leningrad–its sister city and at the same time its greatest rival. St. Petersburg always was (and Leningrad still is) a civilized, elegant place; this is true of both its architecture and its people. In fact, the northern metropolis is courteous and circumspect to the point of being irritating. The appearance of the great capital, on the other hand, is not only incoherent and the behavior of its inhabitants somewhat loutish (on the subway during rush hours Moscovites jostle one another with shameless abandon), but also more unpredictable–

7   The **City Soviet** on Pushkin
Square (previously Strastnaia).
This former residence of the governors
of Moscow was built in 1782. The
statue portrays Prince Iurii Dolgorukii,
the twelfth-century founder of the city.

8   The **first University of Moscow**
in Mokhovaia Street, built in 1793 by
M. Kazakhov.

9   Nikolai Roerich: **Moscow, View of
the Kremlin**, 1903. Oil on pasteboard,
40.7 × 31.7 cm. State Museum of Oriental Art, Moscow.
What we call the Kremlin is simply one
example of a fortress (Russian *kreml*)
around which a town grew up. Moscow's fortress was destroyed several
times by various invaders including the
Tatars, the Poles, and finally the French
in 1812. Today it constitutes the heart
of the city.

10 **Okhotnyi Riad**, one of the historic districts of Moscow that have now disappeared, lay between Theater Square and Tverskaia Street. Until 1922 it was the preserve of poultry and game merchants (*okhota* means hunting) and was the site of many taverns *(traktirs)* and small restaurants. Possibly the unhealthiest part of Moscow, it was the stronghold of the "Black Hundreds," chauvinistic, antirevolutionary organizations of the years following 1905.

11   The coachmen's race was one of Moscow's greatest popular festivals before 1917.

12   Count Nikolai Rumiantsev (1754–1826) was one of the first great Russian art patrons. His collection of books, paintings, maps, coins, and manuscripts has been preserved in Moscow since 1861 in the museum that bears his name.

sometimes surprisingly so. I came across an example of this in my own experience: some years ago, while I was working in Leningrad's Saltykov-Shchedrin Library, choosing exhibition material, I had in front of me two photographic archives devoted to famous poets, one to Anna Akhmatova from Leningrad, the other to Marina Tsvetaeva from Moscow. I confessed to my librarian friend that I felt uncomfortable about the everlasting poses affected by the former throughout her career, and positively intimidated by the totally elusive character of the latter, who alternated between being skinny and plump, her face now chubby-cheeked and now haggard, her hair worn long in one picture and cut very short in another. My Russian friend replied with a laugh, "Ah, there you have the whole difference between Leningrad and Moscow!"

Century after century, time after time, the histories of Moscow and Leningrad have been indissolubly linked. Thus, in the present work it will be impossible for us to speak of one without at least evoking the other. There can be no discussion of symbolism in Moscow without taking into account the influence of Alexander Blok and the St. Petersburg Symbolists. We cannot explain many of the Futurist manifestoes without reference to acmeism, a movement almost wholly confined to St. Petersburg. A survey of music in Moscow cannot ignore

13   The **Kitai Gorod** or "Chinatown" has gone today, but it was in bygone times the largest commercial district in the immediate vicinity of the Kremlin.

the St. Petersburg composers Igor Stravinsky and Sergei Prokofiev, both pupils of Nikolai Rimsky-Korsakov. Just as the poet "[Velimir] Khlebnikov was the direct opposite of [Osip] Mandelshtam," as the Russian-born composer Arthur Lourié says in his memoirs, St. Petersburg is the necessary counterpart of Moscow.

Although we shall have occasion to note that not every innovation stems from these two great cities (the painting of Mikolajus Ciurlionis owes little to either, that of Niko Pirosmanishvili even less), with one or two exceptions it has been necessary to stay within Russia proper and not to make any sorties into

the non-Russian republics, in order to respect the parameters of this book. For example, we have had to pass over the whole *Nova Generatsia* movement that grew up around Mikhilo Semenko and the Ukrainian Constructivistes, as well as the painters David Kakabadze and Lado Gudiashvili, the poets Iashvili and Tabidze, and the film director Nikolai Shengelaia in Russian Georgia. Similarly we have given little or no space to artists who, apart from a few youthful works, created their whole œuvre outside Russia: Alexander Archipenko, Jacques Lipchitz, Ossip Zadkine, Leopold Survage, Vladimir Nabokov—even Igor Stravinsky himself. Neither Vasilli (Wassily) Kandinsky nor Marc Chagall falls into this category, however, since both returned to their homeland during World War I and were given official positions (in Moscow and Vitebsk respectively) by the Bolshevik government.

The characteristic that best distinguishes Moscow is probably a certain sense of excess—comparisons with St. Petersburg bring this out most clearly. The ego-futurism of St. Petersburg seems mannered and flat when set against the immoderate barbarity and gaudiness of Muscovite futurism. The very lovely sphinx shape so dear to St. Petersbury appears tame in comparison with, say, the delirium in stone represented by the grand staircase of Riabushinsky's house, built by Feodor Shekhtel. This makes it easier to understand why the poet Khlebnikov appeared so out of place in the context of St. Petersburg; as Arthur Lourié wrote: "Khlebnikov's behavior was misunderstood in artistic circles in St. Petersburg, where many people found him irritating and accused him of extravagance and folly. The aesthetics of a refined art—refined in the European sense—still enjoyed too much prestige for people to be able to appreciate Khlebnikov's authenticity.... It now looks as if, at that time, Khlebnikov was the shield that art's young extremists used to protect themselves against the [attraction of the] West with its mechanization and evolutionism."

Protecting themselves against the West was a constant preoccupation with Russian artists and writers, particularly those based in Moscow. There is something deliberately non-Western about the neo-primitivism of Mikhail Larionov or Pavel Filonov, the *zaum* incantations (transmental language) of Velimir Khlebnikov, or the boundless and thus paradoxically generous egocentricity of another poet, Vladimir Maiakovsky. The depths of Russia and its remoter reaches find expression in the aggressively innovatice brochures of Alexei Kruchenykh and Olga Rozanova and in the climate of mysticism that underlies Kandinsky's book *On the Spiritual in Art* (1912) or Kazimir Malevich's suprematism. The elegantly decorative orientalism of the *Mir iskusstva* (World of Art) movement and the "Ballets Russes" was matched by another, more fundamental kind of orientalism that ultimately seems less surprising in the theories of someone like Georgii Gurdjieff than in those of the film director Sergei Eisenstein as he pays tribute to the "modes of thought and writing of the venerable languages of the Orient," which had constituted his first vocation. As Eisenstein explained in *Notes of a Film Director*: "the extraordinariness of that mode of thought helped me subsequently to grasp the nature of montage; realizing that it was the normal progress of an internal logic of the emotions, different from what we call logic, helped me find my way around the most secret lodes of the method of my art." There is no doubt that this kind of quest for oriental roots accounts for the love of folk art evinced by the artists and craftsmen in the Moscow suburb of Abramtsevo, by those who collaborated in Vsevolod Meierhold's folk-theater experiment based on fairground theater, as well as by such artists as Larionov, Kandinksy, and Khlebnikov.

In Russia, the first two decades of this century were a time of great intellectual ferment and a restless questioning of values, both of which found expression in a new boldness of thought and in an extraordinary wealth of artistic and literary manifestations. Probably the single most distinctive feature of the period was the unusually high proportion of

women involved in artistic creation. Certainly Paris was aware of this, having already registered a majority of Russians among the women artists working in the French capital. Apart from Sonia Delaunay, however, they were minor figures: Marie Vassilieff, Angeline Beloff, and later Vera Rockline. In Russia that was by no means the case, with painters of the stature of Natalia Goncharova, Olga Rozanova, and Liubov Popova, and such influential poets as Anna Akhmatova and Marina Tsvetaeva.

Was Russia about to "shatter the everlasting thralldom of women," as the French poet Arthur Rimbaud put it? It seemed so, particularly when the revolution brought large numbers of women to the forefront in every field. If they were not all of the stature of the Constructivists Nadezhda Udaltsova, Alexandra Exter, Varvara Stepanova, or the film editor Esther Shub, such writers and artists as Vera Inber, Lidiia Seifullina, Nina Kogan, Vera Pestel, Vera Ermolaeva, and the Ender sisters were at least on a par with their male colleagues.

Here too the Stalinist period tidied things up, banishing some and silencing others (notably Anna Akhmatova), when it did not simply destroy them for disobedience (e.g. Vera Ermolaeva). To borrow the sort of black humor so often

16   The **Bolshoi Theater**.
Built in 1783, the former Imperial Theater was several times destroyed by fire. It was rebuilt in 1856 according to plans by C. Cavos.

17, 18 Until very recent times the single-storied **wooden house** was typical of Moscow architecture.

displayed by Russians themselves, one might say that equality of opportunity brought in its wake equality of misfortune.

The unpopular Russo-Japanese War that led to the violent revolution of 1905 shook men's minds. While politicians like Lenin contemplated changing the world as Marx had wished to do, dreamers like Velimir Khlebnikov worked out utopias meant to change mankind. In 1917 the revolution finally carried the day. One immediate effect of this was to provoke a wave of emigration. Nevertheless, this remained a great moment of hope and enthusiasm in Russia, though the enormous internal and external difficulties faced by the new regime were not really resolved.

In most fields, no real break occurred with the styles in fashion under the tsar, but 1917 did constitute a major break in the world of the fine and the applied arts, which subsequently tended to merge under constructivism and productivism. In fact, the discontinuity was so profound that we have decided to follow the example of the exhibition "Paris–Moscou 1900–1930" and deal with the fine arts in two separate chapters —before and after the revolution. At first the entire avant-garde placed itself at the service of the revolution for purposes of agitation and propaganda, or for organizing celebrations. Then people began to think in terms of developing an art industry. They rejected the fine arts of the pre-1917 period in favor of producing beautiful objects for everyday consumption and sought, through *Lef* (the magazine of the Left Front in Art), an art that would be a "construction of life." In their revolutionary fervor, everyone wanted to cater to the greatest number of people without renouncing what the avant-garde had attained.

It was a case of to each artist according to his talents. While the poet and dramatist Vladimir Maiakovsky composed innumerable propaganda posters called "Rosta windows" after the news agency that ordered them, and Nikolai Kupreanov did illustrations for mass-circulation publications, Vladimir Tatlin, Alexander Rodchenko, Lazar El Lissitzky, Alexandra Exter, Varvara Stepanova, and even such Suprematists as Kazimir Malevich and Ivan Kliun were all busy rethinking everyday objects: clothes, dinner services, furniture, etc. In the early 1920s artists in Russia dreamed more boldly of the future than anywhere else. The fact that their dream turned into a nightmare only makes the whole adventure that much more exciting.

The economic problems and the tensions that followed the Russian Civil

War provoked a second wave of emigration before the mid-1920s. This time music was probably the most affected. After 1924 Sergei Rakhmaninov, Arthur Lourié, Nikolai Obukhov, Nikolai Metner (Medtner), and Vyshnegradsky all joined Igor Stravinski and Sergei Prokofiev in the West (only the last-named returned to Russia in 1934). From the beginning of the 1930s composers either fell silent (Nikolai Roslavets, Alexander Mosolov) or reverted to academic principles (Dmitrii Shostakovich, Aram Khachaturian).

While the NEP (New Economic Policy) served to promote the country's economic recovery, there is no doubt that it reintroduced a certain state of mind allied to artistic conservatism. Maiakovsky's play *The Bedbug* (which Vsevolod Meierhold produced in 1929 with the help of Rodchenko and Dmitrii Shostakovich) poked fun at the *petit-bourgeoisus vulgaris* who had come in again with the NEP. Maiakovsky was wrong: petty-bourgeois vulgarity had never been on the way out. Excessively developed in the brains of Stalinist bureaucrats, this state of mind was soon to break out and impose itself with greater pomp and authority than ever before: profiteering selfishness was to be succeeded by a brutal megalomania evincing parvenu tastes. It would become a matter of putting up with it or disappearing.

The pretentious severity of the palaces and temples of Stalinism was a negation

of the supple, pragmatic realism of an architect like Konstantin Melnikov, a denial of all architectural thinking from Feodor Shekhtel to the *Arkhitektonis*, a retreat from the intellectual boldness of Khlebnikov or the young Vladimir Tatlin. A typical end product was the heavy neoclassical decor of the Taganskaia Metro Station (1948). Stalin's generalized bridling of the country over several decades enabled the spirit of the *petit-bourgeoisus vulgaris* to spread, as it were, by official decree, proving yet again that taste and culture have more to do with environment and education than with class or standards of living.

Serge Fauchereau

19 **Trubetskoi residence**, ca. 1930.
After October 1917, many of Moscow's historic streets and squares were renamed in honor of revolutionary personages and events down the ages. Noble palaces and luxurious private houses were nationalized to provide accommodation for government departments. The former residence of the Trubetskoi princely family today houses the Marx-Engels Institute.

1 Everyday Life

Before the Bolshevik Revolution

From the time of Peter the Great the tsars resided in St. Petersburg, but were crowned in Moscow. The reign of the last Russian emperor, Nicholas II, began most inauspiciously. During the coronation ceremony, which took place in May 1895, an appalling disaster occurred on Khodinsky Field in the western part of Moscow. Drawn mainly by the traditional presentation of gifts, a large crowd had gathered in a place that was not only restricted in area but also rather the worse for the construction work that was going on there. Panic set in, and as a result, some two thousand people were trampled to death. Public opinion blamed the city authorities, and personal accusations were leveled against the governor-general of Moscow, Grand Duke Sergei, an uncle of Nicholas II and a man hated by the people for his ultra-reactionary views, his brutality, and his scandalous private life.

Since the 1870 reform Moscow had been governed by a city council—the municipal Duma—elected by a suffrage based on property ownership. To vote in municipal elections, people had to be Russian citizens, over twenty-five, and local taxpayers. Voters were divided into three categories according to how much tax they paid. The same number of representatives was elected for each category. This limited the voters' choice to property owners, manufacturers, and wealthy merchants. Electoral representation was confined to about 10 percent of the adult population of the city as a whole (in 1916 there were 9,432 eligible voters). The Duma then elected, from among its members, a president and a standing municipal committee; these candidates had to be approved by the Minister of the Interior or by the governor-general. The latter also made sure that the decrees passed by the Duma were in line with current imperial legislation. The powers of the Duma were limited purely to economic and social matters that affected the people of the city. Politics were completely excluded, and the governor-general had the right to leave any decision made by the municipal committee in abeyance.

For all the Duma's obvious efforts, the lot of most Muscovites around the beginning of this century was hardly an enviable one. A population explosion (from 1,038,000 inhabitants in 1897 to 1,762,700 in 1914), due almost entirely to peasant immigration, created difficulties in every sphere of life, most notably in public health, security, and housing. Moscow, together with its suburbs, constituted the capital of the "central industrial region" and as such employed half of Russia's labor force. This powerful

20 Pavel Filonov: **Shrove Tuesday**, 1913. Oil on canvas, 79 × 99 cm. State Russian Museum, Leningrad. The fact that Pavel Filonov, an artist with little inclination to dwell on such mundane amusements, nevertheless devoted a painting to this subject testifies to the importance of the event in the life of prerevolutionary Russia.

21, 22 **Kuznetsky Most** was not a bridge (*most* in Russian) but a district inhabited in the distant past by the smiths *(kuznetsy)* who worked in the arsenals. At the beginning of this century Kuznetsky Most was a street of luxury shops and restaurants– mostly owned by foreigners– and banks. No. 1 was the address of the State Theater Board as well as of the Conservatory.

concentration of the working class soon gave rise to major political as well as social problems.

Each worker received from his employer a record book detailing the terms on which he was hired, his wages, any money docked from his wages in fines, and so on. The length of the working day was governed by a law passed in 1897. It was not supposed to exceed eleven and a half hours, while night shift working was limited to ten hours. Women and children were not supposed to be employed on arduous or potentially unhealthy work. In practice, however, given the level of unemployment and the huge market in unskilled labor, employers rarely abode by these regulations. To be sure, the number of public holidays, both religious and national, varied between eighty and ninety days a year, which went some way toward alleviating the hardship of people's working lives.

The working-class districts were clustered around Presnia Square and stretched as far as Khitrovka, the poorest part of the city inhabited by the homeless, hopeless people whom Maxim Gorky depicted so brilliantly in his play, *The Lower Depths* (1902). The level of overpopulation in these districts was alarming: according to contemporary statistics a workingman had only 2 square meters of floor space and 3 cubic meters of air. A typical house in such districts (usually occupied by several families) was two stories high and built of wood. There was no electricity and the lack of proper drainage turned the Moscow River—the main artery for river traffic—into a stinking, open sewer.

The other main category of Moscow's population consisted of people who

23   Aristarkh Lentulov: **Moscow**, 1913. Metal foil, oil on canvas, 179 × 189 cm. Tretiakov Gallery, Moscow. A city of a hundred churches and a thousand bell towers, Moscow at the beginning of this century was the most Russian city of all the Russias, embodying all the symbols and all the national virtues that survived the ruthless reforms of Peter the Great.

25

24 Mikhail Larionov: **Cinema Impression**, 1907. Oil on canvas, 57 × 70.5 cm. Musée national d'Art moderne, Georges Pompidou Center, Paris. Despite adverse opinions expressed in the "higher spheres," cinematography was a brilliant success in Russia. The movies became one of Moscow's favorite forms of entertainment.

worked in what we would call "the service sector": itinerant tradesmen, who were to be found on every street corner, manservants and maids, waiters and kitchen staff in Moscow's many bars and restaurants, salespeople and apprentices in its stores and innumerable shops. Finally, there were the coachmen (nearly 15,000 of them in 1910), who formed a

class apart, with their own distinctive uniforms, special language, meeting places, and amusements. The coachmen's great passion appears to have been cockfighting, and in Okhotnyi Riad, near the Kremlin, a number of *traktirs* (that characteristically Russian invention, half inn and half café, with the famous Egorov's foremost among

25 During the 1905 Revolution Presnia Street was the scene of bloody fighting between troops and the laborers and artisans who formed most of the local population. It was not until heavy bombardment had destroyed several buildings in the street and in Presnia Square that the government forces managed to dislodge the rebel workers.

26 Moscow possessed a number of racecourses, both permanent and temporary, and horse racing attracted not only the city's "high society" but also representatives of the lowest social classes. There are many passages in classical Russian literature (Alexei Tolstoi, Maxim Gorky, Ivan Bunin) describing the Muscovites' passion for this sport.

27 Despite a relatively dense streetcar network, the horse continued to provide the fastest and most efficient means of traction– especially during the Moscow winter– until the 1920s. Moscow's coachmen were renowned for their bluntness, wit, and inventiveness in the field of bad language.

them) set aside their courtyards for this bloody sport. Although motorized taxicabs made their appearance in Moscow as early as 1907 and the streetcar network covered virtually the whole city by the eve of World War I, the Muscovite's favorite method of transport remained the horse-drawn cab in summer and the sleigh in winter until well into the 1920s.

At that time, Russia was the country with the largest number of horses per head of population in the world. Every morning convoys of *telegas* (peasant carts) would arrive in Moscow to supply its many markets, leaving again at noon. Prices for agricultural produce remained very low; however, despite a definite

boom in 1910–12, triggered by a combination of economic circumstances and government policy, prices of industrial products continued to be expensive for most of the population.

Moscow's "smart districts" (starting from Red Square and the City Hall and following Tverskaia Street and Miasnitskaia Street to Arbat Square) were the domain of the aristocracy and the upper middle class. Hotels like the Metropol and the National, restaurants such as the Slaviansky Bazaar, the Iar, and the Strelnia, and the Eliseev stores were able to satisfy every whim of Muscovites and wealthy tourists alike.

Order was maintained in the city by an army of *gorodovye* (policemen).

28

28   Boris Kustodiev: **Shrove Tuesday**, 1916. Oil on canvas, 61 × 123 cm. Tretiakov Gallery, Moscow. The Orthodox Church insisted on a very strict observance of Lent. As a result, Shrove Tuesday was always celebrated in an exceptionally gay and extravagant manner.

29   One of the city's oldest thoroughfares, **Petrovka Street** owes its name to the Monastery of St. Peter. It used to be a shopping street specializing in ready-to-wear fashions, leather goods, jewelry, clocks, and watches. In 1904 the architect Roman Klein built one of Moscow's largest department stores there for the firm of Muir Merrileas (now Mostorg).

30   Vasilii Kandinsky: **Smolensk Boulevard, Moscow, on a Winter's Day**, 1919. Oil on canvasboard, 26.8 × 33 cm. Tretiakov Gallery, Moscow.

31   Vasilii Kandinsky: **Zubovskaia Square, Moscow**, 1919-20. Oil on canvasboard, 34.4 × 37.7 cm. Tretiakov Gallery, Moscow.
From the two windows of the studio he occupied during the winter and spring of 1919-20, Kandinsky must have been able to see Smolensky Boulevard on one side and Zubovskaia Square and Zubovsky Boulevard on the other. The two streets marked the historic limits of Moscow. Their architecture virtually disappeared toward the end of the 1920s to be replaced by the seven- and eight-storied blocks built there from 1928 onward as part of the first Five-Year Plan.

32   Vasilii Kandinsky: **Red Square**, 1917. Oil on card, 51.5 × 49.5 cm. Tretiakov Gallery, Moscow.
Red Square, the very heart of the city, was the scene of huge demonstrations and popular gatherings in the years following the October Revolution. Like all the artists of the avant-garde, Kandinsky played an active part in these, designing sets and occasional scenery.

33 A funeral procession. The church and religious belief provided a livelihood not only for monks and priests but also for a whole host of employees such as cantors, sextons, and morticians as well as for the beggars who were so numerous in the early years of this century.

34 Until 1920 **Kalanchevskaia Street** contained a number of large private houses belonging to wealthy middle-class Muscovites. Today it links the three Moscow stations lying on either side of Komsomolskaia Square (formerly Kalanchev Square). The photograph shows the extent to which advertising dominated the Moscow street scene. Even Shustov Brandy—an institution at the time—took hoarding space.

35 **Nikolskaia Street** (now 25th October Street) was one of the city center's busiest shopping streets. It contained the offices of Moscow's greatest merchants as well as numerous hotels and restaurants—notably the Slaviansky Bazar, scene of the famous meeting between Konstantin Stanislavsky and Vladimir Nemirovich-Danchenko that gave rise to the Moscow Art Theater. No. 15 was Proofreaders' House, built on the site of the oldest printingpress in Russia, established in the sixteenth century.

Indeed, visitors from abroad expressed surprise at finding one on virtually every street corner. There were a great many police stations, and a special corps of state police, together with the notorious *Okhranka* (security service) kept the peace and supervised *blagonadezhnost* (established moral and political conduct as defined by the governement). The movements of the populace were checked by *dvorniks* (janitors). Each house had its janitor, who was required to keep the tenant list up to date.

In spite of all police precautions, however, political ferment was rife in Moscow, particularly among high-school and university students. Moscow University, founded in 1755, was the oldest in the Russian Empire. It had four faculties: history, philosophy, physics and mathematics, and law and medicine. Two other Moscow institutions enjoyed university status. These were Grand Duke Constantine's Institute of Topography (founded in 1779) and the Technical College. Diplomas from any of these establishments offered real advantages to graduates—a chance, for example, to be ennobled and thus to move up the Table of Ranks that governed the whole of Russian society. The University's autonomy and the question of the curriculum—which was dominated by what students widely regarded as useless disciplines: classics, Orthodox theology,

32

36 Russian market with Jewish merchants. Jews were not allowed to wear their traditional dress within the city of Moscow. Successive administrative measures and police regulations had the effect of shifting the orthodox Jewish population out towards the edges of the Russian empire– mainly to Lithuania and Belorussia.

37 **Bolotnaia Square**, commonly known as Boloto ("mud"), lay opposite the Kremlin on the other side of the Moscow River. From some time in the first half of the nineteenth century until October 1917, it was the site of a "fruit exchange." The prices fixed here each morning were adhered to throughout the city.

38 **Mokhovaia Street** owes its name to the moss *(mokh)* that peasants used to sell here in the eighteenth century for the protection of wooden houses. Today part of Manezhnaia Square, at the beginning of this century it contained one of the buildings belonging to the university (on the left in the photograph) as well as many bookshops and secondhand bookstalls.

33

39 **Russian Students**, ca. 1900.
Moscow had several universities and
colleges of higher education, which
gave it a large student population. They
were the scene of fierce political and revolutionary agitation, often culminating
in violent demonstrations. In his memoirs Vladimir Maiakovsky noted with
some pride that it used to take at least
two companies of mounted cossacks to
disperse demonstrating students.

40 Boris Kustodiev: **The Merchant's
Wife Drinking Tea**, 1918. Oil on canvas, 120.5 × 121.2 cm. State Russian
Museum, Leningrad.
With their distinctive way of life, dress,
and manner of thinking, merchants
constituted a class of their own in prerevolutionary Russian society. Kustodiev's painting caricatures that class
very gently, compared with the merci-
less barbs inflicted by Maiakovsky in his
play *The Bedbug*. Nevertheless, everything here is portrayed as risible: the
subject's corpulence, the petty-bourgeois comfort, the superabundance of
food, even the woman's pseudo-elegant
way of drinking her tea from the
saucer.

НЕГРАМОТНЫЙ тот же СЛЕПОЙ
ВСЮДУ ЕГО ЖДУТ НЕУДАЧИ И НЕСЧАСТЬЯ ·

Church Slavonic–provoked repeated clashes between the student body and the authorities. Until 1918, women could not attend institutions of higher learning; at best, they were allowed to take courses in private schools, segregated by sex, which taught them to be nurses or teachers.

The "provisional regulations" promulgated in 1899, under which all students suspected of subversive activities could be pressed into military service, sparked off a series of student gatherings and demonstrations that culminated in the assassination of Education Minister Nikolai Bogolepov in February 1901. Although no political party's program enjoyed a monopoly hearing in Moscow's schools and universities, young people in general formed a second opposition group—alongside the workers—arrayed against the government and the tsar's autocratic regime. Thus, during the disturbances of the revolution of 1905, for example, strikes spread not only in the factories but also in schools and universities. The Soviet of Workers' Deputies (workers' council), set up in Moscow in October 1905, included a number of representatives from the universities. During the armed uprising decided on by the revolutionary Social Democratic Party and ordered by the Soviet on December 7, 1905

41   Alexei Radakov: **An Illiterate is not Blind...** , 1920. Colored lithograph, 58 × 90 cm.
Propaganda, to be effective, had to be accessible. From the moment of their coming to power the Bolsheviks, targeting their political allies, embarked on a campaign to abolish illiteracy among the most deprived classes of society.

42   Viktor Deny: **The October Hurricane. The Fall of Capitalism in Russia**, 1920. Colored lithograph, 58 × 89 cm.
A repulsive, grasping banker personifying international capitalism became a stock figure in Soviet propaganda.

КЛИНОМ КРАСНЫМ БЕЙ БЕЛЫХ

43   Lazar El Lissitzky: **Down with the Whites with a Red Corner!**, 1920. Colored lithograph, 63 × 52 cm. Propaganda became a formidable weapon during the Civil War. The artists of the avant-garde, united in their support for radical change, placed their talents at the Reds' disposal.

(December 20, according to the Western calendar), there were some ten bloody clashes. Students were seen battling alongside workers against Cossacks and police. The brutal repression that followed ("Soldiers, do not spare your ammunition!" was General D.F. Trepov's order to the guard regiments that came to Moscow as reinforcements)

claimed some 12,000 victims among the civilian population and the insurgents. It also caused extensive material damage, notably in the working-class district of Presnia. (As the center of the rebellion, the Presnia district was subjected to heavy artillery bombardment.) The revolution of 1905 spawned a number of clandestine magazines and newspapers. Among them was *Yuonpel* (Scarecrow), whose savage satire spared neither the government nor the imperial family. Several talented painters (Stanislav Iukovsky, Valentin Serov) worked for the magazine anonymously, contributing documentary and artistic evidence of the tragic events of that year (Nikolai Bauman's burial).

Even at that time, Moscow's press comprised a wealth of titles: in 1910, there were 100 daily newspapers and periodicals covering the whole spectrum of politics. *Moscow News* (possibly the most widely read newspaper) represented the official line, while the rather more literary *Russokol Slovo (Russian*

Word) was the mouthpiece of the liberal opposition (achieving a circulation of 700,000 in 1916). Moscow's publishing industry was likewise in excellent shape, considering the low level of literacy in the country prior to 1918. On the eve of World War I Moscow had more than 200 bookshops.

Generally speaking, culture occupied an important place in the life of educated Muscovites. Theaters, both state-run ("imperial") and private, were numerous, though the former were too often regarded as the private fiefs of court personages (the Romanovs were nearly all interested in the theater, and the Bolshoi in particular was not immune to interfer-

44   Aristarkh Lentulov: **The Victorious Battle**, 1914. Powdered bronze and silver, oil on canvas, 137.5 × 183 cm. Private collection, Moscow. The declaration of war in 1914 unleashed a flood of patriotic and nationalist feeling in Russia. Even Vladimir Maiakovsky and Kazimir Malevich designed propaganda posters in praise of the brave Russian soldiers locked in combat with Teutonic barbarism. Lentulov's painting shows Tsar Nicholas II leading his valiant troops to the hoped-for victory. Such illusions lasted for no more than a few months.

53 A meeting in **Kalanchev Square**.

54 The first Soviet automobile was built in 1927, the first motorcycle a year earlier. These young sportsmen are celebrating their victory at the conclusion of a competition in front of the Lenin Mausoleum in Red Square, which was already a place of pilgrimage for all Soviet people.

artists—particularly those belonging to the avant-garde. According to contemporary accounts, the splendor and excitement that characterized these colorful festivities were in stark contrast to the grim reality of everyday life in Moscow.

The inauguration of the NEP (New Economic Policy) in 1921 brought some improvement in living conditions. Small businesses and street traders reappeared, as did itinerant vendors. But so did the black market, giving rise to a new type of Soviet citizen, the "speculator" pilloried in Vladimir Maiakovsky's play *The Bedbug* and Ilia Ilf and Evgenii Petrov's *The Twelve Chairs*.

Maiakovsky's hatred was also directed against another breed of citizen that emerged from the October Revolution: the new bureaucrats, whose numbers were increasing as the institutions of the new state proliferated. The "anti-intelligentsia" atmosphere, created by propaganda that was sometimes more than heavy-handed, prompted many educated Russians to emigrate. But the task of national reconstruction obliged the authorities to give momentary recognition to the nation's need for *spetsy* (experts)—mainly engineers and technicians, trained under the *ancien régime* —who, however, had to submit to constant "supervision." Thus alongside the workers and peasants—the "intelligentsia" (which also included the civil servants who made up the administration) formed the third constituent element of Soviet society.

The 1920s

In 1923 Moscow numbered some 1,542,900 inhabitants, only 18 percent of whom were Moscow-born, while a large percentage were non-Russian. The city was the headquarters of the Third (Communist) International, or Comintern, as well as being the capital of the Russian S. F. S. R. Many representatives of Asian and European Communist parties lived there (the Chinese even had their own university in Moscow).

Moscow changed little between 1924, the year of Lenin's death, and 1928, the

work), on which no restrictions were placed.

The revolutionary enthusiasm of the capital's population was sustained by huge festivals and parades, and by a ubiquitous propaganda campaign extolling the virtues of hard work and promising an imminent victory for socialism. The organization of the visual side of all these anniversaries and other celebrations was entrusted to the city's finest start of the first Five-Year Plan. A number of new workers' districts were built between 1925 and 1927, and the city was electrified throughout. Outside the center, however, the architectural tone was set by small houses, mostly built of wood. By way of compensation, many green spaces were created in the capital to accommodate "educational leisure sites," "parks of rest and culture," and sports stadiums. The effort put into educating the "new Muscovite"–who was often only recently urbanized–led to the creation of numerous free public libraries and workers' clubs open to all. A great campaign was launched to eliminate illiteracy. The gangs of *besprizornye* (homeless, abandoned children), which had constituted a real problem in the early years after the revolution, disappeared at last from the streets of Moscow.

After ousting Leon Trotsky in 1927, Joseph Stalin steadily strengthened his position at the head of the party secretariat. His decision to abandon the NEP ushered in major changes for Moscow: already in 1926 the great "rebuilding plan for Moscow" provided for the total transformation of the capital's architecture, to bring it into line with the new General Secretary's "monumental and classical" tastes. However, Stalinist architecture proper dates from after 1929–30.

The collectivization of land and the elimination of small-scale private enterprise led to shortages and distress not only in towns but even in the countryside. Bread rationing was reintroduced in 1928; meat, sugar, and cigarettes were rationed in the following year. The population was divided into three–very significant–categories for rationing: workers, technicians, and railway staff (who received the largest rations); civil servants; the rest of the population, excluding coachmen, people who had been deprived of their civic rights, and priests (the separation of church and state having been one of the first decrees passed by the Soviets).

The outward appearance of ordinary Muscovites began to change. They

became drab and uniform, for there was very little variety in textile production. According to eye-witnesses, people started to look sad and preoccupied because of the mounting difficulties of everyday life. Lines appeared in front of shops.

The highpoint of the Stalinist terror was still to come. It built up gradually, reaching its peak in 1937–38. But police surveillance was perceptibly increasing. The representatives of foreign trading companies had been expelled after the abandonment of the NEP, so henceforth foreign visitors were usually on official missions. Entry visas became as hard to obtain as exit visas. From 1928 to 1929, Moscow had the dubious privilege of being the capital of a country that, increasingly, was turning in on itself.

Stanislas Zadora

55   In **Revolution Square** near the Kremlin (it used to be called Resurrection Square) the former Duma, or city council building, housed several departments of the Soviet administration, notably those responsible for finance, taxation, and statistics.

2 The Arts Before the Revolution 1900~1917

The Wanderers

Historians of modern Russian art, both in the Soviet Union and in the West, are in the habit of dating its beginnings to 1863. Camilla Gray, Dmitri Sarabianov, and Valentine Marcadé all—with the best of reasons—cite this date as marking the emergence of a new type of art in Russia. In that year a small group of young painters rebelled against the hitherto unchallenged authority of the St. Petersburg Academy of Arts. The principal result of their action was to establish in Moscow a second center of artistic influence. In 1870 the Traveling Exhibitions Society was founded with the aid of a wealthy businessman named Pavel Tretiakov. A passionate lover of Russian art, Tretiakov was to play a crucial role in furthering its development. The object of the society was to spread artistic awareness beyond St. Petersburg and Moscow by mounting traveling exhibitions to visit other Russian cities. Hence the name—English writers variously refer to them as the "Wanderers" or the "Itinerants"—given to the artists who took part. If the date of its foundation were the sole criterion, the Traveling Exhibitions Society would lie outside the scope of this book. However, the society remained active until 1923, by which time it had organized some fifty traveling exhibitions, which had an enormous influence on our artists.

With the Wanderers, Moscow regained the artistic initiative. In fact, such St. Petersburg painters as Ivan Kramskoi were only too willing to lend active support to their Moscow colleagues in defining the society's aesthetic aims and organizing the exhibitions. The aesthetic ideals of the Wanderers were important not only because they were to affect the next generation of artists but also because they represented a complete reorientation of Russian art, which until then had always followed in the footsteps of the major European schools, principally the French ones.

The Wanderers' first concern was to create a national art detached, as far as possible, from everything foreign—even from impressionism, the new movement that exerted such a fascination throughout the Western world in the last quarter of the nineteenth century. The Wanderers saw themselves as realists, committed to the portrayal of social reality. Their hero was the novelist and independent thinker Count Leo Tolstoi, whose convictions they shared long before the writer set them out plainly in *What is Art?* (1898). It was from Tolstoi that they derived their anti-aesthetic stance and their desire to reach the greatest number of people. From that time onward, Tolstoi declared:

those who will be artists, creators, will no longer be, as at present, a few indi-

56 Mikhail Larionov: **Portrait of Vladimir Tatlin**, 1911. Oil on canvas, 89 × 71 cm. Musée national d'Art moderne, Georges Pompidou Center, Paris. Within the little group of avant-garde artists, liaisons and friendships were often short-lived. Wishing to be regarded as the leader of the group, Larionov demanded recognition of his primacy. Vladimir Tatlin may have been slightly under his influence at this time, but not for long: their ways were to part forever in 1914.

viduals selected from a minority of the population belonging to the wealthy classes or those close to them, but all men of talent from all strata of the population who display artistic gifts and an artistic vocation. Artistic activity will then be open to all. Firstly because the art of the future, far from demanding the complicated technique that spoils works of art today and occasions a great deal of tension and wasted time, will on the contrary call for clarity, simplicity, and brevity – qualities that are acquired not by mechanical training but by the education of taste. Secondly because, in place of today's vocational colleges, which are open only to a few, music and painting will be taught to everyone from primary school upward in the same way as literature and writing, with the result that anyone who, having mastered the rudiments of painting and music, feels himself to have artistic gifts and an artistic vocation may go on to improve himself. Lastly because the energy currently squandered on pseudoart will be employed to spread authentic art among the people.

The Wanderers spent several decades attempting to disseminate their art among a wider public across the country. What made that art "authentic?" In the first place, it strove for clarity, unlike the many Western experiments that the Wanderers rejected as overelaborate. Then there was the fact that its subject matter addressed everyone—and Russians in particular. Hence the high proportion of religious subjects (such as *Christ in the Desert*, 1872, by I. N. Kramskoi and *Golgotha*, 1892, by Nikolai Gai) and historical subjects (such as *The Boiarina Morozova*, 1881–87, by Vasilii Surikov and the famous *Zaporozhian Cossacks Writing to the Sultan*, 1880–91, by Ilia Repin). However, the Wanderers neglected neither portraiture nor landscape. Their greatest landscapist was undoubtedly Isaak Levitan. As regards subject matter, the Wanderers' principal innovation was their acknowledgment of contemporary social reality in references either to the very recent past (serfdom) or to burning current issues (political exile). Repin, surely the most powerful painter of the group, produced the most famous works in this genre: *The Volga Boatmen* (1870) and *They Were Not Expecting Him* (1884), a picture showing the surprise homecoming of a deportee.

The art of the Wanderers, unexceptional though it seems to us today, made an impression on the young artists who were to become the most radical representatives of the Russian avant-garde. As Vasilii Kandinsky noted in his autobiography, *Looking Back*: "While still a child I had been deeply moved by *They Were Not Expecting Him*. As a young man I went several times to make a long, close study of the hand of Franz Liszt in Repin's portrait. I copied [Vasilii] Polenov's *Christ* from memory on a number of occasions, and I was struck by [Isaak] Levitan's *Rowing* with its dazzling monastery reflected in the river." The artists most heavily influenced by the Wanderers were their immediate successors – men like Valentin Serov and Mikhail Vrubel, who made their debuts under the society's auspices. The sadly brief careers of these two great artists had their origins in a rather unusual episode in the history of the Wanderers, namely the Abramtsevo colony.

Serov, Vrubel, and the Decorative Arts in Abramtsevo

In 1874 Savva and Elizaveta Mamontov, a wealthy Muscovite couple with a passion for art, began to assemble a more or less permanent colony of Russian artists on their Abramtsevo estate. The other founders of the Abramtsevo colony were Ilia Repin, Vasilii Polenov, and Valentina Serova, widow of the composer Alexander Serov, who was accompanied by her young son Valentin. They were eventually joined by many more artists, including Viktor and Apollinarius Vasnetsov, Konstantin Korovin (in 1885), and Mikhail Vrubel (in 1889). The members studied Russian medieval and folk art. In addition to painting and sculpture they practiced the applied arts, architecture (the church at Abramtsevo, built in 1880–82, was the joint work of the Vasnetsovs, Polenov, and Repin), and theater. An excellent amateur musician, Savva Mamontov conceived the idea of staging works at his own expense, assisted by his friends. In 1882 he produced Nikolai Rimsky-Korsakov's *Snegurochka* ("The Snow Maiden") at his private opera house. The production marked a turning point in theatrical design, for both set and costumes departed from convention to follow a new ideal based on an intermarriage of folk art and contemporary experiments. It was a lesson Konstantin Stanislavsky had not forgotten when, in 1898, he launched his Moscow Art Theater, which was to be "open to all." To bring about the kind of upheaval he wanted in staging and set design, he called upon the finest painters of the World of Art (*Mir iskusstva*) group: Alexander Benois, Mstislav Dobuzhinsky, Nikolai Roerich, and Boris Kustodiev.

Among the artists close to Mamontov, special mention should be made of Konstantin Korovin and the role he played in the renewal of theatrical design. Unlike the early Wanderers, Korovin was not averse to foreign influences. In fact he was one of the first Russians to take an interest in the Impressionists, whom he had met on a trip to Paris in 1885 (though it was probably Igor Grabar who learned most from impressionism). This open-mindedness made Korovin one of the most listened-to teachers at Moscow's National Art College, to the staff of which he was appointed in 1901. His friend Valentin Serov joined him there in 1903 (but resigned in the wake of the bloody events of 1905). Between them Korovin and Serov taught some of the greatest names of the future avant-garde—artists of the caliber of Mikhail Larionov, Natalia Goncharova, Vladimir Tatlin, Martiros Sarian, Ilia Mashkov, and Robert Falk.

From the beginning Valentin Serov dominated the Wanderers (and even his master Repin). Having made his mark as a draftsman at a very early age, in 1887

Serov emerged as a bold colorist with *The Peach Girl*, a painting that, by Russian standards, was well ahead of its time. The light filling the entire work looks forward to Pierre Bonnard, and the use of large areas of pure color is almost Fauvist. Serov went on to prove himself an enormously skillful artist, but it was toward the end of his life that he produced his most striking works: the portrait of *The Actress Maria Ermolova* (1905), for example, a tall dark figure picked out sharply against a gray background, or that of *Maxim Gorky* (1905), all nervous brushstrokes and movement, with the writer caught in full flow, as it were. Serov enjoyed high esteem among his contemporaries as an incomparable portraitist—as indeed he was: his portraits of the Morozov brothers and of Sergei Diaghilev are astonishing. It was, however, certain particularly bold compositions of his that caught the attention of younger artists. His *Portrait of Ida Rubinstein* (1910) consists of two horizontal bands, one blue-green, the other grayish pink, against which the curiously distorted body of a nude woman stands out, drawn almost without relief in the same grayish pink color. A similar economy of means characterizes *The*

57 Nikolai Roerich: Stage designs for **The Polovtsian Dances** from **Prince Igor** by Alexksander Borodin, 1909. Gouache and distemper, 50 × 74.5 cm. Victoria and Albert Museum, London. Roerich signed many costume and stage designs for the "Ballets Russes." His designs for *The Polovtsian Dances* are some of the more famous.

58   Mstislav Dobuzhinsky: **The Hair-
dresser's Window**, 1906. Watercolor
charcoal, gouache, 19.7 × 21.7 cm.
Tretiakov Gallery, Moscow.
Like many members of the "World of
Art" group, Dobuzhinsky was attracted
by the theater and scenography. His
paintings may also be seen as superb
stage sets.

50

59 Mikhail Vrubel: **Seated Demon**, 1890. Oil on canvas, 114 × 211 cm. Tretiakov Gallery, Moscow.
The demonism so beloved of Symbolists in all countries took on a more human dimension in Vrubel's work in keeping with the ethical climate of late nineteenth-century Russia so familiar from the literary works of his contemporaries.

60 Mikhail Vrubel: **The Demon Carried Away**, 1901. Sketch for the painting of 1902. Watercolor, gouache, and colors on paper, 21 × 30 cm. Pushkin Museum of Fine Arts, Moscow.
Vrubel was probably one of the greatest Russian artists of the late nineteenth century, and his international stature is now widely recognized. He is the most eminent (though not the most typical) representative of what was known in Russia as Art Nouveau.

61 Mikhail Vrubel: **Sadko**, majolica dish, 1899–1900. Abramtsevo Museum, near Zagorsk.
Like other artists of the Abramtsevo circle, Vrubel aspired to a total, homogeneous art that would make it possible for man to surround himself with objects that were not only useful but also beautiful.

62 Mikhail Vrubel: **Spring**, majolica bust, 1899–1900. Abramtsevo Museum, near Zagorsk.

63 Mikhail Vrubel: **The Swan Princess**, 1900. Oil on canvas, 142.5 × 93.5 cm. Tretiakov Gallery, Moscow. Characters from Russian fairy tales and traditional folk art in general were a constant source of inspiration for Vrubel.

Abduction of Europa (1910), a diagonal composition with the shape of the woman and the bull, in brown and bister, floating in a sea of blue dotted with black and white oblongs.

A friend of Serov and a fellow pupil of Repin, Mikhail Vrubel was to go very much further. Vrubel's style was largely formed as a result of a job he began in 1884, restoring Byzantine frescoes in a church in Kiev, and by his enthusiastic study of mosaics in Venice. Under this double stimulus, shape and color in Vrubel's work were fragmented by the effects of light. The tendency can be seen as early as 1886 in *Young Girl in Front of a Persian Carpet*, though it did not constitute his regular manner before 1890. The *Seated Demon* (1890) and the famous *Swan Princess* (1900) both break down the whole picture into tiny polyhedrons of color, lending them a shifting luminosity that was a long way ahead of the experiments of the Futurists. It is probable that Vrubel would have gone on toward even greater abstraction. In his portrait of the poet *Valerii Briusov*—one of his last major works (it was left unfinished in 1906)—the bust of the poet is a monolithic black shape standing out against a background torn by abstract geometrical

shapes. In 1906 the World of Art *(Mir iskusstva)* exhibition presented a whole roomful of works by Vrubel at the Paris Salon d'automne. Vrubel's fantastic world, a distant Slav relation of Gustave Moreau's, created a sensation in Paris. But the painter had already been mentally ill for some years and now had to be permanently committed. He died in 1910, one year before his friend Valentin Serov and the Lithuanian Mikalojus Ciurlionis. In fact the three most important painters of this first decade of the century in Russia all died within a matter of months of each other. Of the three it was Vrubel who, from 1905 to 1910, exerted the most persistent influence on the younger generation. Pavel Tretyakov, who had continued to support the Wanderers, died in 1898, having presented his collection of Russian and foreign art to the city of Moscow four years before. Meanwhile Savva Mamontov had been experiencing financial problems and had to cut down on his patronage. At this point a new figure appeared on the scene and took their place. Sergei Diaghilev, a native of Novgorod who had grown up in the town of Perm, arrived in St. Petersburg in 1890 to study law. Through his cousin Dmitrii Filosofov he met the painter Alexander Be-

nois, with whom he formed what was to be a lasting friedship. In 1891 and 1893 Diaghilev visited the major cities of Europe. He tried his hand at musical composition but quickly decided that he had little talent for it after an opera of his flopped. Turning to the plastic arts, Diaghilev started to organize exhibitions. In 1897 he put on "British and German Watercolorists" and "Scandinavian Painters" in St. Petersburg, and in the following year he mounted the highly successful "Russian and Finnish Painters" in Moscow. The latter included contemporary artists. The Abramtsevo group was well represented, but there were also some lesser-known young friends of Diaghilev: Alexander Benois, Léon Bakst, and Konstantin Somov. The show sealed Diaghilev's reputation as an organizer of exhibitions. It should be noted that, without neglecting the national aspect (in fact he never did neglect Russian art), Diaghilev gave foreign art its due. In that respect he broke with the tradition of the Wanderers.

The break was even more marked among his three St. Petersburg friends, Benois, Bakst, and Somov, and certain younger artists of the same school: Ivan Bilibin, Evgenii Lansere, Nikolai Roerich, and even Mstislav Dobuzhinsky. They reintroduced the taste for elegance, decoration, and festivities depicting Bacchanalian revels, Turkish scenes, minuets, and idealized peasant dances. Such things had long been taboo among the Wanderers. These younger artists loved to evoke the ancient splendors of the courts of Louis XIV or Catherine the Great. Benois fell in love with the palace and gardens of Versailles. Somov sought escape in the eighteenth century, with its crinolines and rococo scrolls. He even went so far as to reinstate the cut-paper silhouette, a genre that had been all the rage a hundred years earlier.

The World of Art and the Golden Fleece Movements

Emboldened by this association with some of the new painters and with such giants of the Abramtsevo colony as Ser-

ov and Korovin behind him, Diaghilev conceived the idea of publishing a sumptuous review, *The World of Art (Mir iskusstva)*, to run parallel with his exhibitions. Having secured the financial backing of Princess Maria Tenisheva and Savva Mamontov, Diaghilev and his cousin Dimitrii Filosofov brought out the first issue in October 1898. The review was very much in the tradition of the beautiful Symbolist and Art Nouveau magazines of the period. From the full-page engraving to the little vignette and even down to the tiniest tailpiece, the whole thing was laid out and produced with the utmost precision and care. All its illustrators from Bakst to Lansere gave the review a luxuriously antiquated look, creating a style that was to impose itself throughout the first decade of the century. (It was the style against which the Futurists were later to react.) In addition to the artists on the staff of the review, *The World of Art* gladly feted the painting of Vrubel and the music of Alexander Skriabin together with folk arts and crafts and modern Russian decorative art. It threw open its columns to the Symbolist writers Fedor Sologub, Alexander Blok, Konstantin Balmont, and Dmitrii Merezhkovsky as well as to the foreigners whom those writers delighted in translating: Charles Baudelaire, Paul Verlaine, Maurice Maeterlinck. As far as art from abroad was concerned, the review cultivated largely Art Nouveau tastes: Pierre Puvis de Chavannes in painting and Charles Rennie Mackintosh and Henry van der Velde in the applied arts. Claude Monet and Edgar Degas put in a brief appearance, but it was only in its last few issues in 1904 that the review turned its attention to the most advanced painting of the period, namely that of the Nabis and, above all, of Paul Cézanne, Vincent Van Gogh, and Paul Gauguin. Nevertheless, in presenting their work *The World of Art* solidly reestablished Russia's dialogue with the West.

The influence of the review was extended through the exhibitions it patronized. These were held annually from 1899 to 1904. Again, international exhibitions alternated with national

54

ones–though with a preference for the latter, where it was possible to promote Benois, Bakst, Somov, Lansere, Dobuzhinsky, Ivan Bilibin, and the rest. The greatest merit of those exhibitions was to mix in with the St. Petersburg artists such Muscovites as Nikolai Sapunov, Pavel Kuznetsov, and the Milioti brothers artists stylistically related to Vrubel, whom those responsible for the *World of Art* so much admired. This brought the two great cities closer together and lessened any rivalry that might have arisen between them. Benois, Somov, and their St. Petersburg colleagues inclined more toward elegance of line and showed something of an addiction to the past in their choice of subject matter, while the Muscovite tendency followed Vrubel in showing more interest in color. The second great merit of the World of Art shows was a certain theatricality of presentation that made it possible to exhibit both painting and applied arts. This not unnaturally pointed the artists concerned in the di-

64   Viktor Borisov-Musatov: **Tapestry**, 1901. Tempera on canvas, 102 × 141.2 cm. Tretiakov Gallery, Moscow. The influence of French painting and in particular of the Nabis on Borisov-Musatov was possibly no more than formal. His art remained profoundly Russian, with all that the Symbolist movement and Symbolist thought implied for creative artists in that country.

rection of the theater. Among the first painters to throw themselves into stage design were Benois and Bakst. The initial successful step toward what was to become famous as the "Ballets Russes" was *Le Pavillon d'Armide*, which was first performed in St. Petersburg on November 25, 1907. Based on a plot borrowed—significantly—from a "rococo" tale by Théophile Gautier, the ballet had music by Nikolai Cherepnin, choreography by Michel Fokine, and costumes and sets by Alexander Benois. It was the highly unconventional character of the latter that took the audience by surprise—as it was to take Paris by storm when the ballet was performed at the Théâtre du Châtelet two years later.

Diaghilev organized two more exhibitions after the review had ceased to appear. Held in 1905 and 1906, they were as carefully staged as the earlier shows. The 1906 exhibition saw the first major public exposure of two newcomers who were to create quite a stir (as well as to remain faithful friends of Diaghilev): Mikhail Larionov and Natalia Goncharova.

The same exhibition contained a large section paying tribute to Viktor Borisov-Musatov, who had died the year before. After training in Moscow, Borisov-Musatov had gone to Paris to pursue his studies under Fernand Cormon and Gustave Moreau, though German painters (Arnold Böcklin) and the frescoes of Pierre Puvis de Chavannes were to make the greatest impression on him. It was from Puvis that the Russian derived his personal style: dark colors, with blue often prominent, laid on without depth to depict peaceful, crinolined figures set in a parklike landscape dating from another age. A typical example is *The Pool* (1902), in which two women are seen beside a body of water. They are looking neither at the water nor at the landscape and appear to have been captured in the middle of some slow, mysterious action like a Maeterlinck drama. The strangeness of the scene is underlined by the muted colors of the work. Borisov-Musatov was to have a great influence on the early work of Pavel Kuznetsov and Ivan Kliun.

1906 was also the year in which Diaghilev created a stir at the Salon d'automne in Paris's Grand Palais, where he presented a dozen rooms. Prepared by Bakst, these rooms contained everything that was important in Russian art, from icons to the experiments of young Mikhail Larionov. Topping the bill as far as the modern period was concerned was Vrubel's work, with which the Western public now had its first chance to become acquainted. Disenchanted since the disappearance of his review and frustrated by the problems he was encountering in theatrical circles in Russia, Diaghilev turned his mind to promoting Russian art outside Russia, particularly since Benois and several of his World of Art friends were prepared to help him in this task. In 1907 and 1908 he organized a series of concerts in Paris devoted to "The Five"—Mili Balakirev, Caesar Cui, Modest Musorgsky, Alexander Borodin, and Nikolai Rimsky-Korsakov. Encouraged by their success, he turned his attention to what was to become the "Ballets Russes."

In the very year in which *The World of Art* ceased publication, another journal appeared. This was *The Scales* (*Vesy*, 1904–9), edited by Valerii Briusov. Primarily a literary review, it was nevertheless illustrated by artists of the stature of Vrubel, Somov, Bakst, Borisov-Musatov, Vasilii Milioti, Maximilian Voloshin (who was a painter as well as a poet), and even by artists very much outside the spirit of symbolism such as Georgii Iakulov and above all Larionov. As for foreign artists, the review published both the German Thomas Theodor Heine and the Frenchman Odilon Redon. However, the chief importance of *The Scales* lay in its role as a promoter of Symbolist literature from Russia and abroad. René Ghil, the journal's correspondent in France, leaped at the chance to disseminate the theories he had put forward in his critical essay *Le Traité du verbe*, according to which sounds and colors correspond to one another. This concept, which he had taken from Charles Baudelaire and Arthur Rimbaud, was enthusiastically received in Russia, not only by the poet Velimir Khlebnik-

65 Mikhail Larionov: **Rain**, 1904–5. Oil on canvas, 85 × 85 cm. Musée national d'Art moderne, Georges Pompidou Center, Paris.
This is a key work as regards our understanding of how Larionov's painting developed. It contains within it the premises of all his later discoveries and theories, notably rayonism.

66 Mikhail Larionov: **Fish at Sunset**, 1904. Oil on canvas, 100 × 95.3 cm. State Russian Museum, Leningrad.
The problem of light was fundamental to Larionov's art. This painting, which is sometimes unjustly regarded as a youthful work, shows early evidence of his preoccupation with it.

ov and the composer Skriabin—who accompanied his symphonic poem *Prometheus* with light projections—but by painters as well. In fact it was to become one of David Burliuk's hobbyhorses. *The Scales* was content to present gifted representatives from among past and present artists without committing itself to a particular tendency. This limited its impact.

A rival review entitled *The Golden Fleece* (*Zolotoe runo*, 1906–9) was very much closer to the contemporary artists. Managed by a wealthy Moscow businessman, Nikolai Riabushinsky, it signaled a clear Western orientation by appearing simultaneously in Russian and French, at least to begin with. It continued to support the World of Art painters (Vrubel, Bakst, Borisov-Musatov, Roerich, etc.), but it also introduced new painters and promoted their work by patronizing exhibitions, as *The World of Art* had done. At the same time its correspondents (Charles Morice, Alexandre Mercereau) served up large helpings of the most recent French art: the sculpture of Paul Gauguin, the theories of Maurice Denis, and virtually a whole issue devoted to Henri Matisse (1909). With Sergei Shchukin and Savva Morozov opening their collections to the public at around the same time, Moscow was now in an excellent position to follow developments in Paris.

Of the exhibitions organized by *The Golden Fleece*, mainly of French and Russian art, several were of crucial importance in setting the future course of art in Russia. The first one, entitled "The Blue Rose," took place in 1907. It brought two painters in particularl to the attention of the public: Pavel Kuznetsov and Martiros Sarian. Kuznetsov had been taught by Isaak Levitan and Valentin Serov, and the latter had brought Kuznetsov's precocious talent to the attention of Diaghilev, who exhibited him in 1906. But it was Kuznetsov's first master, Viktor Borisov-Musatov, who played the decisive role, steering him in the direction of a reflective, dreamladen art—though the younger painter employed purer colors and was possibly less inclined to melancholy. In the

works painted in the period 1905–6 Kuznetsov's characters emerge from a blur of colored lines. Subsequently, having discovered Gauguin on a trip to Paris with Diaghilev in 1906, he adopted a Primitist approach, using sharp angles and bright colors with a marked predilection for blue. Kuznetsov did not voyage to the South Pacific islands as Gauguin did but rather to the steppes on the southern borderlands of the Russian Empire. From his travels among the nomads he brought back exotic scenes—markets, portraits of Kirghiz tribesmen, animals—portrayed by an artist who was acquainted with the latest findings of fauvism and cubism.

A closely related yet even more alien world was portrayed by the Armenian artist Martiros Sarian. His pictures in the "Blue Rose" exhibition bore such titles as *Lovers of a Little Snake, The Oasis, On the Flat Roofs, Man with Gazelles*, and so on. All these Persian and Transcaucasian scenes were handled with the aid of simple shapes and bright colors by an artist who clearly knew his Persian miniatures but was also very probably familiar with the paintings of Matisse, since he had access to the private museum that was Shchukin's apartment.

In 1908, *The Golden Fleece* was the prime mover behind a huge mixed

67 Martiros Sarian: **Date Palm, Egypt**, 1911. Tempera on card, 106 × 71 cm. Tretiakov Gallery, Moscow. Armenia's greatest painter was fascinated by the Orient and its mysteries his whole life long. He made many trips there; in fact Egypt became a place of almost annual pilgrimage for him.

68 Martiros Sarian: **Egyptian Masks**, 1912. Tempera on card, 70 × 80 cm. National Art Gallery of Armenia, Erevan.

69   Pavel Kuznetsov: **The Good Adventure**. After becoming acquainted with Paul Gauguin's work and traveling to the steppes of the Russian Empire, Kuznetsov renounced symbolism in favor of his own form of fauvism between 1910 and 1913.

70   Kuzma Petrov-Vodkin: **The Red Horse Takes a Bath**, 1912. Oil on canvas, 160 × 186 cm. Tretiakov Gallery, Moscow.
This was probably the first work that Petrov-Vodkin executed in his own original style. Nevertheless, it still shows signs of earlier influences from German and French Symbolist painting.

exhibition—the "First 'Golden Fleece' Salon"—in which works by contemporary Russian and French artists were hung side by side. The review set out the objects of the exhibition as follows:

In inviting French artists the *Golden Fleece* group is pursuing a twofold aim: on the one hand, to bring out more clearly, by juxtaposing Russian and Western experiments, the special features of the development of modern Russian painting and its new problems; on the other hand, to stress the features that Russian and Western painting have in common, for despite differences in national psychology (the French are more sensual, the Russians more spiritual) the recent experiments of their young painters share a certain psychological foundation.

The Russian contingent included the "Blue Rose" artists (Kuznetsov, Sarian, Vasilii Milioti, Alexei Utkin, etc.) and two newcomers, Diaghilev's friends Natalia Goncharova and Mikhail Larionov. The latter's aggressively green and pink bathers caused quite a stir, but it was his painting *Rain* (1904) that made the biggest impression. The perpendicular white lines running down this Impressionist landscape lent an extraordinary dynamism to it, as if the artist had had an early intuition of what he was later to call rayonism. The French side of the exhibition included nearly 200 pictures. The few Impressionists (Edgar Degas, Camille Pisarro, Alfred Sisley, Auguste Renoir) were completely swamped by post-Impressionists and Nabis (Cézanne, Gauguin, Van Gogh, but also Henri-Edmond Cross, Paul Signac, Pierre Bonnard, Maurice Denis, and Theo Van Rysselberghe, among others) and numerous Fauves (Matisse, André Derain with his London views, Kees Van Dongen, Othon Friesz, Albert Marquet, and Georges Braque with five paintings from 1906). Georges Rouault was there too, and some young painters as yet in their pre-Cubist phase (including Albert Gleizes, Jean Metzinger, and Henri Le Fauconnier). There was also an important sculptural contribution in which names like Auguste Rodin, Antoine Bourdelle, Aristide Maillol, Camille Claudel, and the Paris-based Italian Medardo Rosso were all represented.

The "Second 'Golden Fleece' Salon" followed in January 1909. A smaller exhibition than its predecessor, it was also more coherent. Only the Fauves (and Rouault, who was close to the Fauves) were retained in the French part of the exhibition. Among these works, those submitted by Braque, which he had painted in 1907–8, already looked forward to cubism. Larionov, Goncharova, Kuznetsov, and Sarian were again the best-represented Russian exhibitors, with Larionov showing his *Fishes*, a painting that sparkles with light. And a new name appeared: Kuzma Petrov-Vodkin, who had recently returned to Russia after several years of study abroad, notably in France, Germany, and Italy. This was before Petrov-Vodkin achieved notoriety with such paintings as *The Red Horse Takes a Bath* (1912).

The "Third 'Golden Fleece' Salon," held from December 1909 to January 1910, presented the usual artists as well as two further newcomers, Ilia Mashkov and Robert Falk. However, it was mainly devoted to Larionov and Goncharova, who now broke away from Western art with paintings inspired by the folk imagery of the *lubok* (peasant woodcut), by primitive icons, by children's drawings, and even by graffiti. Goncharova exhibited coarse peasant scenes in deep colors with abrupt shapes that ignored perspective. In his series of hairdressers (1907–9) and soldiers (1908–9), Larionov showed works that were frankly barbaric. The colors were crude and hastily applied, figures and objects were oversimplified, distorted and quite out of scale: inscriptions were scribbled and even made to come out of people's mouths as in certain medieval paintings. Such work was later dubbed neoprimitivism.

As soon as *The Golden Fleece* disappeared, its place was taken by another review, *Apollon* (1909–17), which was published in St. Petersburg. Slightly less expensively produced, it nevertheless set out to pay as much attention to the arts as to literature. Following what was by now a well-established custom, *Apollon* mounted monthly exhibitions in its own gallery. As far as literature was concerned, Sergei Makovsky's journal adopted a straightforwardly Symbolist line at the outset, though in 1913 it came under the control of the Acmeists (Nikolai Gumilev, Anna Akhmatova, Osip Mandelshtam). Artistically its choices were more eclectic. It welcomed every tendency from the Wanderers to the "Blue Rose" painters, though without promoting the extremes then represented by Larionov and Goncharova. To the review's credit, however, it put on an exhibition of Petrov-Vodkin and showed the work of the Russian circle in Munich (Kandinsky, Alexei Jawlensky/Iavlensky, Marianna Werefkin/Verevkin). It also had the courage to stand up for a painter who had been much neglected, namely Mikalojus Ciurlionis.

Ciurlionis, Kandinsky

Together with Vrubel, Mikalojus Ciurlionis was undoubtedly the most outstanding artist of the first decade of the century. A Lithuanian (at a time when the Lithuanian language was banned), he spent most of his life either in Poland or in St. Petersburg. His original intention had been to follow a musical career, and in fact he left a substantial body of compositions. In 1913, however, disappointed with his studies under Carl Reinecke in Leipzig, Ciurlionis turned to painting instead. He devoted himself to his art with a fierce determination, despite meeting with little success (his work appeared too abstract, too intellectual). Ciurlionis painted series of visionary pictures representing imaginary, timeless landscapes in which pyramids, towers, and ziggurats symbolized a soaring idealism. He drew his inspiration from three sources. The first was music: he sought to transpose its forms and movements to his new medium. The second was folklore and Lithuanian folktales. His third source was theosophy and its derivatives, such as Rudolf Steiner's anthroposophy, which greatly

interested many intellectuals at the time, including Kandinsky, Franz Kupka (of whom Ciurlionis is reminiscent), and Kazimir Malevich, to name only some artists. Ciurlionis died before he was able to exhibit with the Blue Rider group, as Kandinsky aparently wished him to do, and his work has remained largely unknown. *Apollo* continued to back him, and paintings of his were exhibited in Paris and even in London (at the 1913 post-Impressionist exhibition).

At this point we need to step outside Russia for a moment. Following a visit to the Impressionist exhibition in Moscow in 1895, where he had been particularly impressed by Claude Monet's *Haystack*, a young teacher of law decided to take up painting. His name was Vasilii Kandinsky, he was thirty years old, and since it was art from abroad that had attracted him and he had no desire to follow the Wanderers, Kandinsky left Russia in 1896 to learn how to paint in Munich. Munich may seem to have been a strange choice, for its artistic life was dominated not by Monet and impressionism but by Art Nouveau and symbolism. However, it was a very important center and already contained a sizable Russian colony. There Kandinsky met two other Russians—Alexei Jawlensky and Marianna Werefkin—who had also decided to drop everything in order to satisfy their passion for painting. The only difference between Kandinsky and his two compatriots was that the war was to bring Kandinsky back to Russia, while their departure was final.

Kandinsky began his studies under Anton Azbe and continued them under Franz von Stuck. The academic discipline imposed by his masters was a painful experience for Kandinsky. Only gradually did he find his own way toward what he called "the spiritual in art":

For many years I was like a monkey caught in a net: the organic laws of construction paralyzed my will, and it was only with great difficulty and after many efforts and attempts that I knocked down this *wall in front of art*. In this way I finally entered the

domain of art, which like nature, science, or politics is a domain of its own, governed by laws that belong to it alone, and which, in conjunction with the other domains eventually forms the Great Domain that we can only vaguely sense as yet (*Looking Back*).

Much has been made of the influence of theosophy on Kandinsky's ideas, and indeed the phraseology of theosophy almost shines through that quotation. As regards his actual *œuvre*, however, Kandinsky's formal work and his thinking–based on impressionism and divisionism as well as on the Russian folk

art he knew so well (icons, *lubki* arts and crafts, etc.)–were far more important. All this comes across very strongly in the works Kandinsky produced in the early years of the century. Dispensing with models, he readily composed scenes from an earlier age, whether reconstitutions of medieval Russia (*Song of the Volga*, 1906, or *Couple on Horseback*, 1906–7, for example) or episodes from legend (*Night*, 1907). At that time Kandinsky liked to work in dabs rather than in the precise dots or dotted lines of the Divisionists. From 1908 onward he no longer used dabs to form the figures or objects he wished to depict. As his art became less figurative, the little dabs

71 Vasilii Kandinsky: **Composition no. 6**, 1913. Oil on canvas, 195 × 300 cm. Hermitage Museum, Leningrad.

63

grew larger and became shapes. Kandinsky's colors became more and more strident as his shapes grew simpler (e. g. *Landscape with a Tower*, 1908; *The Blue Mountain*, 1908–9; *Railway*, 1909; *Winter Landscape*, 1909) until in 1910 he produced the first abstract watercolor and a series of splendid *Improvisations*. His work eventually departed from nature in order to abstract it and recompose it at will.

In the work of the following two or three years recognizable objects or scenes sometimes emerge from the colored shapes but their presence is unimportant. Kandinsky's art had become *spiritual*. It was at this point (in 1912) that he and Franz Marc brought out the *Blue Rider (Der Blaue Reiter)* almanac, following an exhibition of the same name. Shortly afterward Kandinsky also published a book of poems, *Klänge* ("Sounds"), written in German and illustrated with woodcuts. It would be difficult to define the content of these poems, in which actions are sometimes sketched without being resolved. Everything is highly abstract, but color plays so important a part that we soon realize these are transpositions of his paintings.

Blue, blue soared, soared and fell.
Sharp and thin whistled and burst in but did not pierce.
Reverberations reached into every corner.
Thick brown remained suspended, seemingly for ever.
Seemingly. Seemingly.
You must spread your arms wider.
Wider. Wider...

Recalling Munich during the years 1911–14, an admirer of Kandinsky's, the German poet Hugo Ball, observed in his diary:

At that time Munich was host to an artist whose mere presence there raised that city high above every other city in Germany: Vasilii Kandinsky. Some may find this verdict exaggerated, but it is what I felt at the time.... Indifferent to ridicule and sarcastic remarks, he never committed himself to any form of art without following a new path. Everything about him bespeaks an exceptional harmony—words, colors, sounds—but his ultimate objective was not merely to create individual works but through them to attain a fusion of all the arts (*Die Flucht aus der Zeit*, "Flight from Times").

Kandinsky, though comfortably placed in the artistic life of Munich, of which he was clearly one of the leading lights from 1910 onward, nevertheless remained in close touch with Russia—unlike Jawlensky, Werefkin, and Vladimir Bekhteev (or von Bechtejef, as he called himself in his adopted country). From 1904 onward, Kandinsky frequently took part in exhibitions in Moscow, St. Petersburg, and Odessa, notably with the Moscow Artists' Association. It was in Moscow that he published his first volume of woodcuts, *Poems Without Words* (1904). He occasionally wrote for *Apollon*, among other Russian reviews. *Concerning the Spiritual in Art* was first published in German in December 1911, but Kandinsky made sure that at the same time an abridged version of it was read to the Second Congress of Russian Artists in St. Petersburg. Presented by Nikolai Kulbin, Kandinsky's text was in fact extensively discussed by those attending the congress. And though *Klänge* was first published as a volume in Germany in 1913, the individual poems were known in Russia long before that—many of them, including the one cited above, having appeared with the manifesto *A Slap in the Face of Public Taste* in 1912. Kandinsky also made sure that Russian painting was represented both in the "Blue Rider" exhibition and in the almanac of that name. These contacts were facilitated by Russian artists passing through Munich as well as by Kandinsky's own trips to Russia in 1904, 1912, and 1913—until the outbreak of war prompted him to return to his native land. Meanwhile all trace of figuration had vanished from his pictures. If he did still occasionally compose a figurative landscape, it was in play. From now on Kandinsky's art was pure shape and color.

Kandinsky may also be regarded as having been largely responsible for the exhibitions organized by his friend Vladimir Izdebsky on his return from Munich. The first of these, held in 1909–10, comprised nearly 800 works, half by a wide variety of foreign artists from Giacomo Balla and Georges Braque to Alfred Kubin and Henri Rousseau. Kandinsky was well represented, obviously, as were his friends Jawlensky and Gabriele Münter. The second exhibition organized by Izdebsky a year later included 54 paintings by Kandinsky. Among them were four large *Improvisations* from 1910–probably the ones that had been shown at the first Jack of Diamonds exhibition in Moscow in December 1910, where very few top-class foreign artists were represented. At the second Jack of Diamonds exhibition Kandinsky showed three new large *Improvisations* painted during 1911. This was to be the last exhibition before the revolution. Once again foreign painters were well represented, and they included some major figures: André Derain, Henri Matisse, and Kees Van Dongen among the Fauves Pablo Picasso, Fernand Léger, and Robert Delaunay among the Cubists; and Ernst Ludwig Kirchner, Max Pechstein, Franz Marc, and August Macke among the Expressionists.

The Collectors Shchukin and Morozov

The art magazines, together with these occasional exhibitions, were an important source of information and as such shaped the stylistic development of Russian painters. They would have proved inadequate, however, without a further factor that we have hardly touched on as yet and to which we shall have occasion to return. This was the presence of two large collections of modern art that were open to the public (which explains, incidentally, why it was that Moscow gradually drew ahead of St. Petersburg in this field).

Sergei Shchukin was a wealthy Moscow businessman who, in his forties, began to collect paintings by French artists. He conceived a veritable passion for the latest developments in art. It all began one day in 1897, when on a visit to Paris a friend took Shchukin to the Durand-Rue Gallery. After having exhibited and championed the Impressionists for a quarter of a century, the Durand-Rue Gallery was at last enjoying considerable success. It was now regularly frequented by art lovers, including many discriminating foreigners. That day the gallery was showing Claude Monet.

72 The **Matisse room** in Shchukin's house in Moscow.
Sergei Shchukin, as well as being one of Russia's wealthiest businessmen, was a great art collector and a shrewd patron. In the space of a decade and a half he assembled a fabulous collection of Western (mainly French) painting, notably including works by Paul Gauguin, André Derain, and Maurice Denis, who were hardly appreciated in their own country at the time.

73 Once a week Sergei Shchukin opened his house to the public. Young Russian artists became regular visitors.

Fired with enthusiasm, Shchukin promptly bought a canvas entitled *Lilac in Sunlight (Argenteuil Lilac)* to take back to Moscow and hang in his Znamensky Street home. It was the beginning of his collection and the very first Impressionist painting to enter a private collection in Russia. Other Monets soon followed, as well as paintings by Pissarro, Sisley, Cézanne, and Gauguin. In fact Shchukin became so enamored of the last two artists that he ended up owning the largest collection of their work in his day. From his initial enthusiasm for the work of Monet, Shchukin's taste developed to the point where he became more and more interested in contemporary art. He owned two paintings by Matisse as early as 1904, including *Still Life with Dishes and Fruit* (1901). After that, several of the painter's boldest works found their way to Russia. Shchukin lost no time in making the acquaintance of the artist in person, and Matisse in turn introduced him to Picasso.

Shchukin was not the only important Russian collector. His rival and friend Mikhail Morozov, a textile mill owner who also lived in Moscow (on Prechistenka Street), had begun to collect modern French paintings shortly before the turn of the century. On Mikhail Morozov's premature death in 1903 his brother Ivan felt in honor bound to continue the family collection, in which such artists as Gauguin, Cézanne, Bonnard, and Matisse were eventually represented by at least ten pictures each.

Neither Shchukin nor Morozov was one of those collectors who are interested only in hoarding treasures to impress others. It was with genuine enthusiasm that each of them watched the work of their favorite painters develop. Morosov enjoyed the confidence of Edouard Vuillard, Pierre Bonnard, and Maurice Denis, while Shchukin felt true friendship for Matisse; he called on him every time he was in Paris, corresponded with him, and never gave up trying to get him to visit Moscow.

Thanks to the paintings so generously exhibited by Shchukin, Matisse was the best-known foreign artist in Moscow during the first decade of the century.

Not until 1912–14 did Picasso become a serious challenger. In 1909 *The Golden Fleece* devoted a special issue to Matisse. In that same year Shchukin commissioned a major composition from him: *Dance*. Having seen the preparatory study, Shchukin persuaded the artist to paint the matching *Music*. In other words, we have a Russian collector to thank for two of the twentieth century's most important works of art. In painting these works, both over 4 meters long, Matisse used (as he put it at the time) "the simplest of means... the pink of the bodies, the blue of the sky, the green of the hill." Completed in time to be exhibited in Paris at the 1910 Salon d'automne, the two panels arrived in Russia at the beginning of 1911. Matisse came to supervise their installation in person. It is not hard to imagine what a fuss his patron and his Muscovite fellow artists made of their guest. As for Matisse, he was greatly excited by the Russian icons he saw, and he enjoyed the work of the city's young artists. Shchukin set aside an entire room for the paintings of Matisse (he was to set aside another for Picasso, which Picasso, who hated traveling, never saw). That is why the world's largest and finest collection of Matisse's work is still to be found in Russia; since the revolution it has been divided between the Hermitage in Leningrad and the Pushkin Museum of Fine Arts in Moscow.

By the time the war and then the revolution put a stop to art imports into Russia, Morozov had collected 135 paintings. Shchukin's collection comprised 221 paintings, including 37 by Matisse and some 50 by Picasso as well as dozens by Monet, Renoir, Gauguin, Cézanne, and Derain. Yet the value of these collections stemmed principally from the fact that neither Shchukin nor Morozov was a jealous collector. Both liked to see the public share their admiration—and share it in their own day. They opened their apartments to the public. In a rare interview granted to the French critic Félix Fénéon in 1920, Morozov explained how this worked: "In the days of the tsar I allowed anyone who was interested free access on Sun-

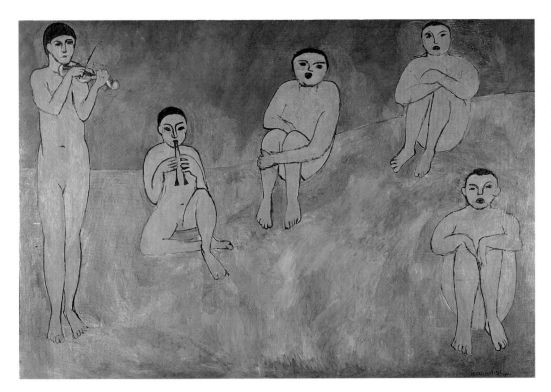

74 Henri Matisse: **Music**, 1910. Oil on canvas, 260 × 389 cm. Hermitage Museum, Leningrad.
In 1910 Sergei Shchukin commissioned Matisse, who was possibly his favorite artist, to paint two large works, *Dance* and *Music*, to decorate his hall. Henri Matisse visited Moscow in the following year to supervise the hanging of what are without doubt the most remarkable works of this period of his career.

75 Henri Matisse: **Conversation**, 1910. Oil on canvas, 177 × 217. Hermitage Museum, Leningrad.
This was one of the last works by Matisse that Sergei Shchukin purchased. The war put an end to a relationship that has no parallel in the history of artistic patronage. The private collections of late nineteenth- and early twentieth-century Western art put together by the Shchukin, Savva Morozov, and S. P. Riabushinsky families were nationalized after 1917. Today most of the works involved are divided between the Pushkin Museum in Moscow and the Hermitage in Leningrad.

day mornings, and subject to certain scarcely tyrannical formalities artists and critics could come on every day except Monday." That was how the young artists who were soon to become giants of twentieth-century art–people like Malevich, Larionov, Goncharova, and Tatlin –were given direct access at a very early stage to the finest painting of the period. We can gain an even better idea of what a visitor to such collections might experience from another passage taken from Fénéon's interview with this astute collector of Western and Russian art:

Since you were in such direct contact with people can you tell me, Ivan Abramovich, which of our painters found most favor with yours?
– Cézanne. I had twenty examples of his genius on display: two *Mont Sainte-Victoires*, the *Girl at the Piano*, a *Jas de Bouffan*, a portrait of his wife, and so on. You know them all, or nearly all. Van Gogh was also much admired. And Derain. Picasso, too, but I had only three of his paintings. The Spaniard [Picasso] and Henri Matisse were better represented in Mr. Shchukin's collection.
– You've mentioned a number of French artists in your museum. Can you complete the list for us?
– Degas, Camille Pissarro, Gauguin (a dozen, mostly of Polynesia), Lebourg, Simon, Henri-Edmond Cross, Maillol (four statues, seven statuettes), Ker Xavier Roussel, Vuillard, Louis Valtat, Lebasque, Marquet, Puy, Guérin, Espagnat, Vlaminck, Flandrin, Friesz, Chabaud, Herbin – I've left some important ones out.... [Indeed he had, and they were among the jewels of his collection: Renoir, Bonnard, Rouault, the American Alfred Maurer.]
– And in the Russian section, who was there?
– Who was there? Well, I had Vrubel, Levitan, Serov, Sapunov, to start with those who are dead; Philippe Maliavin, Korovin, Vinogradov, Golovin, Somov, Benois, Igor Grabar, Kuznetsov, Larionov, Natalia Goncharova, Mashkov, Kuprin, Konchalovsky, Chagall, others....

Futurism: From Hylaea to the Union of Youth

As these treasures were being accumulated and as successive exhibitions marked the advances of the new art, an organized avant-garde began to emerge that was different in spirit and in its methods from the groups of friends who had previously gravitated toward particular journals. This development was connected with the arrival of a number of energetic young artists determined to inject new life into the ways and customs of their elders. Mikhail Larionov has already been mentioned. It is time to take a look at the Burliuk family or rather, to be more precise, at David Burliuk and his brothers Vladimir and Nikolai. The last-named was chiefly a poet, while Vladimir was probably the best painter of the three. There was even a sister who painted–Ludmilla. David himself, who both painted and wrote poetry, was primarily an organizer and a leader of men. The Futurists would always bow to his authority–especially Maiakovsky, whom he met in 1911 when he was still a young art student and whom Burliuk convinced of his poetic talent. The Burliuks came from southern Russia, from the Crimean region once known as Tauris or Hylaea, and this was the name they eventually adopted for their group. The family estate was at Chernianka, and later they would invite their friends Mikhail Larionov, Velimir Khlebnikov, and Benedikt Livshits to visit them there.

In fact the Burliuks were not complete newcomers on the art scene. They had first met Larionov and Goncharova on the occasion of an exhibition called "The Wreath," which they had organized together in Moscow at the end of 1907. Other artists involved were Aristarkh Lentulov, later to become Henri Le Fauconnier's pupil in Paris (1911), and Leopold Survage, who was then still calling himself Stürzwage but was soon to leave for Paris (1908), where he joined the Cubist group around Guillaume Apollinaire. Another unobtrusive "Wreath" exhibitor, Vladimir Baranoff-Rossiné, followed a similar course.

76 Liubov Popova: **The Philosopher**, 1915. Oil on canvas, 89 × 63 cm. State Russian Museum, Leningrad.
A former student of the Paris art college La Palette, Popova long remained faithful to her French masters– Henri Le Fauconnier and Jean Metzinger– while at the same time adopting some of the principles of Russian alogism.

Nevertheless, the "Wreath" exhibition was sufficiently revolutionary for Igor Grabar to protest in the review *The Scales* about artists painting "one with squares, another with commas, and a third with a broom." Undeterred by such criticism, they mounted another exhibition in Kiev less than a year later. This one was called "The Link" and included the three painters from the Burliuk family as well as such artists as Larionov, Goncharova, Baranoff-Rossiné, and Aristarkh Lentulov. Leopold Survage was replaced on this occasion by Alexandra Exter, who came from the Kiev region. Exter was an important recruit, for it was through her that the group received first-hand news of cubism. In 1908 she left to study at the Grande Chaumière in Paris, where Sergei Iastrebtsov (Jastrebzoff, known as Férat) and his sister Baroness Oettingen introduced her to Apollinaire, Picasso, and Braque. Through Ardengo Soffici she also met the Italian Futurists. Until the

war Exter divided her time between Paris and Russia, becoming one of the very first Cubist painters in Russia. After a period under the influence of Cézanne, followed by a period of somewhat rudimentary cubism (1911), she practised a synthetic cubism in the style of Braque (1913–14) before taking up a position closer to futurism, exhibiting with the Italian Futurists in Rome in 1914. It was through her that Larionov and Goncharova got to know Apollinaire and that Lentulov, Linbov Popova, and Nadazhda Udaltsova were able to study under Le Fauconnier and Metzinger.

Burliuk and his painter and poet friends were passionately interested in folk art, primitive art, and children's drawing. (The organizers of Izdebsky's exhibition in 1909 had gone so far as to hang children's drawings alongside works by Braque and Kandinsky, and other exhibitions repeated the experiment; similarly Khlebnikov and Kruchenykh placed their own texts on the same level as those improvised by children.) These interests brought them even closer to Larionov who, as we have seen, during his military service (1908–9) had produced paintings of soldiers and hairdressers in a neoprimitivist style that soon attracted other painters—starting with the Burliuks.

It was while holidaying at Chernianka that the Burliuks and Larionov conceived the exhibition that they called the Jack of Diamonds. Put on with the helpf of Aristarkh Lentulov and Alexander Kuprin, this was held in Moscow in December 1910 and January 1911. It reunited the "Wreath" exhibitors with the addition of Kandinsky and his Munich friends as well as several French painters (Le Fauconnier, Gleizes, L. A. Moreau). But it also gave a great deal of space to three Russian painters—Petr Konchalovsky, Ilia Mashkov, and Robert Falk—and appeared to make a great fuss of them. All three had already spent some time in the West and learnt a great deal there. Their style at that time vacillated between a fauvism influenced by Cézanne and a moderate cubism. The exhibition was also remarkable for the first, as yet unobtrusive appearance of

another famous name: Kazimir Malevich. Larionov and David Burliuk, both
natural leaders, could not agree for long.
The break came in 1911, which is why
the second Jack of Diamonds exhibition
in 1912, athough as we have seen it
included an important Cubist section
(the catalogue lists Picasso, Léger,
Delaunay, and Gleizes), took place without Larionov or Goncharova–or Malevich, who left with them.

However, these artists came together
again on neutral territory in St. Petersburg, where from 1910 the Union of
Youth organized exhibitions of painters
from the two major centers. The Union
of Youth had been launched by a group
of friends who emerged from Nikolai
Kulbin's "Impressionists" group under
the leadership of the painter and composer Mikhail Matiushin and his wife,
Elena Guro, who combined painting
with poetry. Kulbin himself was a high-
ranking civil servant with a burning enthusiasm for modern art. His own work
was only moderately avant-garde, but
he was prepared to listen to every new
idea. Matiushin was a born experi-
menter, passionately interested in problems of color (which in the early 1920s

78 Natalia Goncharova: **The
Washerwomen**, 1911–12. Oil on
canvas, 102 × 146 cm. State Russian
Museum, Leningrad.
Where Mikhail Larionov had his "soldiers" and "hairdressers," Goncharova
had her peasants. These washerwomen
are depicted in the purest Neoprimitivist
style inspired by icon painting and Russian folk art.

71

79 Kazimir Malevich: **Portrait of Ivan Kliun**, 1911. Oil on canvas, 111.5 × 70.5 cm. State Russian Museum, Leningrad.
Ivan Kliunkov, who called himself Kliun, was a friend and disciple of Malevich. His face in this painting, an arrangement of Cubist flat planes, still shows the influence of Fernand Léger.

he was to study systematically with the Ender brothers and sisters at the Ginkhuk). It is a pity that he did not often show his work. Matiushin greatly assisted Burliuk, Kamensky, and Khlebnikov in producing *The Breeding-Ground for Judges* (1910), which was the first literary manifestation of Russian Futurism. It was Matiushin who published its second edition as well as other Futurist writings such as *The Three* and *Roaring Parnassus*. He also published theoretical works such as Malevich's *From Cubism and Futurism to Suprematism* (1916) and his own translation of *Concerning Cubism* by Gleizes and Metzinger. Matiushin became friends with Kruchenykh and Malevich in 1912; and together they created the opera *Victory Over the Sun*, which was produced in 1913 with a libretto by Kruchenykh, sets by Malevich, and Matiushin's own music. Elena Guro, who died prematurely, was a modest but crucial figure in the development of Russian futurism, according to her friends. She painted landscapes with fine lines that occasionally reached the limits of figuration. She also illustrated her own books (e.g. *Camels of the Sky*, 1913).

The Union of Youth organized several exhibitions between 1910 and 1914. It was not only a place where the Burliuk and Larionov groups consented to exhibit together but also a place where new painters emerged. The two exhibitions mounted by the Union in 1911 revealed two major artists, Olga Rozanova and Vladimir Tatlin, both of whom practiced a personal interpretation of Cézanne and cubism. Tatlin showed two famous pictures painted in that year: *The Sailor* and *The Fishmonger*. The second exhibition (December 1911–January 1912) also saw the appearance of the nineteen-year-old Ivan Puni (he later called himself Jean Pougny), who became friends with Malevich and Rozanova, and of Alexander Shevchenko, a Cubist member of Larionov's group. The 1912 exhibition introduced another painter of the first rank and someone who was quite unique on the Russian art scene—Pavel Filonov. Although he participated in

Futurist exhibitions and contributed to Futurist publications, Filonov remained an isolated figure. His densely graphic works were inimitably his own, though his folkloristic subject matter possibly linked him to another isolated figure, Marc Chagall, then living in Paris. The 1913 exhibition revealed Nathan Altman and above all Ivan Kliun, who despite being a Cubist at that time was subsequently to become one of Malevich's finest lieutenants.

Burliuk championed Futurism on his own account and on behalf of the members of his group—principally Khlebnikov, Kruchenykh, Kamensky, and Maiakovsky. All these poets were to a greater or lesser extent painters as well. Maiakovsky in particular produced a number of well executed Futurist compositions, though it was above all as a great graphic artist that he was to reveal himself after the revolution. Nor did Burliuk neglect his own painting; he even experimented with varying the texture of his painted surface by mixing other substances—wax, sand, molten lead —with his paint. The Futurists, not afraid to shock the public, produced manifesto after manifesto and staged repeated demonstrations. They even undertook a lecture tour round the country. To stress their ongoing relationship with artists they had their books (which were always boldly conceived) illustrated by their friends Malevich, Rozanova, Larionov, Goncharova, Tatlin, Filonov, Exter, and the rest. Never have literature and the plastic arts been so closely linked.

Larionov, Neoprimitivism, Rayonism

Outside the neutral territory of the "Union of Youth" Larionov no longer exhibited with Burliuk. The charge he now levelled against Exter, Falk, Konchalovsky, Lentulov, and other friends of the Burliuk brothers was that they were chronic "Cézannists." For his part Larionov no longer wished to have anything to do with the Cubists. So he organized exhibitions in Moscow without

them: "The Donkey's Tail" in 1912 and "The Target" in 1913. Obviously these mainly featured Goncharova and himself, though Malevich—their ally for the present and a painter whose star was rising fast—also received a generous share of space at these exhibitions. They were joined by Tatlin, Shevchenko, and three young recruits: Mikhail Ledentu and the brothers Kiril and Ilia Zdanevich from Georgia. Ilia Zdanevich was not in fact a painter but a poet. Under the name of Elie Eganbury he was writing a monograph on Larionov and Goncharova, which appeared in 1913. There was particularly one young painter, then living in Paris, whose originality interested Larionov. This was Marc Chagall, whose *Death*, painted around 1908, offered a kind of highly colored primitivism that was at the same time Expressionist, unusual, and not unrelated to certain works of Larionov's. In a village in which people and houses are all out of proportion a dead man lies in the road. One person is running away, another mourns, and a third is sweeping while a fourth—who was to come to typify Chagall's world—is a fiddler on a roof.

In the second of Larionov's exhibitions, "The Target," he also showed painted signs, children's drawings, and anonymous drawings gleaned from nonprofessional artists. Lastly he showed the wholly distinctive works of Niko Pirosmanishvili, the "Russian Douanier Rousseau." Larionov had become an enthusiastic fan of the "marvelous, extraordinary Pirosmani" thanks to the Zdanevich brothers. They had got to know Pirosmanishvili in Tiflis—where he still lived, eking out a wretched existence painting signs for shops and nightclubs. The fact of being "discovered" and invited to take part in exhibitions with professional artists did nothing to change his behavior. Ilia Zdanevich noted in his diary how one day Pirosmanishvili had insisted on executing a commission before continuing with the portrait he was working on. "I asked him what the commission was. He showed me a lantern for a shop front on which he was to write an address—Molokane Street and the number of the house. 'You call that a commission?' I asked. 'Of course!' he replied. 'If we don't work on little things, how shall we ever do great things?'" Depending on what commissions he had and what he felt like doing, Pirosmanishvili painted portraits, landscapes, festive scenes, animals, and still lifes with a freshness, strength, and freedom of line such as are possessed only by those who combine a total lack of pretension with enormous talent. Here was the prototype of the kind of art for which Larionov had been searching for years. (Some time later David Shterenberg contrived to recall this artistic effusion in certain of his naive works, such as *The Lunch Party* of 1916.)

The art of Pirosmanishvili seemed closer to primitive art and further from the decadent sophistication of Western art that these men and women rejected. "Besides," Goncharova said (as cited by V. Parkin in connection with the "Donkey's Tail" and "Target" exhibitions), "all art comes from the East; even the very beautiful art of the Stone Age in western Europe has nothing in common with what was done later. Moreover, we must remember that our Stone Age coincided with the flowering of Egypt, India, and

China.... In the West there was civilization; in the East, culture. Our having to fight against Cézanne, Picasso, and occidentalism does not mean we do not need their works." It was the same oriental stance with which the poet Khlebnikov challenged the Italian Futurist poet and publicist Filippo Marinetti. The same attitude is found in Alexander Blok's poem *The Scythians* (written in 1918, possibly inspired by the *Scythian Suite* that Prokofiev had performed in Petrograd in 1916):

Yes, we are Scythians, barbarians from Asia
With avid eyes, slit eyes, herdsmen....

It was another artist, Alexander Shevchenko, who set out the ideas of the neoprimitivist group of which Larionov was the life and soul. He did so in a book called *Neo-Primitivism*, published in 1913, in which it is no surprise to come across such passages as these: "The primitives, icons, *lubki* trays, signs, and fabrics of the East—these are authentic mod-

81 Kazimir Malevich: **Head of a Peasant Woman**, 1912–13. Oil on canvas, 80 × 95 cm. Stedelijk Museum, Amsterdam.
Although the subject of this painting still belongs to Malevich's "peasant," or Neoprimitivist period, the influence of cubism is clearly visible. Note the inevitable shawl worn by countrywomen. This is probably the most interesting painting of what was a transitional period for Malevich.

82 Natalia Goncharova: **The Little Station**, 1911. Oil on canvas, 66 × 74 cm. Private collection, Paris. Locomotion, speed, movement, and machinery were the essence of the Futurist program, to which Goncharova subscribed for a brief period.

els of plastic beauty" or "We, like the primitives and painters of the East, consider that the best work is that which is guided by instinct."

After the soldiers and hairdressers Larionov's art became increasingly barbaric in its graphic style. His *Four Seasons* (1912) are like painted signs, and the Venus in his *Spring* is a disturbing pagan idol in a grayish-beige mist from which only childishly drawn animals emerge.

Goncharova worked in a different style. Her *Peasants Dancing* (1910) and her religious works from the years 1910–11 deal in flat areas of color as if the figures had been roughly cut out of sheets of plain colored paper; they have a massive, clumsy, yet cheerful character. Malevich himself worked in a very similar style in the years 1909–12. Around 1910 (in *The Bather* and *Woman with Buckets*) he painted figures with heavy shapes against more or less simplified backgrounds, often making the hands and feet larger than the head; later, under the influence of a certain kind of cubism (one thinks of Fernand Léger), they assumed geometrical shapes (*Haymaking*, 1911; *The Woodcutter*, 1911). A year later his primitivism had been completely absorbed by his interest in cubism, and abstraction was to triumph (*Woman with Buckets*, 1912 version; *Head of a Peasant Woman*, 1913). His *Knife-Grinder* (1912–13), with its barely intelligible silhouette, is a perfect prototype of cubo-futurism.

Larionov and Goncharova found that, at the very moment when they were practicing their version of neoprimitivism, they felt the need for another type of painting. They also found that they were able to execute works in the two styles simultaneously. According to Eganbury, "rayonism, as preached by Larionov, had been worked out by Goncharova during the winter of 1909–10." In fact, even if there was talk of rayonism in 1910, the first Rayonist works were not seen until 1912. In his manifesto, *Rayonist Painting*, published in 1913, Larionov said this:

> Strictly speaking, rayonism proceeds from the following facts:
> 1) The radiation caused by reflected light forms a sort of chromatic dust in space between objects.
> 2) The theory of radiation.
> 3) Radioactive rays, ultraviolet rays, reflection.

For the Futurists, dynamism and simultaneism stemmed from speed; for a Rayonist, on the other hand, they were due to light and its reflections breaking down and recomposing the subject. In both cases the picture was organized along lines of force and frequently resulted in abstraction. Larionov and Goncharova also studied movement, of course, and sought to render it by showing the same object in many positions. Larionov's *Woman on the Boulevard* (1911) and Goncharova's *Cyclist* (1912) used the same principle of figuration as the famous *Dog on a Leash*

83 Natalia Goncharova: **Portrait of Larionov**, 1913. Oil on canvas, 105 x 78 cm. Ludwig Collection, Cologne. Goncharova could hardly be indifferent to the rayonism of her husband, Mikhail Larionov. Her portrait of the inventor of this new theory of painting reveals the degree of cooperation that existed between the two artists.

84 Natalia Goncharova: **The Cats**, 1911-12. Oil on canvas, 86 × 85 cm. Solomon R. Guggenheim Museum, New York.
This is one of Goncharova's finest Rayonist canvases, skillfully executed in accordance with the strictest principles of the theory.

painted by the Italian Giacomo Balla, also in 1912. And many other painters used the same procedure—Olga Rozanova, for instance, in her *Harbor* of 1912. In such truly rayonist works as *Red Rayonism* (1911) and *Rayonist Sausages and Mackerel* (1912) by Larionov, *The Cats* (1911–12) and *Portrait of Larionov* (1913) by Goncharova, and certain works by Paul-Henri Ledentu, the subject literally bursts forth in sharp-angled beams of light (the opposite of the "spherical expression of light" that interested Delaunay). Larionov was to continue to insist that rayonism was a strictly plastic operation concerned purely with the individual painting:

Rayonism, which may seem like a spiritual, not to say mystical type of painting, is on the contrary essentially plastic. The painter sees the new shapes created between tangible

shapes by their own radiation, and it is them alone that he captures on his canvas. In so doing he attains the zenith of painting for painting's sake, inspired by so-called real things but unable and unwilling to represent them or even to evoke them in terms of their linear existence (*Rayonism in Painting*, 1913).

Larionov was here distancing himself from "the spiritual in art" in the various forms advocated by Kandinsky, Malevich, and Matiushin.

Malevich: From Cubo-Futurism to Suprematism

In such works as *The Knife-Grinder* Malevich had already attained a high degree of abstraction. Just as if suprematism had not yet come of age, so to

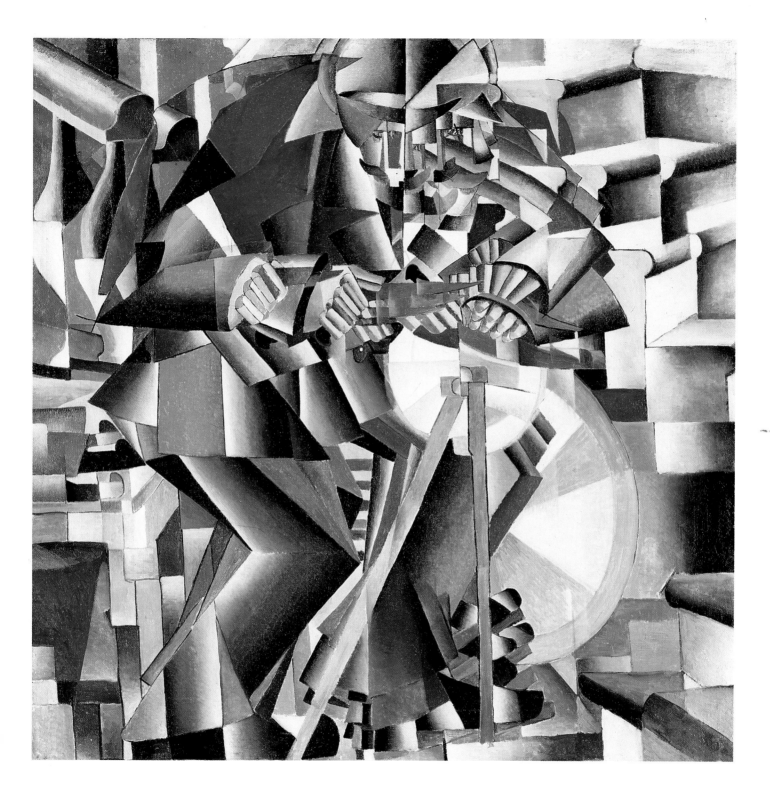

87 Kazimir Malevich: **The Knife-Grinder**, 1912–13. Oil on canvas, 79.5 × 79.5 cm. Yale University Art Gallery, New Haven, Connecticut.

This is perhaps the only purely Futurist painting by Malevich in which the dynamism of movement was obviously the artist's chief preoccupation.

speak, his work was now to enter a new period that lasted barely two years and had to do not so much with cubo-futurism as with what became known as "Alogism." Just as his friend Kruchenykh delighted in associating the most unlikely ideas and words together, Malevich returned to a kind of figuration to assemble incongruous objects amid various inscriptions unrelated to what was represented. Where his *Portrait of Matiushin* (1913) was an arrangement of planes and classic Cubist symbols, *An Englishman in Moscow* (1914; actually a portait of Kruchenykh, who was nicknamed "the Englishman") shows a top-hatted sihouette accompanied by a saber, a candle, a fish, a pair of scissors, three bayonets, a church, a ladder, and the Futurists' distinctive wooden spoon, among other things. The juxtapositions, though they certainly owed nothing to logic and were closer to dadaism than to futurism, were not always gratuitous; there was undoubtedly a key for those in the know. *The Airman* (1914) is probably a portrait of Vasilii Kamensky, who was a pilot besides being a poet. The character is obviously a Futurist, with his top hat and his fork, and if you know that Kamensky once crashed during a display of aerobatics and was badly hurt, the inscription "Apteka" (pharmacy), clearly legible in the picture, acquires an ironic connotation. With his "alogical" works Malevich sowed the last of his wild oats, as it were; his next step towards modernism was to exclude humor.

During 1913 a certain consensus was established among the different Futurist groups and others sympathetic to them. Cubo-futurism stamped a distinctive style on the whole of contemporary avant-garde painting—on Exter, Puni, Rozanova, and Kliun, whom we have met already, as well as on such brilliant newcomers as Liubov Popova, Nadezhda Udaltsova, and, in his early works, Alexander Rodchenko. Notice the extraordinarily large number of women artists who were active at this time. We shall once again find them in the forefront of artistic activity at the time of constructivism. This moment of afflu-

ence—with more and more publications, all in some degree spectacular, drawn up in conjunction with poets—marked an apogee. A measure of agreement between the parties was achieved notably on the occasion of Filippo Marinetti's visit to Moscow and St. Petersburg in January 1914. The snob element and one or two Futurists (the painter Nikolai Kulbin, the poet Vadim Shershenevich) made a great fuss of the Italian poet, but by and large the avant-garde was hostile. Even before Marinetti's arrival Larionov had told a journalist that he ought to be greeted with rotten eggs. In the event Larionov did not carry out his threat but behaved politely, at least, toward the visitor. The most relentless hostility was shown by Khlebnikov, who refused to receive any lesson from a westerner. This attitude never varied throughout his career, and it informs his whole poetic œuvre. Aided by Benedikt Livshits, he distributed an insulting tract during one of Marinetti's lectures. This kind of reaction revealed the extent to which the Russian avant-garde had become conscious of its worth and independence. However, the outbreak of war in that same year, if it did not put a complete stop to this fine flight of creativity, at least slowed it down to a considerable extent.

90 Kazimir Malevich: **Supremus No. 56**, 1916. Oil on canvas, 79.5 × 70.5 cm. State Russian Museum, Leningrad.
Suprematism as conceived by Malevich was far from being just a method of painting: it was a whole profound philosophy expressed by artistic means in which each line and each color had its own special significance.

Despite their avowed suspicion of Paris, Larionov and Goncharova were happy to go there once again in June 1914 for an exhibition of their works put on by Apollinaire. There they found a sizable and comfortably settled Russian colony enjoying *la vie parisienne* (and some of them spelling their names the French way): the Jastrebzov-Férats, Marie Vassilieff, Sonia Delaunay, Léopold Survage, Alexandre Archipenko, Ossip Zadkine, Jacques Lipchitz—and Sergei Diaghilev, who with his team of Russian dancers, artists, and musicians was carving out an impressive niche for himself. Igor Stravinsky's *Rite of Spring*

91   Ivan Kliun: **Suprematism**, 1915.
Oil on canvas, 71 × 89 cm. Tretiakov
Gallery, Moscow.
Even before the *Manifesto of Suprem-*
atism was published, Malevich's new
method found immediate support
among artists. Kliun remained faithful
to the principles of suprematism until
around 1919. Subsequently, events
steered his art in a quite different
direction.

(choreographed by Vaslav Nijinsky with
sets by Nikolai Roerich) had only recently caused a scandal that did him no
harm in terms of publicity. Keen to find
a new type of set for his ballets, departing from the Benois/Bakst line on which
he had relied hitherto, Diaghilev had
asked Goncharova to design Rimsky-
Korsakov's *Golden Cockerel*, which

received its first performance in May
1914. The war forced Larionov and
Goncharova to return to Moscow. He
went into the army; she designed the
sets for *The Fan* by Carlo Goldoni,
which was put on at Alexander Tairov's
theater in Moscow. But when Larionov
was demobilized in 1915 and Diaghilev
summoned both of them to join him,

they went. It was the start of a long and fruitful collaboration, and they never returned to Russia. Other artists drawn back by the war or the revolution were Kandinsky and Chagall, who returned to Moscow in 1914, and Baranoff-Rossiné, who returned in 1917.

By his own account Malevich began his Suprematist works in 1913–at the same time, in other words, as he was painting the alogical works we have just been looking at. The radical simplicity of suprematism came to him like a sudden inspiration, he said: a black square on a white ground, a black cross on a white ground, a black circle on a white ground.... The famous black square did undoubtedly appear in the sets for the opera *Victory over the Sun*, which was produced in St. Petersburg in December 1913. But it was not until 1915 that Malevich actually began to talk about suprematism. His manifesto *From Cubism to Suprematism: The New Pictorial Realism* came out in 1915 and 1916 before being republished in 1916 in a heavily revised edition as *From Cubism and Futurism to Suprematism: The New Pictorial Realism*. It opens with this abrupt declaration: "All painting of the past and present prior to suprematism (sculpture, verbal art, music) was in thrall to the form of nature and awaited its liberation in order to speak in its own language and not depend on reason, meaning, logic, philosophy, psychology, the various laws of causality, and life's technical changes." Malevich thus eliminated not only all figuration from painting but also all human intervention, whether individual or social, and all technical intervention. He was left with an art untouched by the outside world and unrelated to it: suprematism. While rejecting all that had gone before him, Malevich did acknowledge certain merits: "Honor is due to the Futurists, who banned the painting of female thighs, portraits, and guitars in the moonlight. They took a very big step, rejecting the flesh and glorifying machines." However, "futurism's attempt to produce a purely pictorial plastic art as such was not crowned with success: unable to renounce the figurative

aspect as a whole, it merely destroyed objects with a view to capturing the dynamic aspect.... The Cubo-Futurists gathered all objects in the town square, smashed them, but did not burn them. A pity." Speaking in his own name in the second version of his manifesto, Malevich offered glimpses of a certain mystical quality that was to grow in importance over the years: "I transfigured myself into the zero of forms and went beyond that to the zero of creation, that is to say towards suprematism, towards the new pictorial realism, towards non-figurative creation. Suprematism is the start of a new culture: the savage is conquered as was the ape." When Malevich exhibited his *Black Square on a White Ground* at the "0.10" exhibition in 1915 it caused a mighty scandal, even among defenders of the avant-garde. Malevich protested:

> The square is not a subconscious form. It is the creation of intuitive reason.
> The face of the new art.
> The square is a royal child full of life.
> It is the first step of pure creation in art. Before it there were only naively ugly things and copies from nature.

Very quickly, however, Malevich found painters embracing his austere system: Kliun, Rozanova, Popova, Puni, and his wife Boguslavskaia. Moreover, he was himself to emerge from this elementary geometrical shape uniformly painted black (and its successor, *White on White*) to introduce color and combinations of various geometrical shapes. The career of the Suprematist movement was just beginning–with Malevich as its leader and chief thinker.

Tatlin Versus Malevich: The Last Glimmers of Futurism

That same year saw the emergence of another major figure who would have to be reckoned with: Vladimir Tatlin. On his return from Paris in 1913 he had started a series of polychrome reliefs incorporating various materials that

92 Vladimir Tatlin: **Assemblage of materials**, counterrelief, 1915-16. Wood, iron, various materials, 100 × 64 cm. Tretiakov Gallery, Moscow. After his trip to Paris in 1913, Tatlin gave up easel painting altogether. Believing that beauty lies in simplicity and that all painting, even abstract painting, is endowed with a decorative element that inevitably leads to prettiness, he decided that nature itself supplied the best materials for any kind of creative activity. The period of reliefs and counterreliefs proved of great importance in the emergence of the theory of constructivism, with its wealth of manifestations in every field following the October Revolution.

could be applied to a wall or fixed in a corner (Picasso and Braque also went in for this kind of thing). And when Ivan Puni organized the "Tramway V: Futurist Exhibition" in Petrograd in 1915 (St. Petersburg having changed its name in 1914), it was not Malevich who was the star with his *Portrait of Matiushin* or his alogical works but Tatlin with his reliefs. One wonders whether he already had the idea of detaching the work from the wall completely and turning it into a kind of flying machine. The exhibition also included works by Popova, Exter, and Udaltsova that were likewise influenced by Parisian cubism and yet intensely dynamic as well as works by Rozanova and Kliun at the height of their Cubo-Futurist and before their Suprematist phase. It was not until December 1915 that Malevich, exhibiting alongside these same artists, showed his first Suprematist works, much to the detriment of Tatlin, from whom the *Black Square* stole the limelight. Puni subsequently contrived to reconcile the two trends in his Suprematist reliefs of 1915–17, just as he reconciled abstraction and alogism by painting a plate and a hammer on a geometrical canvas. The

simplicity of the elementary shapes was probably very close to suprematism, while the gesture was perhaps not so close to the unwitting dadaism of the contemporary Tiflis group made up of Kruchenykh, Terentiev, and the Zdanevich brothers. A hammer coupled with the color red was capable of evoking work, reconstruction; as for the empty plate against a plain ground, its meaning was only too obvious in 1918, the famine year that followed the revolution.

While Tatlin and Malevich were dividing artistic opinion in the years immediately preceding the revolution, a third important figure was able to make his mark. Kandinsky had arrived in Moscow in December 1914; Rodchenko and Varvara Stepanova lived in his flat for some time in 1915, and David Burliuk rented a studio not far away. But Kandinsky did not involve himself in the artistic world beyond participating—with a discretion quite foreign to artists like Malevich and Tatlin—in two exhibitions, one in April 1915 with Altman, the Burliuks, and Goncharova and Larionov just before they left Moscow for Paris, and one in Petrograd in December 1916 with Malevich and Popova, among others.

In 1916 Tatlin organized an exhibition in Moscow under the title "The Store." Wanting it to be Futurist in inspiration, he took advantage of his role to refuse Malevich's Suprematist works and accept only his Cubo-Futurist and alogical submissions. The other exhibitors included Kliun, Popova, Rozanova, Udaltsova, Puni, and Exter. In retrospect the most memorable thing about this exhibition was the appearance of a young artist who did not feel obliged to opt for one or other of the two local masters. His name was Alexander Rodchenko, and he showed some graphic works that were notable for their very obvious use of ruler and compasses. (This was a technique he was not yet using in his oil paintings, which at that time were still very Cubo-Futurist, an example being his *Two Characters* of 1916.)

In spite of the war and the fact that some of the Futurists were absent from

Moscow, artistic life went on. An example in a rather different domain was the volume entitled *War*, a series of Suprematist collages in bright colors illustrating the poems of Kruchenykh. *War* was one of the finest books to come out of Russian futurism. Also in 1916 Alexandra Exter did the sets and costumes for Innokentii Annensky's *Famira Kifared* at the Tairov Theater; and in the following year she worked on Wilde's *Salomé*. Her abstract sets were well received and marked the beginning of a brilliant career in the theater and the cinema. The last important exhibition before the revolution was the Jack of Diamonds show early in 1917, where Futurists and Suprematists hung side by side: the Burliuk brothers, Malevich, Kliun, Rozanova, Exter, and so on. But possibly the most curious project of the years 1916–17 was the "Picture Café" that Tatlin was commissioned to decorate with the aid of Georgii Iakulov and Rodchenko. Contemporary accounts and photographs conjure up an interior with its walls irregularly encrusted with jumbled geometrical shapes breaking up the uniformity of the rooms and adorned with mechanomorphic figures (probably Iakulov's contribution). It was in this setting that Maiakovsky upbraided an audience he found overly inert:

> You people sitting here
> with your backs to the walls,
> glued
> to the wallpaper...
> you who tremble
> at the sight of a knife,
> you boast of being the guardians of a
>   great era...

The Futurists, having invoked the kind of revolution they wanted, afterwards claimed to have precipitated it. The revolution and then constructivism did not find it easy to put futurism on the shelf, as it were. As a state of mind it was tenacious and was forever being reborn. In 1919 it tried for an official rebirth as *Komfut* (Communist futurism). In 1921 Maiakovsky, as an artist and poet in the service of the revolution, was still occasionally referring to himself as a *komfut*. And so numerous were the formerly

Futurist artists and poets involved in *Lef* that they also formed a separate organization known as MAF (the Moscow Association of Futurists), which for a time published books under its own imprint. There is even, in what is now the Costakis Collection, a large watercolor drawing by Kliun dated 1925 that, but for a certain purist influence, takes us back twelve years to the heyday of militant futurism. It shows a portrait of Kruchenykh taken from a photograph (reproduced in Markov's *Russian Futurism* as plate 31) together with, among a variety of other objects, a trapped rat called Pushkin; among the inscriptions we find the initials MAF and, in the center, *dyr bul shchyl*, the most famous *zaum* line of which Khlebnikov and Kruchenykh said in *The Word As Such* (a 1913 brochure illustrated by Malevich and Rozanova) that it "contained more Russian national character than the whole of Pushkin's poetry." This was empty nostalgia. The irrepressibly cheerful Futurists were by now fossils from a bygone era, whose turn it might be one day to take Pushkin's place.

Serge Fauchereau

87

3 The Arts After the Revolution 1917~1930

The Reorganization of Art and Education

The vast majority of the Russian intelligentsia experienced the revolution —both that of February, 1917, and the Bolshevik-led one of October, 1917—as the tangible realization of their dreams and aspirations. The great majority of artists greeted the revolution with genuine enthusiasm. Aware of its promise to change utterly every field of human activity, they saw it as a full and final break with the hated past. "*Complete renewal*: seeing to it that our false, filthy, tiresome, hideous existence becomes henceforth fair, clean, lovely, and happy," declared Alexander Blok in January 1918.

As far as the avant-garde was concerned, approval of the revolution was immediate and virtually unanimous. Vladimir Maiakovsky called it "his" revolution, and many saw it as the concrete embodiment of their work hitherto. As Vladimir Tatlin put it, "the political events of 1917 were prefigured in our art in 1914."

The first few years after the revolution placed avant-garde artists in a highly privileged position. They filled all the key posts in the new system of cultural administration. The People's Commissariat of Education (Narkompros) was headed by Anatolii Lunacharsky; David Shterenberg directed the Department of Fine Arts (IZO), with Vladimir Tatlin in charge of its Moscow branch; Vsevolod Meierhold directed the Theater Department; Vasilii Kandinsky, Olga Rozanova, and Ivan Puni (Pougny) sat on IZO committees, and Alexander Rodchenko was given the job of director of the Museum Bureau and Purchasing Fund. After the reform of art education advocated by Narkompros in 1918, the avant-garde virtually had the field to itself. In the very difficult situation in which the young Socialist republic found itself in the period 1917–22 (civil war, foreign intervention, an economy geared entirely to the war effort), the alliance between Soviet power on the one hand and the artists of the avant-garde as unconditional supporters of the revolution on the other became a natural one; even if their visions of the future diverged, they appeared to have the same aim, namely the revolutionary transformation of their country.

Their energy and enthusiasm served the interests of power even though the avant-garde itself, true to its original ideology, was driven by a fierce spirit of anarchism. In fact many artists contributed to the review *Anarchy* between February and April, 1918; Tatlin, Kazimir Malevich, Nikolai Punin, Nathan Altman, and Nadezhda Udaltsova did so regularly. And from the "Futurists' Café," next door to the anarchist headquarters in Duritvovka Street, Maiakovsky and

95 Kazimir Malevich: **The Red Cavalry at Full Gallop**, 1918–28. Oil on canvas, 90 × 140 cm. State Russian Museum, Leningrad.
Reverting to painting after his trip to Poland and Germany in 1927, Malevich adopted a fresh style, in an attempt to apply the theories of suprematism to a certain kind of figuration. This painting, which is extremely difficult to date, was very probably shown at the exhibition that marked the tenth anniversary of the October Revolution.

Burliuk issued their *Manifesto of the Flying Federation of Futurists* in March, 1918, calling for "the separation of Art and State" and "the transfer of control of institutions to the artists themselves." However, during this brief period even Nestor Makhno, the leader of the Ukrainian anarchists, was momentarily in alliance with the Bolsheviks.

The chief difference between the avant-garde—especially the Futurists —and the Soviet authorities had to do with the conception and function of culture in the revolution and in relation to the new ruling class, the proletariat. The break seemed to be complete: "The revolution destroys the old forms of social life. We are destroying the old forms of art: we are revolutionaries, and we are in step with the revolution" (Nikolai Punin). In the past the bourgeoisie had created its own art and its own culture to serve its own class interests. The proletariat as the new ruling class must therefore have a new culture.

This affirmation appeared self-evident to all the artistic tendencies and groups that sprang from October, 1917, as it did

to the authorities, but the slogan was interpreted differently by each. This led to a polarization of opinion within the avant-garde, and among academic artists, as official cultural policy crystallized. In the years 1918–22 the polemical battles were still conducted freely and were open to everyone, just as museums and exhibitions were, though the avant-garde tended to monopolize the discussion from its privileged position in the institutions. The various groups that made up the avant-garde at the time and that were soon to be bracketed together as "leftist art" were in fact far from homogeneous. But two options united them: "hatred of the past and an aesthetics that favored form over content."

The Futurists saw all the art of the past as nothing but a useless burden as far as

creating the art of tomorrow was concerned. "From today, with the abolition of the tsarist regime, *we have ended art's existence* in the warehouses and repositories of the human spirit: palaces, galleries, exhibition halls, libraries, theaters." So said Maiakovsky in the *Futurists' Gazette* in March, 1918 (decree no. 1 on the democratization of the arts). The art of the past was merely a kind of feudal hangover–unnecessary and even noxious to the proletariat, which must think in terms of a new life and a *new art*. This brought the problem of form to the fore: art could serve the revolution only if, aesthetically speaking, it was itself revolutionary. The realistic representation of man or object was an outmoded aesthetic form, declared one of the theorists of Futurism, Nikolai

97, 98 Liubov Popova: **Dynamic Construction** (recto-verso painting), 1919. Oil on canvas, 159 × 124 cm. State Gallery of Painting of the USSR, Moscow.
Large-scale geometrical compositions – studies of optimal relations between form and color– were a feature of Popova's final period of easel painting. After 1922 she concentrated almost entirely on applied art, which she regarded as more useful from the social point of view.

91

99 Nathan Altman: **Petrokom-
muna**, 1921. Oil on canvas, 104 ×
88.5 cm. State Russian Museum, Leningrad.
Just after the revolution, Altman, Marc
Chagall, and David Shterenberg formed
a separate group, working and exhibiting together. They embraced the Bolshevik cause unreservedly–indeed, with
positive enthusiasm–and accepted important posts in the new Soviet cultural
administration.

Punin. Art no longer aimed to convey reality, whether mental or physical. The attention of the artist was henceforth directed toward studying the specific properties of his materials. For the Futurists, as we have seen, this was not a new problem. All they had to do was to continue the experiments begun by the poets on the autonomy of art ("the word as such"). In terms of painting, these experiments meant that they must seek autonomous plastic values in a reorganization of the painted work–and they led straight to the complete abandonment of easel painting.

Malevich, for example, though he arranged an exhibition of non-objective and Suprematist art in Moscow in 1919 and took part in a number of projects, appears to have given up painting altogether from 1918 onward in order to devote himself to theoretical reflection, to teaching, and to fresh experiments.

Agitprop, Proletkult

The notion of the democratization of art, which the Futurists also preached, was capable of realization in large-scale projects in the field of revolutionary propaganda–Agitprop, as it was called for short. Between 1917 and 1922 all major holidays, anniversaries of events connected with the revolution, and congresses were given monumental sets. For the first anniversary of October, 1917, a number of artists including Altman, Puni, Shterenberg, Malevich, and Tatlin conceived a vast spectacle for Moscow and Petrograd, plastering both cities with abstract diagrams and colored panels and setting up dynamic rhythms punctuated by flags and inscriptions. The monumentality of the undertaking quite alarmed the few foreign visitors present. They saw it (with every justification) as representing the end of a world.

The art of propaganda, mass art, and the solemn erection of monuments dedicated to the revolutionaries of past ages created an atmosphere of ongoing celebration that the Futurists adored. Revolution, for them, was a continuous

dynamic process. It was an end in itself. Propaganda trains and boats left Moscow decorated by avant-garde artists. The Russian Telegraph Agency (Rosta) placed in its display windows the famous posters of which Maiakovsky was such a master. Art had left the palaces and museums and come down into the street. There are few examples of Futurist painting from this period: artists preferred to work in the more accessible fields of poster design, typography, and street decoration.

The Futurist utopia, accepted and encouraged even during the difficult period of war communism (1918–21), lost much of its attraction in the eyes of the authorities once the Bolsheviks were victorious on all fronts and it was time to give the Soviet state its definitive shape.

The avant-garde was not alone in wanting to carry out a "cultural revolution," although the privileged position it enjoyed within IZO and in education meant that it was uniquely well placed to do so. It found a worthy adversary in the Proletarian Organization for Culture and Education (Proletkult). Founded in 1906 and revived in October, 1917, this was the only cultural institution to escape the tutelage of Lunacharsky's People's Commissariat of Education. At its first congress, held in September,

100 Nathan Altman: **Material Assemblage**, 1920. Oil, enamel, plaster,
glue, sawdust, 83 × 65.5 cm (oval).
State Russian Museum, Leningrad.

1917, Proletkult stressed the need for complete autonomy vis-à-vis the state administration. The simple propositions on which the organization was based enabled it to attract large numbers of adherents, at least until 1920. Those ideas were put forward by Alexander Bogdanov, who was the movement's theorist even before October, 1917. Basically they were that the proletariat, in its struggle against the bourgeoisie, needed to organize its forces with the aid of a class art that would be collectivist in spirit in line with altered socio-economic conditions. In opposition to the

Futurists, the partisans of Proletkult denied the autonomy of art and of the creative process. They saw culture as being only one arena for an ideological struggle to be fought on strict class lines.

Lenin was among the first to criticize the stance taken by Proletkult. In his famous letter to the party Central Committee of September, 1920, he remarked, "Under the cloak of proletarian culture workers are being offered bourgeois philosophical ideas (Mach) while in the field of art an attempt is being made to foist ugliness and distortion upon them." The Futurists saw Pro-

letkult as the antithesis of a revolutionary art. "Changing the subject is trivial!" wrote an indignant Punin, criticizing Proletkult's "addiction to the past." However, a partial synthesis of Futurist ideas and those of Proletkult was soon to give birth to constructivism, the most original movement to come out of the Soviet avant-garde.

Tatlin and Malevich

The Futurist revolt, with its anarchist determination to deny tradition wholesale, found itself at cross purposes with the ideas of the Bolshevik leadership. Lunacharsky defended the avant-garde, at least at the outset. He was editor-in-chief of the review *The Art of the Commune*, in which the Futurists published their most virulent attacks on their adversaries. But even he tried to mitigate their destructive impulses by prescribing "a teaspoonful of antidote" (*The Art of the Commune*, no. 4). Lenin himself joined in the argument by professing his disgust at "this nonsense that seeks to destroy and reject what is beautiful purely on the grounds that it is old. We must preserve the beautiful, draw inspiration from it, *develop* the finest traditions of our existing culture instead of trying to *invent* a new culture at all costs." The debate was not entirely theoretical, now that the state, as sole patron of the arts, distributed all commissions and also allocated studios, materials, and even food.

The "dictatorship" of "leftist" artists was possible only in quite specific historical conditions. It corresponded to the heroic period of Soviet Communism. When the New Economic Policy or NEP was introduced in March 1921 a certain return to order began to make itself felt in every sphere of social life. Initially there was a polarization of artistic attitudes and ideologies, with the party and state authorities acting as supreme arbiters. This confrontation between "leftist" artists on the one hand and "academic" artists on the other was not of course something that came about suddenly. Its beginnings date back to 1919, when in the case of certain artists rejection of the traditional forms of art became transformed into a desire to create a fresh ideological basis for art, while in others the defense of traditional form became an ideology in itself.

In fact it was a question of defining the function of art in society and the artist's role in the formation of a new culture. The last occasion on which the entire avant-garde presented a united front was the Tenth State Exhibition, entitled "Non-Objective Art and Suprematism."

102 Liubov Popova: **Composition**, 1921. Gouache, varnish on paper, 31 × 32 cm. Private collection, Moscow. Popova's formal explorations of the dynamic tensions of colored masses within a painting were no doubt prompted by what she had learnt from Kazimir Malevich. They provided the theoretical basis for the lessons that she herself gave at this time at the new academy of arts known as Vkhutemas (Higher State Workshops for Art and Technology).

103 Konstantin Iuon: **The New Planet**, 1921. Tempera on card, 71 × 101 cm. Tretiakov Gallery, Moscow.
103 Konstantin Iuon: **The New Planet**, 1921. Tempera on card, 71 × 101 cm. Tretiakov Gallery, Moscow.
In the early 1920s, despite enormous economic difficulties, many artists and intellectuals saw communism as the one and only answer to all the world's problems. For them it symbolized universal happiness.

From that time on the paths of the former friends diverged. Malevich continued his Suprematist experiments, extending them to architecture and the applied arts, while at the same time pursuing his theoretical reflections–initially in Vitebsk and from 1923 in Petrograd (renamed Leningrad in 1924).

Tatlin, true to his theory concerning the "culture of materials," gave a fresh, universal dimension to the synthesis of the arts. His *Monument to the Third International* was to have been "built of iron and the revolution," which according to the artist would become the mate-

rials of contemporary classicism, comparable to marble in the past. The *Monument to the Third International* was the first attempt to combine purely artistic forms with purely utilitarian ones. This approach lay at the origin of Constructivist thinking.

The Applied Arts and the Search for New Forms

In 1918–19 the development of Suprematist theory drove Malevich to look beyond problems of color and surface.

matist thinking and to invade other aspects of everyday life. "The harmonization of architectural forms... will necessitate the replacement of existing furniture, crockery, clothes, and posters. I anticipate that the movement of architecture will significantly possess a Suprematist harmony of functional forms."

Today there seems to be no doubt that Malevich's utopian architectural projects exerted an influence at the design level on the work of young Soviet architects, even though they never resulted in an actual building. On the other hand the design projects worked out with his disciples, notably Ilia Chashnik and Nikolai Suetin, went into mass production. This was particularly true of the porcelain that became the glory of the famous Leningrad factory.

Suprematism did not set out to create a new civilization. What it sought to do was to rethink the world: "In treating art as an emotional perception of the world, he [Malevich] treated it as an activity that aimed at understanding rather than at knowledge" (Punin).

Constructivism, Inkhuk

The Moscow Constructivists found Malevich's "idealism" unacceptable. They were mainly interested in an immediate application in terms of material. His work was soon seen as being of purely laboratory interest and his institute regarded as a monastery. These charges finally led to its closure in 1926. The problem of "plastic construction," of the mutual relations between form and content and color and line, where construction was opposed to traditional composition, was a shared preoccupation of such artists as Exter, Popova, Rodchenko, Puni, and Rozanova.

The upshot of these pictorial experiments was seen at the " $5 \times 5 = 25$ " exhibition in Moscow in 1921, where five artists contributed five works each. The exhibition is generally thought to have represented the point of no return for easel painting within the Russian avant-garde. It showed works by Liubov Popova, Alexander Rodchenko, Alexander

104 Kazimir Malevich: **Arkhitekton Gota**, 1923. Plaster.
The cube, the principal element of Malevich's *arkhitektones*, is a three-dimensional square– the starting point of the Suprematist system. The *arkhitektonis* symbolized the "new world" for Malevich.

White became the sole representation of infinity while the surface, having come out of the frame, could wander freely in space. "We can no longer speak of Suprematism in painting. Painting has already come full circle; the very idea of the artist is a thing of the past. A true artist is an inveterate workman who constructs and arranges fresh symmetries in the creation of nature."

This new theory found embodiment in plaster constructions that Malevich called first *Planits* and then *Arkhitektonis*. The cube on which these were based was simply a three-dimensional extension of the square, the starting-point of the Suprematist system. Malevich believed that his *Planits* and *Arkhitektonis* would embody a New World, endowed with "an original form of meaning and awareness."

This was how architecture–in the broadest sense of the term–came to occupy a dominant position in Supre-

Vesnin, Varvara Stepanova, and Exter that were described as "series of experiments materializing construction." Popova's works analyzed the relationships between color and surface and between space and dynamism. Exter's examined the role of color contrasts and rhythms. Rodchenko exhibited three monochrome canvases–red, blue, and yellow–and defined "color as such," which he understood as a "pure and absolute" element aiming at the total *identity* of color.

Rodchenko's red canvas showed that painting had gone as far as it could go. "To continue along this path would be pure speculation, the antithesis of creation," concluded Nikolai Tarabukin, one of the most eminent art critics of the period. This analysis led directly to the total abandonment of easel painting (the last picture, Tarabukin declared, had been painted in 1920) and to a renewed questioning of the function of art and the usefulness of works of art.

All these theoretical debates and experiments took place within new cultural institutions such as Inkhuk (Institute of Artistic Culture) and Vkhutemas (Higher State Workshops for Art and Technology), which in 1927 changed its name to Vkhutein (Higher Artistic-Technical Institute). The job of organizing Inkhuk, the object of which was to analyze art in a Communist society, was initially given to Vasilii (Wassily) Kandinsky. Kandinsky already held several official posts–at the Academy of Sciences, of which he was vice president, at IZO, and at the Central State Bureau of Museums and Acquisitions. Yet he still found time to paint (producing *In Gray* in 1919 and his Moscow series) and to teach.

Kandinsky's "idealist and spiritualist" positions having failed to find any supporters (he left Russia a few months later, in 1921), Tarabukin took over the job of reorganizing Inkhuk by bringing in a number of theorists of the Proletkult school such as Boris Kushner and Boris Arvatov. He also secured the collaboration of the artists Rodchenko and Stepanova and the architects Nikolai Ladovsky and Moisei Ginzburg.

Inkhuk, born of a merger between the Free Studios and the Moscow School of Applied Arts, was given university status. The teaching body included Rodchenko, Tatlin, Ladovsky, Popova, Udaltsova, El Lissitzky, and the Vesnin brothers. Structurally the Institute represented a negation of any kind of academic hierarchy among the arts. All faculties, whether on the production or on the artistic side, enjoyed equal rights, and contacts and exchanges were possible between them. In fact it actually overturned such a hierarchy qualitatively by having a "foundation" faculty to give all students a general artistic education.

Underlying Vkhutemas was the plan to get rid of the gulf separating art from industry and artists from the masses. This was one of the ideas that motivated the Constructivists. As early as 1919, replying to Maiakovsky's poem *The Poet is a Worker*, Osip Brik wrote in *The Artist and the Commune*:

> In the Commune everyone is a creator–not in dreams but in life, ... Artists must know how to do the job of art, how to execute the work: to paint pictures and make sets, to paint ceilings and walls, do drawings, produce posters and signs, build monuments to order. They carry out specific, socially useful tasks.... Such work gives the artist the right to place himself on the same level as other groups of workers.

The artist thus became a worker like any other. Granted, he worked in his own specific sphere, but the product of his work, purged of all aestheticism, had to be *useful* and serve the everyday needs of life and society.

Constructivist doctrine was founded on two basic theoretical texts: Naum Gabo's and his brother Anton Pevsner's *Realist Manifesto*, published in 1920, and *Constructivism* by Alexei Gan, which dates from 1920–21. The *Realist Manifesto* argued that "the art of today must finally break with all the conceptions of the past, with literature, anecdote, and decoration, and like an engineer building a bridge construct... our objects with the precision of a pair of

compasses." According to Gabo and Pevsner, sculpture must renounce volume. Depth was the only sculptural form measuring *space*, while kinetic rhythm gave expression to real *time*, time and space being the essential factors of life. Art could do no more than reproduce them. Gan's approach, though different in many respects, also preached rationality: "Nothing fortuitous or uncalculated, no blind taste or arbitrary aesthetic dictates. Everything must be thought out technically and in a functional manner."

It was the technical revolution, involving a radical change in both materials and technology leading to large-scale mass production, that constituted the focus of interest for the Constructivists. "Modern technology has revolutionized not only social and economic development but also aesthetic development," wrote Lazar El Lissitzky. According to the Constructivists, however, a true technological revolution could come about only in the wake of a genuine social revolution, making possible an alliance between technology and art. Artists would

105 Vasilii Kandinsky: **In Gray**, 1919. Oil on canvas, 129 × 176 cm. Musée national d'Art moderne, Georges Pompidou Center, Paris.
One of the few paintings dating from Kandinsky's Soviet period. Having been made responsible for education and the reorganization of cultural life, Kandinsky found it impossible to get his theories and methods accepted and left Soviet Russia in 1921.

99

106 Alexander Rodchenko: Photomontage for Vladimir Maiakovsky's **Pro
eto** 1923. Ludwig Collection, Cologne.
Photomontage was one of the ideal me-
dia for the implementation of Constructivist theory. Rodchenko was a master
of this new technique, creating several
hundred examples. In fact until recently
he was known only as a photographer:
his pictorial work is still largely un-
discovered.

107 Lazar El Lissitzky: **Prun 12 E**,
1920. Oil on canvas, 57.9 × 42.7 cm.
Busch-Reisinger Museum, Cambridge,
Massachusetts.
These "projects of affirmation of the
new in art" were among a hundred
utopian examples of global ambitions
fostered by the revolution. The *prun*
grew out of suprematism. Rejecting its
mystical aspect, El Lissitzky sought to
apply it in a tangible way to his theories. He believed the *prun* would "free"
painting from "the prison of the canvas" and, by integrating it with architecture, give it a fresh dimension.

then move "from the easel to the machine," as Nikolai Tarabukin put it.

In response to Gan's book Stephanova and Rodchenko drew up the *Program of the Productivist Group*. This document showed how constructivism had moved on to ideological problems, formulating a theory of production as creation and so automatically settling the question of the function of art:

> Our task consists in imparting a Communist meaning to the material labors of construction.... We shall carry out that work with the backing of scientific hypotheses. We shall stress the duty to achieve a synthesis of ideological and formal elements in order to turn laboratory work into practical activity. Our ideological options are as follows: our course is based exclusively on the theory of historical materialism. Influenced by the practice of the Soviet Government, we resolve to translate our experiments from the abstract into reality.

Productivism placed emphasis on the role of organization in the fields of production and ideology. This conception could not help but be a totalitarian one, since the aim was to intervene in every aspect of life in order to produce objects that should be useful and in conformity with their prime purpose. A work of art was as logical as a machine. Art in production and technological change in social revolution thus led automatically to the transformation of ways of thinking. The idea of enveloping all the arts in one—the art of constructing a new way of life—came to constitute the ideological foundation of constructivism. It must have been influenced by the political slogan of the time about the need "to build socialism." Everyone could unite in one great shared work of creation. "We are all creators," El Lissitzky said. If the Constructivists made *creativity* one of the kingpins of their ideology, it was because, unlike *creation*, it was not a matter for the artist alone.

In evolving a creative mode of perception the Constructivists sought to place the spectator in a situation where he was actively participating. They believed

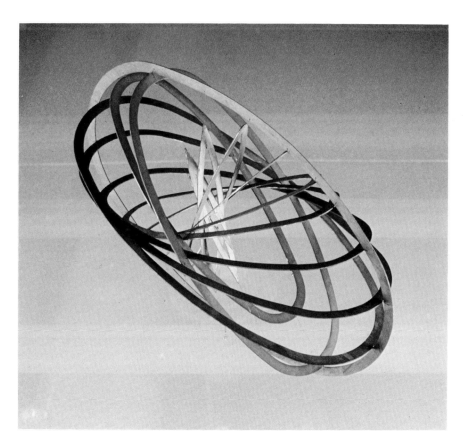

that, by applying the procedures of art to everyday life as a whole and adopting a creative approach to cultural phenomena, they had brought together the necessary conditions for changing men's minds. In abandoning the painted canvas but retaining the experience of painting, the Constructivists were able to engage in new forms of artistic expression that were more accessible to the masses: photomontage and typography, architectural and industrial projects, fashion, furniture design, and scenography for stage and screen.

Virtually all the artists in the Constructivist circle practiced photomontage, using it for poster design, book illustrations, scenery, and publicity displays. "We mean by photomontage the use of photography as a plastic resource," wrote Gustav Klutsis. "The combinative arrangement of the photograph replaces composition of an image by drawing." In photomontage the photograph is used both as a "treatment element" and as a "representation element." The con-

108 Alexander Rodchenko: **Sculpture in Space**, 1921. Wood and metal, 59 × 68 × 59 cm. Private collection, Moscow.
The painter, photographer, and sculptor Rodchenko, one of the leading theorists of constructivism, was possibly the most fertile artist working in Russia in the 1920s. Having abandoned easel painting as a "petty bourgeois art form," he sought to make his prolific output of direct use in daily life. His aim was always the same: to build socialism.

101

109 Mikhail Matiushin: **Movement in Space** (white ground), 1917-18. Oil on canvas, 124 × 168 cm. State Russian Museum, Leningrad.
The influence of the musician, painter, and theorist Matiushin within the Russian avant-garde was great, particularly on Kazimir Malevich, his friend and colleague at the Leningrad Institute of Artistic Culture.

structivists—and in particular Rodchenko, El Lissitzky, and the Stenberg brothers Georgii and Vladimir—were greatly attracted by the possibilities of this new technique, notably its efficacy, which derived from its documentary value, and its expressiveness ("a power of effect on the spectator impossible to achieve through graphic representation" was how Klutsis put it).

The same concern to awaken creativity among the masses led the Construc-

tivists to look again at the problems of reading in everyday life and hence to concern themselves with typography, which they invariably approached from the plastic standpoint. El Lissitzky, for example, used the same spatial arrangements in his typographical compositions as he used in his own *Prouns* —Suprematist-inspired canvases that he defined as an intermediate form between painting and architecture. Similarly Rodchenko, in his experiments in

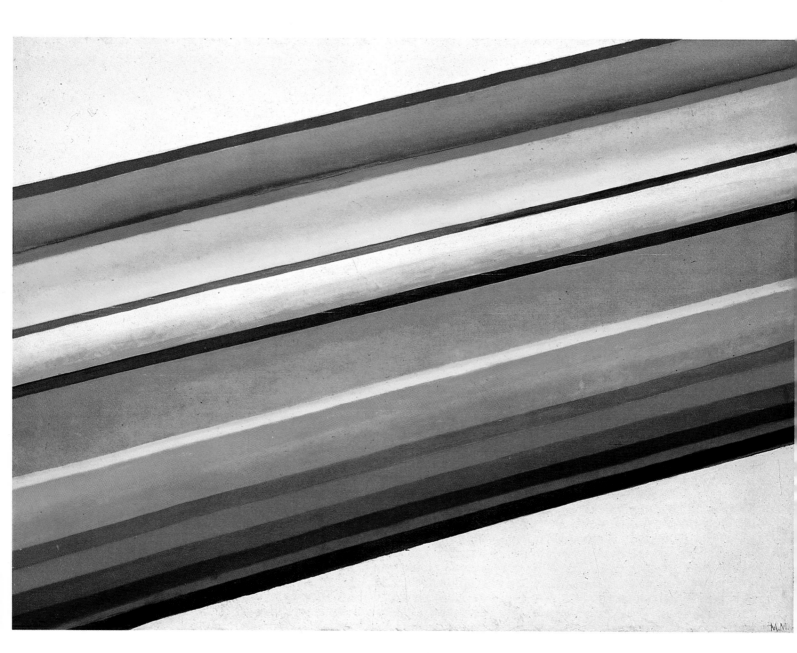

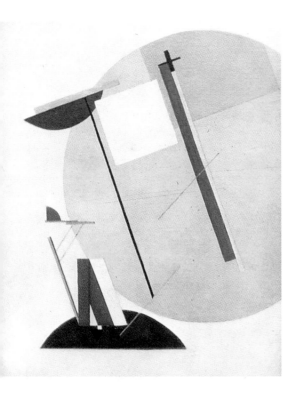

the fields of books, posters, and photomontage, applied the same principles that had formerly governed his painting. The aim of introducing art into industry and so creating a wholly new mode of existence prompted the Constructivists to extend their activities into such spheres as fashion, furniture, and porcelain. Soviet design was undoubtedly born at Vkhutemas, where the individual faculties kept in constant touch with factories. The metallurgy faculty, which Rodchenko headed, devised models for railway cars, streetcars, and furniture for workingmen's clubs. The textile faculty, where Stepanova, Exter, and Popova taught, produced fabrics and garments. Utility, economy, and functionalism governed all these experiments. Unfortunately the level of Soviet industrial development was then incapable of satisfying the Constructivists' demands, and their monopolistic claims to organize all aspects of life, including production, placed them in ever worsening conflict situations. The everyday life that they sought to change so much eventually proved stronger than their utopia.

The Elimination of the Avant-Garde

The battle against "leftist" art and subsequently against "formalism" went through several stages as the situation in Soviet Russia itself developed. Until 1922 the avant-garde enjoyed immense power. Its attacks on "addiction to the past" and on every aspect of academic tradition (the Moscow branch of the Academy of Arts was closed down for a while in 1918!) met with no real resistance. The artists of the left were seen as unconditional partisans of the revolution. They had also been the first to adopt the political language of the Bolsheviks in their declarations. All this made them seem unassailable during the Civil War years. The proletariat was led by a minority, namely the Communist party; in the same way the arts must be entrusted to their most enlightened representatives, namely the avant-garde. With the advent of peace and the introduction of the New Economic Policy the situation changed: "socialism in one country" could appeal to national tradition as well.

In 1922 the artists of the Traveling Exhibitions Society, true to the pictorial manner of their illustrious predecessors, merged with the Union of Russian Artists to found the Association of Painters of Revolutionary Russia (AKhRR). A manifesto signed by Nikolai Kasatkin, Alexander Moravov, Abram Arshipov, and Isaak Brodsky defined its outlook clearly: "We regard it as our civic duty to reproduce in an artistic and documentary fashion the greatest moments of our history seen in their revolutionary dimension. We shall portray the everyday life of the Red Army soldiers, workers, peasants, and the heroes of the revolution and of labor. We shall give events their true image, rather than the freakish abstractions that are discrediting our revolution in the eyes of the international proletariat." Many of the AKhRR artists were products of the Moscow Academy (e.g. Boris Ioganson, Terpsikhorov, N. Maliutin, Kasatkin, and Mitrofan Grekov). The Association became an active organizer of "mis-

110   Lazar El Lissitzky: **Prun 3 A (Prun 62)**, 1923. Oil on canvas, 71.1 × 58.4 cm, County Museum of Art, Los Angeles, California.

111 Alexander Deineka: **Textile Workers**, 1927. Oil on canvas, 170.4 × 194.4 cm. State Russian Museum, Leningrad.
A former student of the Vkhutemas and one of the founders of the OST group (the Society of Easel Painters), Deineka embodied the Constructivist-inspired dream of the industrialization and technical progress of Soviet society.

112 Alexander Deineka: **The Defense of Petrograd**, 1928. Oil on canvas, 210 × 230 cm. Central Museum of the Armed Forces, Moscow. Ten years afterward, the October Revolution had already achieved the status of myth. Deineka's treatment of the subject–sober, economical, and devoid of triumphalism– resembles a propaganda poster.

105

sions" in factories and among the troops; it also mounted regular exhibitions and was active in propaganda. Its method, dubbed "heroic realism," was concerned essentially with content and occasionally with titling; the pictorial system used never stepped outside the bounds of the figurative traditions of the nineteenth century. The AKhRR enjoyed official backing from 1924, and by the end of the 1920s it had become the country's largest artistic organization. It eventually swallowed several other groups to become, in 1930, the Federative Union of Soviet Artists and later the Union of Painters, Sculptors, and Graphic Artists.

113   Alexander Labas: **The Airship and the Orphanage**, 1930. Oil on canvas, 160 × 80 cm. State Russian Museum, Leningrad.
Like Alexander Deineka, Labas was a member of the OST group. He too introduced into his painting motifs associated with industrialization, tinged with a certain romanticism.

Around the mid-1920s, however, realism still enjoyed a certain freedom of interpretation, despite its adoption as the official style. In 1925 a number of former Vkhutemas students, led by Alexander Deineka, Iurii Pimenov, and Petr Villiams/Williams, founded the Society of Easel Painters (in Russian, OST). True to their master, David Shterenberg, and still imbued with Constructivist illusions, they took their subject matter from the city, industrialization, and the dynamaic nature of modern life. Their paintings portrayed machines, sportsmen, movement, and the like, using fragmented composition, contrasting colors, and sharp-edged rhythms. Two other members of OST–Alexander Tyshler and Alexander Labas–worked in a more imaginative vein, incorporating dream elements handled with a certain lyricism.

The former Jack of Diamonds artists Petr Konchalovsky, Alexander Kuprin, Aristarkh Lentulov, and Robert Falk, having regrouped in the Association of Muscovite Artists, continued their experiments bearing on French post-impressionism. Pavel Kuznetsov and Martiros Sarian (both still under the spell of the East), Kuzma Petrov-Vodkin, the sculptors Vera Mukhina and Alexander Matveev, and the graphic artists Vladimir Favorsky, Vladimir Lebedev, and Mikolai Kupreanov worked within the Union of the Four Arts. Their style did not change radically. All that appeared to interest them was the professional problems specific to each form of art. Just occasionally, though, for incidental reasons, they would take their subject matter from Soviet reality, an example being Petrov-Vodkin's *Death of the Commissar*, which was painted for the tenth anniversary of the foundation of the Red Army.

At the same exhibition Kazimir Malevich showed his *Red Cavalry at Full Gallop*. Recalled abruptly from Berlin in 1926 after his one-man show but banned from teaching, Malevich returned to figuration while still trying to preserve his Suprematist convictions, at least as far as colors were concerned. Those convictions had doubtless been

114 Kuzma Petrov-Vodkin: **Death of the Commissar**, 1928. Oil on canvas, 196 × 248 cm. State Russian Museum, Leningrad.
This occasional work— it was painted for the anniversary of the Red Army— nevertheless reflects Petrov-Vodkin's current preoccupations. It shows him true to his lyrical symbolism and to an advanced degree of formal experimentation with problems of space.

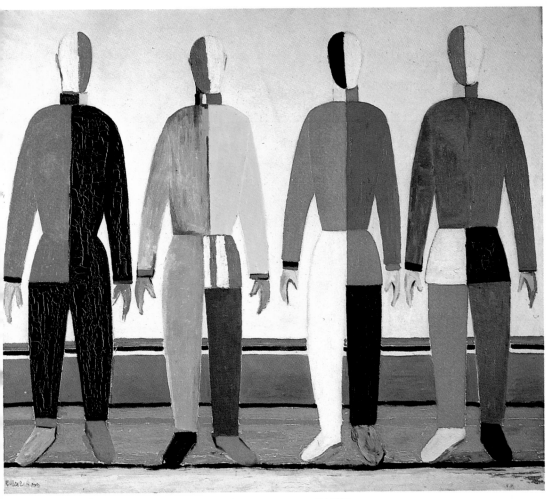

115 Kazimir Malevich: **The Athletes, Suprematism within an Outline**, 1929. Oil on canvas, 142 × 164 cm. State Russian Museum, Leningrad.
In the late 1920s, before the canons of "Socialist realism" were fully elaborated, certain artists enjoyed relative freedom of creation on condition that they respected figuration in their works. Malevich painted a whole series of remarkable pictures at that time. In most of them Suprematist colors were applied to peasant themes or to the human figure, with the face left featureless, in the manner of Chirico.

enhanced by the lessons of Mikhail Matiushin, his colleague at the Leningrad Institute. Collectivization, which was destroying the whole peasant culture so dear to Malevich, prompted his "peasant" series of paintings, which are full of symbolic references of a nostalgic nature *(Man Running, Arrest, The Red House)*. Painted between 1928 and 1930, these pictures adhered to the pictorial principles of "organic culture" as devised by Matiushin. Another major

116 Pavel Filonov: **The Formula of the Petrograd Proletariat**, late 1920s. Oil on canvas, 154 × 117 cm. State Russian Museum, Leningrad. Filonov's "formulas," executed in accordance with the principles of "analytical art" (his own invention), were totally uncompromising. Banned from teaching and given no commissions, Filonov lived in virtually complete isolation from 1928.

figure from the city that had now been renamed Leningrad, Pavel Filonov, continued to evolve his analytical method as expressed in innumerable "formulae" on universal subjects: the proletariat, world revolution, capitalism, imperialism, spring, and so on. Silenced in 1925, he continued to work in almost total isolation.

The era of imagination and the creative dream was nearing its end. It is enormously tempting to try to represent the

first ten years of Soviet art by picking out two symbolic works by a single artist, Vladimir Tatlin. The works are the *Monument to the Third International* and his flying machine, the *Letatlin*. The dreams and enthusiasm of the revolution as a universal phenomenon embodied in the projected tower end up, ten years later, as Icarus' dream of taking flight for freedom.

Stanislav Zadora

117   Isaak Brodsky: **Lenin at Smolny**, 1930. Oil on canvas, 190 × 287 cm. Tretiakov Gallery, Moscow. Brodsky occupied a rather special place among the realist painters of the 1930s in that his portraits of the great revolutionary leaders and eminent Soviets, in spite of or possibly because of his exemplary realism, occasionally came in for criticism. Done from photographs, his paintings were distinguished by their extreme "verism" and almost obsessive concern with detail.

4 Literature

Realism: From Tolstoi to Gorky

As the twentieth century opened, the most famous and the most widely read Russian writer, both in his own country and abroad, was undoubtedly Leo Tolstoi. Born in 1828 and without a serious rival since Dostoevsky's death in 1881, by 1900 he already had half a century of literary activity behind him. Yet his productivity and his combativeness were undiminished. Indeed, from the 1890s on he rejected the religious authorities as well as the political authorities—notably the censor. His stance made him the implicit spokesman of a burgeoning discontent throughout tsarist Russia.

In 1898 his book *What is Art?*, which summarized his aesthetic and social ideas, produced a powerful impact on Russian intellectual circles. In fact it is impossible to exaggerate the importance of this book. Many of the ideas contained in it were to crop up again not only in most of the debates but in most of the official programs dealing with art and literature in tsarist Russia and subsequently in the Soviet Union during the early part of this century. In *What is Art?* Tolstoi saw himself as the prophet of what he called "the art of the future."

[It] will not consist in imparting sentiments accessible only to certain members of the wealthy classes, as is the case at present: it will be an art realizing the highest religious awareness of the men of our time, and that alone. The only works that will be regarded as art will be those conveying the universal feelings that prompt men to unite in brotherhood or the universal feelings capable of uniting all men. Only that kind of art will be singled out, accepted, commended, and propagated. As for the art that conveys feelings arising out of the religious teachings of another time, ecclesiastical, patriotic, or voluptuous art, art that expresses feelings of superstitious awe, pride, vanity, or hero worship, art that arouses an exclusive love of one's own people or sensuality, such art will be considered bad and harmful and will be condemned and scorned by public opinion. And as for all other manifestations of art, those expressing feelings accessible only to certain persons, they will be seen as negligible and will be neither rejected nor welcomed. Moreover, the sole judges of art will not be the class of wealthy people, as is the case today, but the people as a whole. Furthermore, for a work to be recognized as good and to be commended and propagated, it will have to satisfy the requirements not of a few people in identical, often artificial circum-

118 Georgii Iakulov, cover of **The Poets' Spring Salon**, 1918.
The Poets' Spring Salon is typical of the joint collections published in the years immediately following the revolution. Every school is represented here: symbolism by Briusov, Balmont, Blok, and Sologub, acmeism by Gumilev, Akhmatova, and Mandelshtam, and futurism by David Burliuk, Maiakovsky, and Kamensky; also included are such independents as Kliuev, Esenin, and Tsvetaeva.

111

119   The last portrait of **Leo Tolstoi**, taken on July 31, 1908.
After Dostoevsky's death in 1881 Lev Tolstoi was regarded as the greatest Russian writer of his day. His influence was considerable, even outside intellectual circles. However, the authorities were suspicious of his sympathetic attitude toward certain forms of anarchism.

stances but of all men, of the great human masses in the natural conditions of labor.

Art and literature as thus defined, created by everyone for everyone, were the very antithesis of symbolism, which at the time was felt to be the exclusive preserve of a minority of decadent aesthetes. Equally reprehensible in Tolstoi's view was academic work, which he denounced as stemming from a desire for profit and for glory in the eyes of the ruling classes. It is also clear that such a definition already went some way toward a dictatorship of majority taste, as both the proletarian writers and Andrei Zhdanov were to recall at a later date. That is not to say that Tolstoi, who was fundamentally opposed to authoritar-

ianism of any kind, would have approved of either.

At the turn of the century, then, the old writer was still active. As well as essays Tolstoi continued to produce novels: *Resurrection* was completed in 1899 and *Hadji Murad* in 1904. He also had plays produced: *The Living Corpse* in 1900 and *Everything Stems from It* in 1910, the year of his death. His passing marked the end of an era in Russia. It was no accident that the great aesthetic debates did not begin until 1910.

A friend and admirer of Tolstoi—who incidentally returned the compliment —was Anton Chekhov, another writer who bestrode two centuries. Despite weak health and intrigues, the little Moscow doctor continued until the end of his short life to write short stories (*In the*

120 **Anton Chekhov and his wife, the actress Olga Knipper**, in 1901.
During his brief career Anton Chekhov (1860-1906) wrote a substantial number of short stories and plays. The universal success his work enjoys today should not delude us into thinking that the writer was always successful in his lifetime.

121 **Leo Tolstoi and Anton Chekhov**, 1901. State Literature Museum, Moscow.
Tolstoi and Chekhov had a genuine respect for each other, notwithstanding their widely differing approaches to literature. Here they are photographed together on holiday in the Crimea in 1901.

Ravine, for example) and above all plays, including *Three Sisters* (1900) and *The Cherry Orchard*, which Konstantin Stanislavsky produced in Moscow shortly before the writer's death in 1904. Chekhov, who never lost his popularity, was to exert considerable influence, although unlike Tolstoi he had little inclination for theory. Petr Kropotkin was able to demonstrate in his *Ideal and Reality in Russian Literature* (given as lectures in 1901 and published in Russian in 1907) that from Pushkin to Chekhov, taking in Dostoevsky and Tolstoi on the way, every great Russian writer had been fundamentally opposed to the regime and concerned about the extreme poverty of the people.

But the writer who was to come to symbolize the twentieth century was Maxim Gorky. After an unhappy childhood and extensive wanderings, during which he did a variety of jobs, Alexei Maximovich Peshkov significantly adopted the pseudonym "Gorky" ("the bitter one") to sign his books. A self-educated man, he first gained attention in the 1890s with his stories of vagrants.

122   This picture is actually a montage, adding **Maxim Gorky** to the photograph of **Tolstoi** and **Chekhov** and so completing the trio of the most famous Russian writers of the early years of this century.

These social outcasts, whether victims or rebels, were to earn him real notoriety in 1902 when Stanislavsky produced his play *The Lower Depths* in Moscow. Already in *Foma Gordeev* (1899) Gorky shows us a man breaking with the wealthy and becoming a vagrant through his rejection of hypocrisy and money, while in *The Three* (1902) he uncompromisingly portrays the vices of society on the basis of three examples. The generosity informing Gorky's work was what accounted for his great success: "It is the living we must love," says the wise old Luka in *The Lower Depths*. A convinced revolutionary, Gorky was arrested in 1905. He was freed the following year and went to live abroad. It was during this time that he became friends with Lenin. In exile he wrote *Mother* (1906–7), which both revolutionary militants and admirers of realism hailed as an exemplary work.

Beginning in 1902 and for some ten years thereafter, Gorky gathered a group of writers round him. Works were published under the imprint "Knowledge" (*Znanie*) by Gorky himself (even during his exile), Leonid Andreev, Ivan Bunin, and Alexander Kuprin, to name only the best known. Ivan Bunin started out as a poet before proving himself a major naturalistic novelist with *The Village* (1909), in which he describes a gallery of characters living in a drab, dismal rural environment. Possibly his finest book is *The Gentleman from San Franciso* (1915), which portrays a rich and powerful man whose life is as empty as those of the people he exploits. Alexander Kuprin, whose works included *Moloch* (1896) and *The Pit* (1912), resembled Gorky in his denunciation of social injustices, notably the living conditions of factory workers and the no less inhuman conditions in which prostitutes plied their trade. Leonid Andreev made his mark in 1902 with a play (*Thought*) and a story (*The Abyss*). Andreev went beyond naturalism to examine man's inner depths, the unconscious part of his being. His best known work is *The Story of the Seven Who Were Hanged* (1908), an account of the last moments of seven revolutionaries.

Symbolism Between St. Petersburg and Moscow

The reaction to this powerful wave of realism was an equally important Symbolist movement that began to manifest itself in the last years of the nineteenth century. According to its leading figure, Valerii Briusov, this amounted to a veritable renaissance in Russian literature: "The renaissance occurred around

123 **Ivan Bunin** (1870–1953) began his career as a poet, devoting himself to the novel only after the publication of *The Village* in 1909. His best-known book, *The Gentleman from San Francisco*, dates from 1915. Shortly after that he emigrated to France, where he continued to write, winning the Nobel Prize for Literature in 1933.

1890. Russian lyricism owes it in part to a profound study of the modern poetry of the Western peoples, chiefly Britain and France. The young Russian poets endeavored, as they examined the poetry of the English pre-Raphaelites and the early French Symbolists, to take the latter's discoveries in the fields of ideas and meter and adapt them to their own literature." In a country whose intellectuals all spoke French as their second language (a tradition that went back to the court of Catherine the Great), Charles Baudelaire and his Symbolist progeny were rapidly discovered, assimilated, and translated. But the younger genera-

116

tion also rapidly became acquainted with the British and American authors then fashionable in Paris: not only the pre-Raphaelites but also Edgar Allan Poe, Oscar Wilde, and Walt Whitman. Later the German Friedrich Nietzsche joined the list of influential personages. The Russian Symbolists were great travelers. They loved going to Paris, of course, but they also visited Italy and Germany; Andrei Belyi went to Africa, and Konstantin Balmont actually wrote his book *Serpentine Flowers* on a trip to the pre-Columbian sites. Each of them saw it as his duty to make the writers he admired known in Russia: Fedor Sologub translated Paul Verlaine, Dmitrii Merezhkovsky and Konstantin Balmont translated Poe, and Briusov translated Emile Verhaeren, Maurice Maeterlinck, René Ghil, Wilde, and many others.

The whole Symbolist movement had the great merit that it introduced new themes and a fresh atmosphere into Russian literature–though at the risk of "going over the top." In Sologub's case, an excessive admiration for Baudelaire led him to delight in the morbid and the demonic. Here he is in a poem of 1894:

O death, I am yours. All around
I see you alone. Loathsome to me
Are the paths of this earth.
Men's exaltations pass me by;
Their battles, feastings, fairs
Are so much din in the dust.

The exaggerated aestheticism of these poets sometimes made their work difficult to read, once the contemporary craze had run its course. "I am the slave of my dreams," wrote the poet Zinaida Hippius in 1896, and she was only one of many poets who fled into their ivory towers to escape the problems of the moment. In fact "The Tower" was what the great scholar and poet Viacheslav Ivanov called his St. Petersburg apartment where meetings were held every Wednesday to discuss religion, esoterism, and poetry–a long way off, the participants liked to think, from the rifle fire of the 1905 Revolution. Here is a typical poem by Balmont entitled *The Valleys of Dream*:

I shall go into the valleys of dream
Where flowers lean and bloom.
Out there, out there where the Moon
Dives down giant chasms.

The moon dives across the sky
In one unending leap.
The secret valleys of dream
Breathe a dense opium.

Out there a strange string sounds
Unbrushed by the bow.
The soul in the valleys of dream
At the heart of the limitless wave.

Such writers were content with abstraction, with dreams and wreaths of smoke, as it were–all the whorls of Art Nouveau and the "modern style," all the nebulosity of a certain kind of literary impressionism.

Later some of the younger poets reacted sharply to all these languorous leitmotivs. Nikolai Gumilev, for example, wrote: "Konstantin Balmont, so fragile, so disembodied in his first period, came to love things more and more passionately and to place the music potentially concealed in them above all else. His epithets did not aim at pre-

117

cision; it was their sound he was after, not the concept they covered...."

As well as absorbing these foreign influences Russian symbolism was also rooted in the kind of mysticism—more Asian than Slav in origin—that has always been ready to crop up in Russian philosophy and literature. In this sense the biggest influence at the beginning of the century was undoubtedly Vladimir Soloviev. A philosopher who wrote poetry on the side, Soloviev began to expound his views in a book published in France in 1889 with the title *La Russie et l'Eglise universelle* (Eng. trans.: *Russia and the Universal Church*, 1948). In contrast to Merezhkovsky and Ivanov, his basic religiosity did not prevent him from being open to the idea of revolution. This meant that poets such as Alexander Blok always remembered the lesson he taught. Here is a typical quatrain from Soloviev's work:

Pan-Mongolism, the uncouth name
Yet sounds sweet to my ear.
As if it presaged
A lofty destiny divine.

It is significant that Blok took the first two lines as an epigraph for his famous poem *The Scythians*. Pretensions to a non-Western cultural specificity were common in the early part of the century —among the Futurists, for instance, notably Velimir Khlebnikov. As for Soloviev's particular philosophy of religious syncretism, traces of it may be found in Nikolai Berdiaev and even in Lev Shestov and Petr Uspensky.

After 1900 there was a reaction within symbolism itself. At the prompting of the Belgian poet Verhaeren, with whom he was in regular contact, Briusov began to introduce more urban, down-to-earth themes as well as a certain unanimism into his own poetry. Ophelia is no longer the pale, pre-Raphaelite heroine floating among flowers; she is a despairing city girl who hurls herself from the window of an apartment block:

The crowd shivered and, being curious, paused
About the body bleeding in the dust....

Then life resumed its noisy, painted course,
Automobiles and streetcars fleeing in the distance.

This state of mind corresponded to the arrival of a new generation of Symbolists that included Maximilian Voloshin, Alexander Blok, and Andrei Belyi. Blok did relatively little foreign traveling (Germany, Italy, France), but the other two poets certainly kept up the Symbolist tradition. Belyi spent several years abroad, notably in Switzerland where he stayed with Rudolf Steiner, whose anthroposophical teachings influenced his work. Voloshin, forced into exile for involvement in political agitation in Moscow, spent the years 1910–17 in Paris, where he became a well-known figure in Montparnasse. He was often to be seen in the company of the Italian and Mexican artists Amedeo Modigliani and Diego Rivera, painting having always been almost as strong a passion with him as poetry.

Alexander Blok rapidly became the most famous of the Symbolists (today he is the only one who still retains a large readership). A friend of Merezhkovsky and Hippius, in 1904 he met the Moscow poets Briusov, Balmont, and Belyi (who was to become his friend). The same year saw the publication of his first collection, *Verses about the Beautiful Lady*. The title was symptomatic: Blok was to spend his whole life pursuing a "beautiful lady," who was alternately an earthly creature of the flesh and some kind of goddess, a reincarnation of Soloviev's Sophia (Divine Wisdom) and later a personification either of salvation or of revolution. In 1909 she still preserved her Symbolist langor:

How narrow is the circle of our being;
Since all roads lead to Rome, we foresee
The past extending into a future
That will repeat itself endlessly, slavishly.

And I like the rest know what awaits me

As I march down my darkening road:
To worship her once again, She who
    reigns in the highest
And whom I shall yet betray here on
    earth.

Mystical symbolism here reached its apogee. It was at this point that Blok wrote: "The sun of naive realism has set; nothing whatever can now be imagined outside of symbolism. That is why writers, even very gifted ones, can do nothing with art if they have not been baptized by *the fire and spirit of symbolism*. Racking one's brains to think of fresh inventions does not yet mean being an artist, but being an artist means standing up to the winds of the world of art, a world utterly different from this one." Blok seems to have been attacking the groups of artists associated with the smart reviews and the fashions they promoted: *The Scales*, Sergei Diaghilev's *World of Art, The Golden Fleece*. Yet he himself contributed to the most influential of them, namely *The Scales* (1904–9), which Briusov edited. *The Scales* distinguished itself from the others by the attention it paid to things French, both in the fine arts and in literature. Its French correspondent was the poet René Ghil, whose theories (a development of Baudelaire's *correspondances*) were propagated by Briusov and created something of a stir in Russia—notably among such Futurists as Khlebnikov and Matiushin. Blok felt that aesthetic affectations were out of place after the violent events of 1905.

The "fresh inventions" over which people were "racking their brains" may have been a reference to Belyi's experiments in the field of language. It was in his prose rather than in his investigations into verse structure that Andrei Belyi (real name: Boris Bugaev) was most innovative. In the early years of the century he wrote a sequence of rhythmic prose pieces that he called *Symphonies*. In his desire to get as close to music as possible he ended up using words more for their sound than for their meaning. It was a thoroughly Symbolist preoccupation, but Belyi took it so far that sometimes sound was all that

was left; there was no meaning. In this he anticipated the experiments of the Futurists. The formalist linguists of the 1920s acknowledged their debt to his pioneering work. Viktor Shklovsky wrote in his *Theory of Prose* (1929) that "the new Russian literature would have been impossible without the *Symphonies.*" Belyi continued his prose experiments in a series of novels published

126 Cover of the review **Apollon**, 1911, No. 2.
Apollon was published from 1909 to 1917. Symbolist at first, it very soon came under the influence of Nikolai Gumilev and the Acmeists. In 1910 it brought out a special French issue, put together by the poet René Ghil. The review also championed the painter and composer Mikalojus Ciurlionis.

127 This photograph, taken before the revolution, shows a highly disparate group.
Left to right, seated: Alexei Remizov and Fedor Sologub; **standing**: Andrei Belyi, Boris Pilniak, Alexei Tolstoi, and Benedikt Livshits. Remizov, Belyi, and Tolstoi were to emigrate to Paris and Berlin, though only Remizov remained in exile. Sologub was persecuted after the revolution and died of a broken heart; Pilniak and Livshits were "liquidated" under Stalin.

before and after the revolution, notably *Petersburg* and *Moscow*. His rhythmic effects and playing on words (the reader is sometimes reminded of Joyce's *Finnegans Wake*) irritated some commentators after the revolution. Possibly the harshest verdict was Trotsky's: "Belyi searches words as the Pythagoreans searched numbers for a second, private, hidden meaning. That is why he often finds himself up a blind alley" (*Literature and Revolution*, 1923). In fact Belyi was preparing ground that would be explored systematically by the Futurists and, after them, by such novelists as Boris Pilniak and Evgenii Zamiatin.

Here we must mention a remarkable writer, Alexei Remizov, who was to exert a similar influence. He made his debut in the principal Symbolist reviews, but his preoccupations were slightly different. Instead of working on the musicality of the sentence, Remizov interested himself in the structure of literary narrative. Shklovsky wrote in *Zoo* (1923): "One day he told me: I don't want to go on beginning novels with 'Ivan Ivanovich was sitting at the table' .... Just as a cow eventually consumes the last blade of grass in a meadow, literary subjects become exhausted, methods wear out and disappear." Tired of the usual tricks of novel-writing, Remizov decided to upset the applecart. As early as 1905 his novel *The Pond* surprised critics with its unusually dis-

jointed construction. It is a family saga made even more somber by the chaotic way in which it is narrated, by the mingling of fantastic elements with realistic descriptions, and by a style laden with archaisms and neologisms. The atmosphere of pessimistic chaos reaches its nadir in *Sisters of the Cross* (1911), one of the blackest and cruellest works in the whole of Russian literature. It presents a series of piteous and violent characters who appear to embody everything mean and contemptible in society. Yet it is not for them that Remizov shows contempt but for the very respectable wife of a general: "She has neither murdered nor robbed and will never murder or rob because all that she does is eat." So neither the mysticism of Blok and Belyi, nor the diligent versatility of Briusov, nor the grim vision of Remizov prevented a whole section of the Symbolist movement from joining the Realists in their denunciation of society's evils. Most of them wished to see major changes, and some of them wanted an actual revolution.

Futurism

The movement known as Russian futurism began in painting before it manifested itself in literature. In 1907–8 Mikhail Larionov painted a number of unashamedly barbaric canvases that defied perspective, insulted good taste, and represented a complete rejection of the color games of the Impressionists and the elegant decorations of the Symbolist painters. But there was one writer who shared this same, radically new state of mind around the same period. His name was Velimir Khlebnikov. However, the Symbolists to whom he showed his poems did not take him seriously. He had to wait until 1910 before he found someone who would print such a work as his *Conjuration by Laughter*, an explosion of verbal virtuosity detonated from a single word. In this poem Khlebnikov, who had a wide knowledge of folk culture, had in mind the spells of sorcery, the magic formulae employed by the shamans or medicine-men who

held sway in the remoter reaches of the country. Russia was indeed a vast land encompassing all kinds of religious groups from whirling dervishes, who spun themselves round and round in search of ecstasy, to the flagellants of the Khlysty sect. And in this disturbed and restless period of its history prophets, charlatans, and mystical sects abounded and proliferated—just as they had in France before the revolution in 1789.

Velimir Khlebnikov applied his universally inquiring mind at an early age to a passionate study of mathemat-

128 Portrait of Velimir Khlebnikov by Nikolai Kulbin, 1913. State Russian Museum, Leningrad.
Khlebnikov (1885–1922), who as a keen Slavophile changed his first name from Viktor to Velimir, was a native of Astrakhan. The Futurists, following Vladimir Maiakovsky's lead, unanimously hailed him as their master and the greatest of their number.

129 This photograph, taken in 1914, shows four characters from slightly different backgrounds. Saltykov-Shchedrin Public Library, Leningrad.
Left to right: the Acmeist poet Osip Mandelshtam, who had published his first collection, **Stone**, the year before; the poet and critic Kornei Chukovsky; the illustrator Iurii Annenkov, who was to make a name for himself with his work in Blok's *The Twelve* before throwing himself into theatrical costume design; and the Futurist poet Benedikt Livshits, who published *The Wolves' Sun* in that year.

ics, history, mythology and folklore, and philology, among other subjects. He was also a proud Panslav, hostile to any systematic transposition into Russian culture of methods borrowed from abroad. It was in this spirit that he changed his first name Viktor to the non-Latin Velimir. Khlebnikov was an independent—yet the Futurists were always to hail him as their master.

The story really begins in 1908, when another young poet, Vasilii Kamensky, decided to publish one of Khlebnikov's poems in his review *Spring*. It was through Kamensky that Khlebnikov made contact in the following year with the Burliuk brothers, Elena Guro, and Mikhail Matiushin. The group's first public appearance together came with the publication in 1910 of an illustrated

allmanac or joint anthology printed on painted paper and entitled *The Breeding-Ground of Judges*. The moving spirit behind this was the painter and poet David Burliuk, the great organizer of the Russian avant-garde from now until the revolution; the contributors included David's brothers Nikolai and Vladimir (also both painters and poets), Elena Guro, Kamensky, and Khlebnikov. The volume contained a number of Primitivist poems by Kamensky extolling nature and the simple life in the manner of his novel *The Cabin*, which was published in the same year. But the most astonishing contribution was Khlebnikov's: in *Marquise Desaix* periods overlap and objects and inanimate beings exchange roles; in *The Crane* a giant bird composed of metal parts destroys the world;

while *The Menagerie* grieves over the lot of animals kept in confinement.

Shortly after this publication, which in its presentation broke completely with symbolism's customary elegance, the group was joined by three newcomers, the poets Vladimir Maiakovsky, Alexei Kruchenykh, and Benedikt Livshits. These men could also count on the sympathy of certain painters whom Burliuk met at the Jack of Diamonds exhibition, notably Mikhail Larionov, Natalia Goncharova, and Kazimir Malevich. As we have seen, when David Burliuk met Maiakovsky and admitted him to his circle of friends, Maiakovsky was just eighteen years old. A student at a Moscow art school, he had already served two prison terms for political agitation but had not yet published anything. It was Burliuk who convinced him of his talent for poetry.

In 1912 this small group of friends, who had begun to call themselves "Hylaea" (the ancient name of the Crimean region where they spent their holidays), published in Moscow what amounted to the first manifesto of Russian futurism, *A Slap in the Face of Public Taste*. The violent nature of this work was further underlined by its being bound in sackcloth. "We alone are the face of our time," declared the four signatories, David Burliuk, Khlebnikov, Kruchenykh, and Maiakovsky. They went on to wipe out the past, which was now "incomprehensible"; it was necessary to "chuck Pushkin, Tolstoi, etc., etc. overboard at the present time." Then came a string of insults aimed at all their elders from Gorky the Realist to Briusov the Symbolist: "Wash your hands if you have been in contact with the tacky muck of the books written by all those countless Leonid Andreevs. All those Maxim Gorkys, Kuprins, Bloks, Sologubs, Remizovs, Averchenkos, Chernys, Kuzmins, Bunins, etc., etc." In order to revitalize their obsolete language the new poets, scorning any idea of literary fame and thumbing their noses at public incomprehension, committed themselves to "increasing the volume of the poetic vocabulary with the aid of arbitrary, derived words." This statement lay at the basis of *zaum*, a transmental language made up of words that were either wholly invented or derived from existing roots (as distinct from the free verbal association and onomatopoeia of the Italian Futurists). The manifesto closed with a sort of excuse for any residue of "good sense" and "good taste" that might have survived in the writings of the signatories. Among the texts that followed it was not so much the very restrained, almost Acmeist poems of Livshits nor the extracts from Kandinsky's *Klänge* (included without the author's permission) but once again the pieces by Khlebnikov that seized the reader's attention by virtue of their novelty—from *The God of the Virgins*, a fairytale of pagan Russia, to a sort of nursery rhyme that already made extensive use of *zaum* language.

The other two newcomers, Kruchenykh and Maiakovsky, did not go unnoticed. Alexei Kruchenykh, who went on to become the most radical of the Futurists, already displayed his distinctive manner: lines with neither punctuation nor capital letters, chaotic stresses, and even spelling mistakes (which he maintained were an integral part of the writer's personality). Maiakovsky's contribution was a kind of urban poetry that offered an apocalyptic vision of the city not far removed from what we find in

130 **The Three**, illustrated by Malevich, brought together texts by Velimir Khlebnikov, Alexei Kruchenykh, and Elena Guro. Guro, who was married to Mikhail Matiushin, had died prematurely in that same year (1913).

the contemporary works of the German Expressionists:

A dull rain lashed the eyes
And behind
The neat
thought-threaded wire
netting
an eiderdown.
Lightly
resting
thereon,
the feet of the rising stars.
But the death
of the streetlamps,
tsars
with gas crowns,
made more distressing
to the eye
the hostile redolence of the street-
girls...

The *Slap in the Face of Public Taste* provoked a major literary scandal. those like Briusov and Gorky who looked kindly on the rise of a nonconformist younger generation were irritated. On the other hand it is not clear why the Acmeist group then in process of formation escaped vilification, though admittedly Gumilev had defended Khlebnikov and his friends on several occasions. In February, 1913, Gumilev wrote in the review *The Hyperborean*: "The group of writers that formed to publish this collection necessarily inspires confidence both by its indubitably revolutionary character in the verbal domain and by the lack of any quality of meanness in its vandalism. It devotes most of its attention to stylistic problems and is trying to restore to words the strength and freshness they have lost through use." That was an extremely tolerant reaction to the spirit of deliberate provocation that motivated these poets. Never mind: their movement was launched.

Meanwhile another group had appeared in St. Petersburg toward the end of 1911 whose members called themselves Ego-Futurists. In that year the best-known member of the group, Igor Severianin, had published a volume entitled *Electric Poems*. However, despite the title his poetry was closer to decadentism and the affectations of

Oscar Wilde than to true futurism. Among the Ego-Futurists, mention should be made of Vadim Shershenevich, who translated Marinetti's manifesto in 1914 and was one of the Italian Futurist's few fans in Russia. The critic Kornei Chukovsky commented revealingly: "Where the Ego-Futurists saw in their dreams young princes on diamond-studded thrones, Kruchenykh said of himself: 'I am a beast of burden, a donkey in a field.'"

Futurist Theories and Works: *Zaum*

The Hylaea group are nowadays described as Cubo-Futurists by analogy with the works of their painter friends, Larionov, Goncharova, Tatlin, Malevich, Rozanova, and Exter, who readily illustrated their publications. It helped to foster close relations between the two groups that the poets Guro, Kamensky, Maiakovsky, Kruchenykh, and of course the Burliuks themselves also painted and drew. A stream of manifestos and other publications, both collective and individual, began to appear. In 1913 and 1914 Khlebnikov and Kruchenykh published a series of important manifestos asking radical questions about grammar, punctuation, and spelling:

1) We have ceased to view the structure and pronunciation of words in accordance with the rules of grammar, seeing letters only as *orientations*. We have dislocated syntax.
2) We have begun to invest words with meaning *in accordance with their graphic and phonetic character*.
3) We acknowledge the role of suffixes and prefixes.
4) For the sake of the freedom of individuality we repudiate orthography.

It was because of this emphasis on individuality that the Futurists published their works by cyclostyle duplication, which in addition to the illustrations reproduced the poet's own handwrit-

124

131-135 **Tay li tay**, 1914. Private collection, Paris.
This spectacular volume, calligraphed and hand-decorated by a team consisting of Alexei Kruchenykh, Velimir Khlebnikov, and Olga Rozanova, was published in an edition of only fifty copies.

136-138 Produced entirely by hand, this last edition of Alexei Kruchenykh's and Velimir Khlebnikov's *Game in Hell*, 1913 was illustrated with lithographs by Olga Rozanova and Kazimir Malevich (the first edition was illustrated by Mikhail Larionov and Natalia Goncharova).

ing. The result was some of the twentieth century's handsomest and most inventive books, in which text and image form a perfect synthesis. The most spectacular among them were generally the books and brochures of Khlebnikov and Kruchenykh. Together they produced, among others, *Worldbackwards* (1912, with illustrations by Goncharova, Larionov, Tatlin, and I. R. Rogovin), *Half-Alive* (1913, with Larionov), *Game in Hell* (two editions in 1913, with Malevich and Rozanova), *Forestal Sound* (1913, with Rozanova), and *Tay Li Lay* (1914, with Rozanova). Alone, Kruchenykh published *Old-fashioned Love* (1912, with Larionov), *Hermits* (1913, with Goncharova), *Explosiveness* (1913, with Nikolai Kulbin, Goncharova, and Malevich; a second edition with Rozanova), and *Pomade* (1913, with Larionov), while Kruchenykh published *Creations* (1914, with D. Burliuk) and *Selected Poems* (1915, with Pavel Filonov). In these books, spelling and typography are often far from orthodox: the poems in *Worldbackwards* and the first edition of *Explosiveness* were printed with a rubber stamp, in different colors, and in a more or less chaotic fashion; quite often they are straight reproductions of the author's handwriting. Possibly the finest example in this style is *Tay Li Lay*, in which the handwritten text is closely entwined with motives designed by Olga Rozanova—or Velimir Khlebnikov's *Selected Poems*, calligraphed by Filonov. The illustrators showed themselves no less inventive, whether the style they adopted was Primitivist (Goncharova in *Game in Hell*), Futurist (Rozanova in *Explosiveness*), or Rayonist (Larionov in *Oldfashioned Love*). Larionov's lithographs appliqued on pages of gilded paper *(Pomade)*, for example, or Goncharova's cut-paper collages *(Worldbackwards)* are a very long way from the Symbolists' highly aesthetic editions printed on luxury paper. Perhaps the most astonishing of all was the slightly later *Transmental Book* (with the Russian word for "book" being deliberately misspelt) that Kruchenykh published in Moscow in 1916. His collaborators

included one Aliagrov (actually the linguist Roman Jakobson) but more importantly Olga Rozanova, Kruchenykh's wife. She contributed a series of linocuts on colored paper, inspired by playing cards, that blended futurism and primitivism; she also did two remarkable collages, one of which—on the cover—is simply a red cut-paper heart with a

139 Cover of **Pomade**, 1913. State Literature Museum, Moscow, and Martin-Malburet Collection, Paris. Published by Alexei Kruchenykh in 1913, *Pomade* was the prototype of the Futurist book. Designed in a small format, handwritten, and incorporating spelling mistakes and *zaum* language, it was illustrated with Primitivist drawings by Mikhail Larionov.

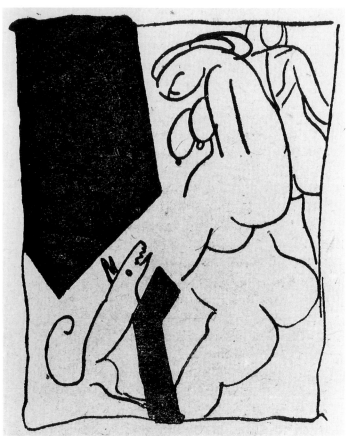

big white button fixed to it. It looks as if it has just been torn off some garment!

The two friends Kruchenykh and Khlebnikov did not have a monopoly in inventiveness. Any list of the finest books to come out of Russian futurism must also include Maiakovsky's *Vladimir Maiakovsky, Tragedy* (1914), illustrated by David and Vladimir Burliuk, and the famous *Tango with Cows* by Kamensky. In the latter the poems are printed on paper painted with large, brightly colored floral designs that contrast sharply with the deliberately barbaric black-and-white illustrations by the same two Burliuk brothers. The list must also take in—among many other works—the many compilations and almanacs published by the Futurists between 1910 and the early years of the revolution. In addition to *The Breeding-Ground* and *A Slap in the Face...* we must mention *The Three, The Missal of the Three* (1913), *First Journal of the Russian Futurists, Burst Moon, Roaring Parnassus* (1914), *The Archer* (1915), and *Masters of Moscow* (1916).

Among the many formal inventions of the Futurists, the one that has provoked the most discussion and which we must examine in rather more detail is *zaum*. It has been suggested that Elena Guro was the originator of this transmental language that reaches beyond words. Certainly her interest in lullabies, counting-rhymes, and children's language steered her in that direction. Her *Finland* (in *The Three*), for example, roughly translated, goes something like this:

Lula, lola, lala, lu
  Lisa, lola, lula-li.
    The needles whirr, whirr,
Ta-hi-hi, ti hi hu-hu.

    Is it a forest—is it a lake?
Is it that?

140 Mikhail Larionov, **Portrait of Vladimir Burliuk**, 1907.
Oil on canvas, 133 × 104 cm. Musée des Beaux-Arts, Lyons. Larionov and Natalia Goncharova on the one hand and the Burliuk brothers on the other were the twin powerhouses of the early days of Russian Futurism. Their alliance was short-lived, however.

141 This self-portrait of **Vladimir Burliuk** (1886–1917) is typical of the illustrations that filled the pages of such Futurist publications as *Roaring Parnassus* and *Mares' Milk* (1914). Their obvious affronts to common sense and distortions of the laws of perspective were calculated to provoke the bourgeoisie.

142 Drawing by **David Burliuk**. The painter and poet David Burliuk (1882–1967) was also the chief organizer of Futurist demonstrations and publications in the years before the revolution. Everything about him was characterised by a blend of audacity and naivety, of primitivism and easy grace.

143 Kazimir Malevich, **An English-man in Moscow**, 1913-14. Oil on canvas, 88 × 57 cm. Stedelijk Museum, Amsterdam.
Alexei Kruchenykh's friends used to say he looked like an Englishman, and it was thus that Malevich painted his portrait, complete with such recognizably Futurist attributes as top hat and wooden spoon. The other incongruous objects in Malevich's painting make it more Dadaist (before its time) than Futurist– which perfectly suited the flamboyant personality of this daring, disconcerting poet.

130

Alas, Anne, Lisa, Marie,
Hhei–rran!
Tra-deri-deri... du
Rollay–koolay–niyay-ay...

Kruchenykh and Khlebnikov were also interested in the child's world, its myths and language (they even published in collaboration with children). But their use of *zaum* went much further. "Speech and thought cannot keep up with the experience of inspiration," they maintained. "That is why the artist is free to express it not only in ordinary language, but also in a personal language." They meant: in the same way as the painter was now acknowledged to have the right to express himself in non-figurative forms. *Zaum* must be used

- when the artist produces images that have not yet assumed a definite form inside him or outside;
- when it is not necessary to name an object but only to suggest it: names of characters, towns, imaginary lands;
- when one experiences a loss of composure, hatred, jealousy, rage;
- when there is no need for language, in religious ecstasy, in love, to convey interjections, exclamations, murmurs of pleasure, the prattle of a child....

Of the Futurists, only Maiakovsky made little use of *zaum*. Kruchenykh not only used it; he allowed his natural bent for provocation to push him into overusing it. In 1914 the Futurists undertook a national tour. One can imagine the effect on a provincial audience as, with their faces painted all the colors of the rainbow, dressed in outlandish costumes and sporting a spoon or fork in their buttonholes, the performers went through elaborate rituals in reciting their *zaum*–which they insisted contained more poetry than the whole of Pushkin! The one who made the most judicious use of *zaum* was Khlebnikov. In his fantasy play *Zanguesi*, which Tatlin staged just after the poet's death in 1922, the animals and gods, being beyond human conventions and human understanding, express themselves quite naturally in *zaum*. Eros, for instance, addresses us in words that are clearly not our own:

Mara-roma
Biba-bool!
Oox, koox, ail!
Raydaydeedee, deedeedee,
Piri-paypi, pa-pa-pee!
Chogui guna, gaynee-gann!...

Otherwise, however, Khlebnikov uses ordinary language in the play, managing to disjoint it or on the contrary to make it sing with extraordinary lyricism. When Zanguesi delivers a monologue, for example, or when he is struggling in an everyday context to which he is not adapted, we know that this is Khlebnikov talking about himself:

A butterfly entering
The room of human life,
I shall leave the flourish of my dust
On the stern windows, a prisoner's autograph
On fate's hard panes...

As always, it is not the inventors and the masters who merit censure but the bad imitators who simply copied a method of working. It was they–not Khlebnikov nor Kruchenykh–whom Chukovsky attacked: "We love *zaum* language. We love *tsia tsints tsviliu tsints*. We know that no poetry is possible without *zaum* language. But what is one to make of a generation that needs no other language, for whom this one is enough? There is a surprising decline in intellectuality here, an extraordinary impoverishment of the life of the emotions."

Russian futurism reached its zenith in the years 1913–14. It was in the latter year that Maiakovsky's play *Vladimir Maiakovsky, tragedy* was performed in St. Petersburg. A great many books appeared, and the Futurists regularly shocked the public with their demonstrations and tours. Other Futurist groups emerged. There were the Ego-Futurists, of whom the leading figure was Igor Severianin, and close to them there was the short-lived "Mezzanine of Poetry" in Moscow. A much more interesting group was Centrifuge, which emerged in Moscow toward the end of 1913. Two poets who made their debut with

144 **Vladimir Maiakovsky** in 1910.
Maiakovsky was only twelve years old when, in 1905, he first became involved in revolutionary agitation in Georgia. Moving to Moscow in the following year, he was twice arrested on political charges during his student years. It was David Burliuk who, by his own account, opened the young man's eyes to his vocation by assuring him, after seeing his first poem, that he possessed genius.

Centrifuge in 1914 went on to become famous. They were Boris Pasternak *(A Twin in the Clouds)* and Nikolai Aseev *(Nocturnal Flute)*. Centrifuge books tended to be less ambitious aesthetically, but some mention at least should be made of two very handsome publications: *The Gardeners Beneath the Vines*, poems by Sergei Bobrov with illustrations by Natalia Goncharova (1913), and the Cubist-influenced *Weak Foundations*, poems by Ivan Axenov illustrated by Alexandra Exter (1916).

Many painters managed to visit Paris before World War I, but few Futurist writers ever left Russia–unlike their Symbolist elders. However, books and reviews reached them from abroad and kept them abreast of what was going on. They very soon heard about Italian futurism, but since they already had their own version of futurism, strongly tinged with primitivism, they were not prepared to acknowledge that the Italians had in any way beaten them to it. They were even less prepared to pay allegiance to Marinetti. In 1913 Khlebnikov and Kruchenykh denounced the Italians as "loud-mouthed braggarts and mewling artists incapable of speech." As we have seen in Chapter 2, when Marinetti visited Moscow in January, 1914, to propagate his message, it was Larionov who first triggered hostilities before the entire Burliuk group rejected the visitor. Khlebnikov and Livshits even distributed an extremely violent pamphlet attacking "the Italian big shot." Thus rejected by the Russian Futurists, Marinetti left in some disappointment.

Other European avant-garde movements reached Russia only very fragmentarily. In January, 1914, Alexander Smirnov, a friend of the Delaunays, gave a lecture at the Stray Dog nightclub in St. Petersburg on the subject of simultanism and the book *La Prose du Transsibérien* by Blaise Cendrars and Sonia Delaunay: "Everyone clearly liked the book very much," Smirnov wrote to his friends in Paris. And in 1915 the almanac *The Archer* published an interview with Ezra Pound, which was complemented by several examples of Pound's Imagist poetry.

Acmeism as a Reaction Against Futurism

The Futurists were not the only ones to reject symbolism. In fact at the height of the Symbolist movement and arising out of the same French heritage, the Hellenist Innokentii Annensky introduced a dissident note. Annensky occupies much the same position in Russian poetry as Paul-Jean Toulet does in French poetry, owing the bulk of his reputation to the work collected in a volume that was published in the year after his death. In the Russian's case this was *The Cypress Chest*, published in 1910. Annensky was reacting against the imprecision and overdecoration of symbolism; he wanted a verse form that was less musical, perhaps, but more tightly wrought; he sought genuine content clearly expressed. Mikhail Kuzmin was moving in the same direction when he made this recommendation in the review *Apollon* in 1910: "Be logical in your plans, in the structure of the work, and in syntax; be a skilled architect as to detail and as to the whole.... Love words as Flaubert did, be economical with your means and sparing of your words, be precise and true, and you will discover the secret of a wonderful thing: the beautiful lucidity that I shall call clarism." Kuzmin's own poems were written in the same slightly oldfashioned spirit as prompted certain contemporary painters–Konstantin Somov, for example–to recreate the eighteenth century on their own terms.

In reviving some of its predecessors' ideas, acmeism took them a lot further. The movement emerged in 1912, bringing together around Nikolai Gumilev a number of poets who already enjoyed a certain reputation. They included Anna Akhmatova, Osip Mandelshtam, and Sergei Gorodetsky. At the very beginning of 1913 Gumilev published *Acmeism and the Symbolist Inheritance* in the review *Apollo*. It was a kind of manifesto. After speaking of the decline of symbolism, Gumilev went on to ridicule the Futurists (though he had welcomed certain of their publications, particularly

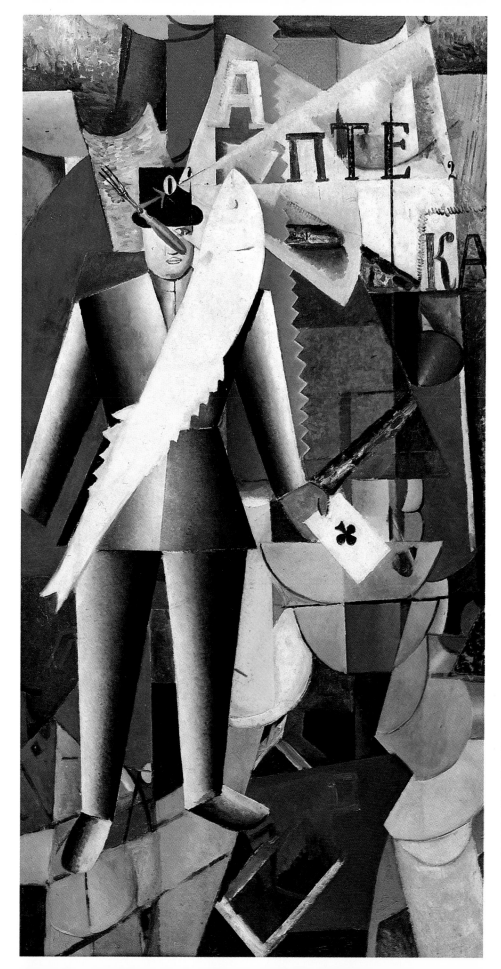

145 Kazimir Malevich, **The Aviator**.
Oil on canvas, 124 × 64 cm. State
Russian Museum, Leningrad.
Malevich was closely associated with the
Futurists, who for their part were great
admirers of both his works and his theories. Just as the cryptic title **An Englishman in Moscow** conceals a portrait of his friend Kruchenykh, the
painting entitled **The Aviator** is in fact
an "alogical" portrait of Vasilli Kamensky, who as well as being a Futurist
poet was a pioneer of Russian aviation.

those of Khlebnikov) and then to announce: "Here, to replace symbolism, is a new movement that, whatever name we give to it—whether acmeism (from the Greek *acme*, the highest degree of something, the flower, the culmination) or adamism (a virile conception of life, a clear view of life)—is a movement that in any case calls for a better balance between subject and object than symbolism represented." Gumilev named François Rabelais, William Shakespeare, François Villon, and Théophile Gautier as the four ancestors that acmeism chose for itself (almost the same choice, incidentally, as Ezra Pound arrived at in London). The tangible, sensual world of acmeism was very much opposed to symbolism. Gorodetsky said bluntly: "As far as the Acmeists are concerned, the rose is once again beautiful in itself, on account of its petals, its scent, and its color and not on account of its hypothetical resemblance to mystical love or anything else." And Mandelshtam, in *The Dawn of Acmeism*, said much the same thing: "The supreme ambition of the artist is to exist. He looks for no paradise beyond that of being." On the other hand, the Acmeists felt more attracted to the Middle Ages than to the modern world and all its technology that so fascinated the Futurists. They were fierce individualists. Here is Gumilev again:

I am polite to modern life,
But there's a barrier between us.

Acmeism received a warm welcome, particularly since it included a number of impressive figures in its ranks. Only the Futurists churlishly lumped them together with the old Symbolists in their manifesto *Go to the Devil* (January, 1914). Gumilev was not only a prominent poet and a respected critic; he was also a man of action and a great traveler. He was temperamentally too domineering to be likeable all the time. Only one man's friendship for him proved indestructible, and that man was the poet Osip Mandelshtam.

Mandelshtam distinguished himself at a very early age with some near-perfect verse:

The fall invariably goes with fear,
And fear itself contains the feeling of emptiness.
Who is dropping rocks on us from above?
Does rock refuse the yoke of dust?

And you once paced the paved courtyard
Like a monk in wooden shoes.
Flagstones and vulgar musings hold in check
The thirst for death and the motions of melancholy.

A curse, then, on the Gothic sanctuary
Where the ceiling deceives you as you enter
And no bright fire burns in the hearth.
Few dedicate their lives to eternity,
But should the moment make you anxious, then
Your fate is terrible, your dwelling built on sand.

One occasionally senses a certain arrogance in these poets with their lofty speech. Paradoxically, one is at the same time aware of fear of an imminent fall, a kind of fascination with failure. In the work of Anna Akhmatova, another major poet of acmeism who kept a small court around her, intimist accents nevertheless creep in. Individualists though they were, none of these poets overlooked contemporary events. Here is what Akhmatova wrote with great prescience in 1914:

Terrible times are on the way. Soon
We shall have fresh graves all over,
Expect to see famine, earthquakes,
Pestilence, and eclipses of heavenly bodies.

The importance of acmeism is due in equal measure to the fact that certain independent poets of quality such as Marina Tsvetaeva and Vladislav Khodasevich came within its orbit. And we must acknowledge the influence it was to have later on such poets as Nikolai Tikhonov, Eduard Bagritsky, and Pavel Antokolsky. It was the last literary movement of note before the revolution.

Writers in the Revolution

The great flowering of literature and the arts that Russia experienced on the eve of World War I was in stark contrast to the economic stagnation and social discontent that prevailed throughout the country. Defeat in the war against Japan and the crushing of a revolution in 1905 had only made matters worse. Nothing had prepared Russia for the war to which the tsar (apparently quite unaware of the real situation) committed the country in 1914. The revolution that convulsed Russia in 1917 was to reveal as great a disparity of positions among writers as among the rest of the population. Many were hostile to it or became so during the early years. The period 1917–22, during which the country was plunged in Civil War, saw a great wave of emigration. Of the big names of realism, Bunin and Kuprin emigrated to France and Andreev to Finland; only Gorky sided with the revolution and became the most influential Soviet writer. Except for Valerii Briusov, Alexander Blok, and Andrei Belyi, the Symbolists were opposed to the Bolsheviks. Konstantin Balmont, Zinaida Hippius, and Dmitrii Merezhkovsky left for France and Italy (in 1924); Fedor Sologub did not emigrate but remained in opposition; Maximilian Voloshin took refuge in the Crimea and stayed there until his death, painting and writing poems in which he voiced his attachment to Russia through all her sufferings and in all her tragedy:

> Sad, infanticide Russia,
> I shall die in the depths of your caves,
> I shall slip into a pool of blood,
> But I shall never quit your Calvary...

The attitude of the Acmeists is difficult to pin down in simple terms. None of its three main representatives emigrated (only Tsvetaeva and Khodasevich going to live in France). But nothing in their individualistic philosophy prepared them for an easy adaptation to the new regime. After only a few years, which Gumilev had spent working with Gorky on a reorganization of the literary world in the wake of the revolution, the disagreement between them and the new regime was such that Gumilev, having been accused in 1921 of involvement in a counter-revolutionary plot, was executed (despite Gorky's intervention; moreover, the poet's involvement would seem to have been very much less compromising than his judges believed). It was a death he had forecast in several moving premonitory poems. After that, Anna Akhmatova and Osip Mandelshtam lived in internal exile, and were progressively less well received. The former was persecuted at first, but then was rehabilitated and enjoyed high honor in the 1960s; the latter, less happily, died as a deportee of the Stalin regime in 1938.

The division was less clear-cut than it appeared. It was not a case of the emigrés on one hand and those who stayed on the other. As we have seen, some of those who stayed were not supporters of the revolution and remained passive. Even among the emigrés, we have to distinguish between the militant anticommunism of some (Ivan Bunin, for example) and the noncommitment of others (notably Alexei Remizov). We must also include those who went into exile in the early days of the revolution and then asked to be allowed to return: Alexei Tolstoi and Ilia Ehrenburg both returned in 1923 and became official writers. Life was not easy for the artists living abroad. In his book *Zoo*, Viktor Shklovsky recounted what life was like in Berlin in the early 1920s. There were even some who returned at the height of the Stalinist era: Alexander Kuprin in 1938 and Marina Tsvetaeva in 1939 (though she committed suicide in 1942).

Apart from Gorky, the major writer of the revolution was Alexander Blok. He earned the title with a single, violent, inspired poem, *The Twelve*, written in 1918 and telling the story of a group of Red Guards wandering through the city. They are twelve in number like the Apostles (in fact they are joined at the end of the poem by Christ himself), and for all their mediocrity and their misdeeds they embody and portray the revolution in progess:

146 Alexei Remizov (1877–1957) was a curious writer who combined something of both symbolism and modernism from his very earliest works, such as *The Pond* (1905) and *Sisters of the Cross* (1911), both permeated by a dark pessimism. He was also a gifted illustrator. In 1921 he emigrated to France, where he continued to work in total isolation.

147 **Au sans pareil**, 1923. Jacques Doucet Library, Paris.
In his illustrations for Alexander Blok's poem *The Twelve*, illustrations that were conceived under the influence of revolutionary events, Iurii Annenkov portrayed the chaotic clash of two worlds: the collapse of a bankrupt westernized world and the as yet uncertain world of the revolution. Annenkov's style owes as much to cubism as to popular caricature.

148 **Baron von Wrangel's Manifesto**, 1920. Poster. State Literature Museum, Moscow.
This poster is a work of satirical propaganda by the popular poet Demian Bednyi (1883–1945). Bednyi went on to become one of the most prominent of the proletarian poets.

Proudly, they proceed on their way,
Behind them a mangy dog,
Before them, red flag
In hand, moves a shadow,
Invisible to all eyes.

In *The Twelve* Blok reconciled revolutionary mysticism with historical event, the symbol with the most trivial anecdote. Shortly afterwards he wrote another major poem, *The Scythians*, before concentrating on prose, though without abandoning his revolutionary commitment.

We have said nothing as yet about the Futurists in the revolution. That is because they present a very special case. They all welcomed it, in fact, and joyfully joined in it. Trotsky, in *Literature and Revolution* (1924), offered a dual explanation for this:

The proletarian revolution in Russia broke out before futurism had had time to throw off its childishness, its yellow shirts, and its excitement and before there had been an opportunity for it to be recognized officially—that is to say, turned into a politically inoffensive artistic school with an acceptable style. The seizure of power by the proletariat took futurism by surprise at a time when it was still being persecuted! This circumstance pushed futurism in the direction of the new masters of existence, especially since coming toward the revolution and establishing contact with it were made easier for futurism by its philosophy—that is to say, by its lack of respect for the old values and by its dynamism.

The dual explanation—historical and psychological—is doubtless correct, yet it makes altogether too light of the genuine desire to change society that motivated all the Futurists from Maiakovsky down. Looking back on the event in his autobiography, the poet wrote: "October. To join or not to join? The question never arose, either for me or for the other Moscow Futurists. This was my revolution." Maiakovsky promptly devoted his enormous talent to singing the praises of the revolution, educating its adherents, and rallying the undecided. Here he is in 1918:

Scatter the plumes of smoke above the
    Winter Palace,
that macaroni factory!
Armed with rifles, we reach another
    day,
and we think:
We'll tell those oldsters where to get
    off.
Eh what!
Turning your coat
Is nothing, comrades!
Now turn yourselves—inside out!

That did not mean that Maiakovsky was about to renounce works in the tradition of his poems *A Cloud in Trousers* and *The Backbone-Flute*, which were mainly about himself. In 1921, he published two poems that represented the

two poles of his work: the epic *150,000,000* and the lengthy intimist poem *I Love*. Actually his finest poems in the 1920s reconciled a highly personal inspiration with social utterance in the form of revolutionary sermonizing. On the other hand he now proceeded to branch out: he wrote propaganda verse and committed theater (*Mystery Bouffe*, 1920), he went back to painting (the Rosta windows) and took up film-making, and he went on lecturing and reporting tours round the country and subsequently abroad as well.

Kruchenykh returned to Moscow after an interlude—more Dadaist than Futurist—in Tiflis (later Tbilisi) in 1916–19, where he participated in the 41° group founded by Ilia Zdanevich (later known as Iliazd) and Igor Terentiev, together with such excellent local painters as Lado Gudiashvili. (Kruchenykh's dadaism was somewhat in advance of that of the rest of the movement.) Vasilii Kamensky's route was similar. In Moscow they joined forces with Maiakovsky. The Burliuks had disappeared during the war, David having left for Japan, from where he later went on to America. As for Khlebnikov, he was definitely for the revolution. In fact he worked as a correspondent with the Red Army and for the telegraph agency (Rosta). He was unable to give up his itinerant way of life, however, and continued to write and publish all over the place, still enjoying the admiring friendship of Maiakovsky and his circle. Physically ill-equipped for the new living conditions imposed by war, blockade, and famine, he eventually died of exhaustion.

Maiakovsky and the Left Front of the Arts

Under the influence of painters and theorists and at the benevolent instigation of Anatolii Lunacharsky, the man responsible for the cultural aspects of the revolution, futurism began to change after 1917 and to commit itself to the service of the greatest number. In 1923 Maiakovsky helped to found the review *Lef*, in which a manifesto

announced that "futurism has become the Left Front of the Arts" (hence the title of the review). The word "futurism" was to be replaced by "constructivism": "The basic position of *Lef*: against fiction, against aestheticism and psychologism in art, for propaganda theater, skilled journalism, reporting.... One of the watchwords, one of the major conquests of *Lef* is the de-aestheticization of the applied arts, constructivism. Its poetic supplement is the poem of economic agitation, publicity." Propaganda and the desire to educate are indeed ever present in Maiakovsky's work—even when he is at his most autobiographical, as in *About That* (1923):

> If you do not beat her
> the mare of everyday life will not
>   budge an inch.
> It is just that, in place of spirits and
>   good fairies,
> today's guardian angel is the tenant in
>   the army tunic.

Lef was the most important review of the 1920s. In addition to Maiakovsky and some of his close friends (Kruchenykh, Kamensky), contributors included such

eminent writers as Boris Pasternak, Isaak Babel, and Nikolai Aseev, theorists such as Viktor Shklovsky, Osip Brik, and Sergei Tretiakov, and many Constructivist (soon to be known as Productivist) artists such as Alexander Rodchenko, Liubov Popova, and Varvara Stepanova. In 1922 the Moscow Association of Futurists (MAF) was founded, and for three or four years it worked in close agreement with *Lef*. Its *éminence grise* was Kruchenykh, and its wellwishers included the painter Ivan Kliun (see Chapter 3, "The Arts After the Revolution"). During the second half of the 1920s, futurism's old associates failed to adjust to the new situation. Kruchenykh's anarchism was too deep-seated; unable to renew himself, he dropped into the background and was thus eventually forgotten. Kamensky, trying desperately to adapt, squandered his talents in ever fainter echoes of his long poem *Stenka Razin*. In the years during which Stalin was gradually consolidating his power, fresh talents appeared. Kornelii Zelinsky emerged as a theorist of Constructivism. Ilia Selvinsky composed narrative poems and, as a supremely skillful versifier, wrote reports such as "How a light bulb is made." Other poets set about

describing the life of the people in the revolution. Eduard Bagritsky did this in his *Ballad of Opanas* (1926), the story of a poor peasant caught up in the turmoil of the Civil War. Bagritsky's first collection, *South-West*, came out in 1928. Among the young poets encouraged by Maiakovsky mention must be made of Semen Kirsanov, who made his

150 **Vladimir Maiakovsky and Lilli Brik**.
Maiakovsky met Osip and Lilli Brik in 1915. She was to become, if not the only, certainly the great love of the poet's life, the one that featured most often in his work. It was to her, for example, that he dedicated the long poem *I Love* in 1922. The troubled love affair of Maiakovsky and Lilli Brik, long a taboo subject in the Soviet Union, reminds one of the adventures of the protagonists of Abram Room's film, *Bed and Sofa*.

151 His poetry having met with the approval of Lenin himself, **Maiakovsky** in 1922 was almost an official spokesman for revolutionary literature. He traveled extensively in that capacity in the years that followed. Here in Berlin he must have come across a number of old acquaintances who had preferred to make their escape, whether permanently or only for a period.

152 **Boris Pasternak**, 1922.
Although it was with his late novel *Doctor Zhivago* that he achieved world renown, Boris Pasternak (1890–1960) is regarded primarily as a poet– one of the finest in the Russian language. Certainly it was as a poet that he made his debut with the Futurist group Centrifuge.

debut in *Lef* in 1924 at the age of only eighteen, and particularly of Mikhail Svetlov, whose poem *Grenade* (1926) was to enjoy lasting popularity. But the best-known name is probably that of Boris Pasternak. Temporarily abandoning the lyricism of *Life, My Sister* (1922), in 1927 Pasternak published two long poems glorifying revolutionaries: *The Year 1905* and *Lieutenant Schmidt*. In them he achieved a vehemence and a staccato rhythm that were very reminiscent of futurism:

> Stooping over the sleds,
> The pine trees blow
> Thinly and sigh.
> Look, lights...
> The district.
> The friendly refuge of the ispravnik.
> Trains are still running.
> All talk is of the call to arms.
> The strike marches snarling
> Over city pavements.

Old and New Trends

The immediate aftermath of the revolution was not marked by any abrupt reorientation of literature under the influence of rigid directives. These came in only gradually after the death of Lenin in 1924. Before that anxiety and social ferment created an atmosphere favorable to fresh experiments. Opoiaz (the Society for the Study of Poetic Language) was a group born during the war. Close to the Futurists, it continued its work during the 1920s and forged links with the Constructivists under the influence of Brik and Shklovsky. Roman Jakobson was the driving force behind another group, the Moscow Linguistic Circle. Another writer whom we must mention was his friend Iurii Tynianov. Both Jakobson and Tynianov contributed occasionally to *Lef*, though Tynianov was better known for historical novels such as *The Death of Vazir Mukhtar* (1929), written for the hundredth anniversary of the death of the writer Alexander Griboedov, who had been murdered in Persia while serving as ambassador there. Apart from these quietly unobtrusive workers, there were two groups that got themselves talked about, namely the Imaginists and the Serapion Brothers.

The Imaginists would probably have fallen into oblivion had they not included among their number a poet of the very first rank. Sergei Esenin made a name for himself in Petrograd during the war as a peasant poet whose talent dazzled the salons. At first he was influenced by Nikolai Kliuev, himself a peasant poet who expected the revolution to lead the country back to the land. (In this Kliuev was doomed to disappointment, and the ill humor he displayed as a result got him into trouble and eventually earned him exile under Stalin.) In 1919 Esenin moved to Moscow and joined the Imaginists, a bohemian group that existed from about 1919 to about 1921. Notable members of the group were Anatolii Marienhof and Vadim Shershenevich, who frequented such literary cafés as "The Stable of Pegasus" in Moscow and conducted themselves in a mildly scandalous manner. In this period Esenin liked to pose as a "hooligan," as in his most famous poem, *Confessions of a Hooligan* (1920):

It's deliberate, my going about
    uncombed,
With my head set like a kerosene lamp
    on my shoulders.
In the darkness I like to shed light
On the leafless autumn of your souls.

The other Imaginists strove in vain to copy Esenin's images. They were always too artificial. In Esenin's work the images seem to occur spontaneously, each one perfectly at home in the poet's rural, sentimental world:

It's as if our stable, to get warm,
    Squats down in front of the brazier of
      the dawn.

It is that kind of poetry rather than his "revolutionary" verses or his drama *Pugachev* that has made Esenin one of the most widely read writers in the Soviet Union today. Torn mentally by his own contradictions and with his health undermined by drink, Esenin committed suicide in 1925–an action that Maiakovsky was to condemn in a famous poem.

The Serapion Brothers (the name is taken from the title of one of E.T.A. Hoffmann's collections of tales) began

to make their presence felt from 1921 in various statements and anthologies. Though the group lasted for no more than a few years, it is remembered because of the many fine writers who made their début under its aegis. They caused offence at the time by choosing to hold themselves aloof from any kind of political commitment. The youngest of them, Vladimir Pozner, elaborated later: "They did not codify, never demonstrated, and proclaimed nothing except the primacy of art and its total

154 **Sergei Esenin with his wife, Isadora Duncan.**
Esenin's whole life contained elements of a *poète maudit* myth: his peasant origins, his violent drinking bouts around the world, his marriage to the dancer Isadora Duncan, who no more spoke Russian than he spoke English, his literary triumphs, and finally his romantic suicide in 1925 at the age of thirty. Isadora was strangled to death by her own flowing scarf caught in the tire of a moving car.

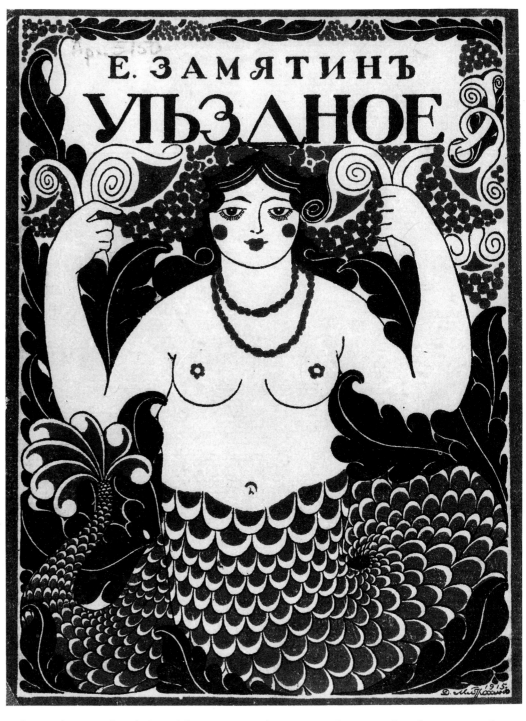

Е. ЗАМЯТИНЪ
УѢЗДНОЕ

155 Evgenyi Zamiatin, **The District**, 1919.
An engineer by training, Zamiatin was working in a British shipyard when his first collection of stories, *The District*, was published in 1919. The book's cover was designed by the artist Dmitrii Mitrokhin.

independence of politics." The writers involved were a very mixed bunch. They had met at the House of the Arts —thanks to Gorky, who encouraged them. Another thing they had in common was that several of them acknowledged Evgenii Zamiatin as their master, a writer who was shortly to provoke a serious row over his novel *We* when it was offered for publication in 1924. Notable Serapion Brothers were the novelists Konstantin Fedin (*Cities and Years*, 1924), Vsevolod Ivanov (*Armored Train 14-69*, 1922), Mikhail

156   Vsevolod Ivanov, **Armored Train 14.69**, 1923. State Literature Museum, Moscow.
Ivanov (1895-1963) came to prominence– helped by Gorky– with his short stories on the subject of the Civil War, of which *Armored Train 14.69* was the most successful. The book was published in 1923 with a cover designed by Iurii Annenkov.

157 It was Gorky who first revealed the talent of **Isaak Babel** (1894-1941). The inspiration for the stories collected in Babel's *Red Cavalry* (1926) came from the writer's war experiences. He nonetheless came under attack from official "Socialist realism." Like Boris Pilniak, Osip Mandelshtam, Benedikt Livshits, and so many others he was to disappear in Stalin's jails.

Pilniak likewise made his debut at an early age. The revelation came in 1922 with *The Naked Year*, a discontinuous account of the early years of the revolution that showed the influence of Belyi and Remizov. For Pilniak too the change of cultural policy was to prove fatal.

Alongside these newcomers, who are today often dubbed "fellow travelers" (in relation to orthodox Communist writers), older writers such as Mikhail Prishvin and Alexander Grin continued to produce work. Some even produced their best work at this time: Alexei Tolstoi (*Nikita's Childhood*, 1921), Sergei Sergeev-Tsensky (*Transfiguration*, 1923), Alexander Serafimovich (*The Iron Flood*, 1924), and Ilia Ehrenburg (*Zhulio Zhurenito*, 1922). And of course there was Maxim Gorky. Out of favor with the regime, he spent the years 1921–28 living in Sorrento, Italy, before making a triumphal return to Russia. It was during that period that he wrote several of his best-known books: *My Universities* (1923), *The Artamonovs* (1925), and *The Life of Klim Samgin* (1927).

158 During the prerevolutionary period **Ilia Ehrenburg** (1891-1967) consorted in Paris with Amedeo Modigliani, Diego Rivera, Maximilian Voloshin, and other artists and writers of Montparnasse. Returning to Russia, he achieved the status of an official author and left a large and varied body of work.

Zoshchenko (*Respected Citizens*, 1927), Nikolai Nikitin (*Vomiting Fort*, 1922), and Veniamin Kaverin (*The End of Khaza*, 1926). To these names must be added that of an excellent poet, Nikolai Tikhonov, who published his first collection, *The Horde*, in 1922.

Among the writers whom Gorky helped to get started we must not forget Isaak Babel, though he was not one of the Serapion Brothers. He made his debut in Gorky's review, *Chronicle*, but it was not until several years later—some of them spent as a war correspondent with the Red Army—that he made a name for himself with the short stories collected in 1926 as *Red Cavalry* and *Odessa Tales*. During the 1930s Gorky's patronage did not shield him from attacks by the champions of "Socialist Realism." He ceased publishing after 1935, was arrested in 1939, and disappeared in 1941. Much the same sad fate befell another writer who was very influential during the 1920s: Boris Pilniak.

The traditional novel continued to attract young writers who were interested in psychology and social realism. One of the finest of these was Leonid Leonov, author of *The Badgers* (1925), and *The Thief* (1927) with its almost Dostoevskian central character. Another novel in the Dostoevskian tradition was *Envy* (1927) by Iurii Olesha.

Satire provided a rich literary vein, as in the picaresque escapade of the *Rastratchiki* (1927) by Valentin Kataev and *The Twelve Chairs* (1928) by Ilf and Petrov. Other satirists of note were Mikhail Zoshchenko, whom we have already mentioned, and Mikhail Bulgakov. Actually the latter came to prominence with *The White Guard* (1925), a realistic novel about a counter-revolutionary family in the Ukraine, but subsequently, in the stories collected in *Devilry* (1925), for example, and in such plays as *Zoika's Apartment* (1926), he moved towards a kind of satire that he liked to color with fantasy. (H. G. Wells was a big influence in Russia; one thinks of Zamiatin's *We* and Alexei Tolstoi's *Aelita*.)

Protelarian Literature and Social Control

The chief preoccupation at this time, however, was proletarian literature. After 1917 the aim was to promote a culture for everybody and created by everybody—proletarian culture, or Proletkult for short. The theorist of Proletkult was Alexander Bogdanov. It soon had its own review and its own publishing houses, with ramifications throughout the country. Between 1917 and 1920 such writers as Briusov, Belyi, Gumilev, and Zamiatin taught in Proletkult workshops. In Moscow the proletarian group called itself the Forge and in Petrograd the Cosmists. When the proletarians denied the value of all bourgeois culture, their reaction was of course a very blinkered one. It was not the view of Lenin or of Trotsky—and even less of Lunacharsky. In 1920 Proletkult was brought under the People's Commissariat of Education, and later it was sup-

pressed. But proletarian literature certainly did not fade into the background; on the contrary, it reorganized itself to such effect that in the 1920s it very often dominated the scene. Some of its finest creations were novels: *Chapaev* (1923) by Dmitrii Furmanov, *Cement* (1925) by Fedor Gladkov, *Defeat* by Alexander Fadeev, and of course the popular *And Quiet Flows the Don* by Mikhail Sholokhov, the first volume of which appeared in 1927. The poetry of this trend was probably less remarkable, apart from a few works by Mikhail Svetlov and Alex-

159 **Mikhail Bulgakov**
(1891–1938) made his debut as a realist with the novel *The White Guard* (1924) before turning to the fantastic. His famous tale *The Master and Margarita* is a curious blend of the two genres. Like Evgenii Zamiatin and Boris Pilniak, Bulgakov was regarded with growing suspicion by official literary circles from the late 1920s onward.

160 **Alexei Tolstoi** (1883-1945) made his debut with a collection of poems, though it was as a novelist and essayist that he made his name. Having emigrated to France after the revolution, he decided in 1923 to return to his country, where he became a thoroughly "official" writer and published a huge and diffuse œuvre.

161 Cover of **Maiakovsky Alive**, 1930.
This book, published soon after the poet's death, is an act of homage by one of Maiakovsky's oldest friends, Alexei Kruchenykh. As his companion on some of the Futurists' wildest escapades, Kruchenykh presented a different image of Maiakovsky from the one that the Stalinist regime was preparing to impose on the dead poet. A nostalgic hangover from the Futurist era, Kruchenykh was already a forgotten man.

ander Bezimensky; its "duty bard," Demian Bednyi, commanded a large audience in his day.

The *Lef* group (the review was renamed *New Lef* in 1927) regarded proletarian literature with an extremely critical eye. Tretiakov published a series of articles in which in the name of "facts" and of a necessary literature of facts he attacked the most famous proletarian novels *(Cement, Defeat)* as deeply "addicted to the past." The First Congress of Proletarian Writers in May, 1928, speaking through Fadeev and Iurii Lebedinsky, issued a vehement riposte, confident of having the authorities and the public on its side. It attacked not only the fellow travelers (Pilniak came in for particular criticism) but also the writers of the *Lef* group, whom it accused of sterile intellectualism. Under critical fire from all sides, Maiakovsky's

group was eventually forced to merge with the RAPP (the Russian Association of Proletarian Writers).

In 1929 the RAPP ruled the literary scene. According to such theorists as Leopold Averbakh it was the duty of the writer to obey "social control" and to place himself at the service of the Five-Year Plan as a "shock worker." This led certain writers (Valentin Kataev, Vera Inber, Kornelii Zelinsky, Mikhail Zoshchenko) to extol the work done by political prisoners and common-law prisoners in digging a canal from the White Sea to the Baltic. It was two of the best-known "fellow travelers," Pilniak and Zamiatin, who provoked the greatest outcry. Even before the book had been published in the Soviet Union, Pilniak allowed a Russian edition of his novel *Mahogany* to appear in Berlin. This kind of thing had been permitted for several years and was not in fact unusual. However, *Mahogany* was not authorized to appear in the Soviet Union because it was unacceptable to the censor, so its prior publication abroad was seen as an act of bravado. A campaign was mounted against Pilniak, who was expelled from the Writers' Union. The writer subsequently tried very hard to secure a pardon. He fitted his novel into a wider project devoted to the Five-Year Plan and entitled *The Volga Falls to the Caspian Sea*, and in 1934 he went so far as to disown as "evil" such works as his travel book *The Roots of the Japanese Sun* (1926). A similar mishap befell Zamiatin, also in 1929, though he reacted with greater dignity. An abridged version of *We* was published in an emigré review in Prague. Zamiatin denied responsibility but was blamed nonetheless and had to resign. In 1931, after addressing an open letter to Stalin, he was allowed to emigrate to Paris—an act of largesse for which he no doubt had Gorky's patronage to thank.

This disciplining of two major writers augured badly. Yet the man who was to draw a line under this period was someone who in principle inspired greater confidence than these fellow travelers, namely Maiakovsky. The aims of *New Lef* having been repudiated, Maiakovsky was obliged to reject them himself and join the Russian Association of Proletarian Writers. "We must work under the direction of Communist proletarian circles," he declared. "We must use every means of involving ourselves with the masses." Even so, a retrospective exhibition of his work over twenty years was unenthusiastically received, as was his play *The Bath-House* (1930). He too embarked on a poem in praise of the Five-Year Plan, though he never completed it. On April 14, 1930, five years after Esenin had done the same, Maiakovsky committed suicide. Intellectual weariness, the depressing effect of constant criticism, a personal emotional crisis, disillusionment over the way things were going in the country—none of these explanations can account on its own for Maiakovsky's cruel discouragement; probably they all contributed to it. Whatever provoked it, the disappearance of this pillar of Russian literature marked the end of an era—and the start of a new one.

Serge Fauchereau

5 The Theater

"When we get to Moscow..." Chekhov's three sisters dreamed—and stayed at home. But other young people, theater-lovers from Penza, Kiev, and Vladikavkaz, did make the trip to Moscow frequently—and for good reason. A modest guide to Moscow's theaters, published in 1926 under the imprint of "The City Administration," makes very exciting reading, confirming as it does that every phenomenon in the history of the theater existed simultaneously in the Russian capital at that time. In the space of a few days theatergoers could see everything from the most innovative experiments to productions dating from the early years of the century. The whole story of how theater evolved internationally was, in a manner of speaking, narrated within the compass of three Moscow streets or boulevards: Tverskaia, Nikitsky, and Sadovaia. People who were there at the time actually witnessed events that have since become subjects of controversy and debate for generations of historians.

Stanislavsky and the Moscow Art Theater

On June 21, 1897, a momentous meeting took place at the "Slaviansky Bazar" restaurant in Moscow's Nikolskaia Street. The two men involved were Vladimir Nemirovich-Danchenko—drama-turgist, critic, and music teacher—and Konstantin Alexeev, owner of a goldsmith's workshop and a great lover of the theater. Alexeev, who already had a certain reputation as an actor with the company run by the Society of Art and Literature, had adopted the pseudonym Stanislavsky. Between them the two decided to open a new theater in Moscow. News of their decision spread fast. Many saw it as just another whim on the part of the wealthy businessman: "Our Moscow moneybags is determined to bury the body of Melpomene," was one comment.

The theater—originally described in its title as "artistic and popular" but later simply called "The Moscow Art Theater" —was inaugurated on October 14, 1898, with a performance of *Tsar Fedor Ivanovich*. The play evoked Moscow's glorious past "in a lively, human way"–the Cathedral of the Archangel, the aristocratic boyars in their long robes, all the street life of yesteryear with its balalaika players, itinerant salesmen, and babas. The dense foliage of the trees occasionally concealed the actors from the audience. At nightfall, candles were lit and cocks crowed. During preparations for the production the company made numerous sorties into the country to purchase antique furniture, material, and costumes. Their efforts and enthusiasm bore. fruit. "You could gaze at the sets for hours," wrote one young actor to

162   Fedor Shekhtel: design for curtain and stage, 1901.
For its fifth season the Moscow Art Theater moved into new premises and had fresh sets made. The curtain with the silhouette of a seagull became the theater's emblem.

149

163 Anton Chekhov reading **The Seagull** to the actors of the Moscow Art Theater.
The play was first performed in St. Petersburg, where it was not a success. The Moscow revival two years later was a triumph.

his wife. The actor's name was Vsevolod Meierhold. Meierhold had hoped to land the principal part, that of Tsar Fedor, but it was feared that his highly distinctive appearance might spoil the show. The tsar was played by another actor. However, Meierhold did get a part in *The Seagull* by Chekhov, which the theater put on later in the same year (December 14).

We do not know precisely what Stanislavsky and Nemirovich-Danchenko talked about for eighteen hours, but the theater's program and credo were clear from the very earliest productions. The curtain was to be sober and movable, the orchestra that played in the intervals was done away with, and sets and costumes were designed specially for each play. But the spirit of innovation went deeper than that: the intention was to replace the eighteenth-century idea of

theater, based on the performances of the actors, by a theater based on the scenic ensemble. The star actor or "lead" had been able to make the spectator forget all the imperfections of the direction. One of the best-known legends of the nineteenth-century theater told how Pavel Mochalov, playing Hamlet at the Little Theater one night, neglected to remove his felt boots. So powerfully did his performance grip the audience, however, that nobody even noticed. Konstantin Stanislavsky believed that a production must be designed as a whole. It must constitute an overall scenic composition in which no detail, no role was insignificant, however small it might be. Each performance must be approached in the same artistic spirit. Stanislavsky introduced a new concept into the Russian theater: that of the director. Hitherto the director's role had

150

been confined to positioning the actors on the stage. From now on he was the driving force behind each performance. In fact he was a kind of artistic dictator.

Given the radical nature of this reform, the Moscow Art Theater naturally had its critics. In particular it had to face a number of broadsides fired in defense of the actor. The principle of the unity of performance was realized, as the Moscow Art Theater saw it, by echoing real life. The stage must be so disguised as to cease to be one. Many might find absurd an approach that sought to do away with the theater as a representational space. But such was indeed the historical role of Stanislavsky, for whom the word "theatrical" rang false. He hated any kind of pose, any kind of exaggerated, repetitive mimicry used to "express emotion"; he abhorred all trivial accessories, all sets "looking like a dentist's waiting room in a small German town and supposed to represent Othello's bedchamber." Stanislavsky endeavored to rid the theater of falsity in

164 The Muscovite merchant Konstantin Alexeev—better known by his pseudonym, Konstantin Stanislavsky—was one of the greatest theoreticians of twentieth-century theater.

165 V. Simov: set design for **Three Sisters** by Anton Chekhov, Moscow Art Theater, 1901–2, directed by Konstantin Stanislavsky.
Stanislavsky's aim was to create a total, perfect illusion of real life. The sets played as important a part in this as did the acting. He gave the most careful attention to every detail.

houettes of the players the form of a bas-relief. The theater became virtually motionless; only the music "moved slowly." Stanislavsky was very enthusiastic at first, not realizing that the novelty of this kind of production was based precisely on the negation of his own principles.

Before embarking on its fifth season the Art Theater purchased a building in Kamergusky Passage in Moscow. Before long Muscovites were calling it "Art Theater Passage," while the building became known as "Chekhov House." Chekhov himself saw only *The Cherry Orchard*, which was produced in the year of his death. He little expected that his theater would be renamed the Maxim Gorky Theater in the early 1930s by decree of the Soviet authorities.

The theater in Kamergusky Passage set itself the task of "serving Russia" by staging the great classics of Russian literature: Tolstoi, Saltykov-Shchedrin, Dostoevsky, Turgenev, Gogol, and Griboedov. However, possibly under the influence of the masquerades that were so popular with Moscow's acting community during Lent, a new theater of "lesser forms" emerged in the auditoriums of "Chekhov House." The "Bat" nightclub—the name was probably a skit on *The Seagull*—was started by Nikita Baliev in 1908. Its first home was in a building inhabited mainly by actors of the Moskova company, but in 1909 it moved into the tallest building in the city, Nirensee House, just off Tverskaia Street. Its repertoire, based essentially on parodies of Moscow Art Theater productions, was to be a source of inspiration to young actors as well as to the great avant-garde directors of the future.

At the same time Stanislavsky was continuing his theoretical studies of acting. Around 1912 these studies eventuated in the elaboration of his famous "method," which is still taught today in drama schools throughout the world. According to the rules of the "method," work on a production began with a collective playreading. Guided by the director, the actor sought to identify with the character he embodied, to feel his past and his present as well as his relations with the other protagonists. Mastering the text came later. Psychology and the subconscious governed the whole quest, and the actor was expected to capture the nature and mind of his character almost intuitively. Rehearsals were frequently interrupted by Stanislavsky's famous "No, I don't think so," and the actor was obliged to have another shot at identifying his character's precise state of mind. A whole range of exercises based on psychology and on yoga (then very fashionable in Moscow) helped the actor to develop his creative intuition. The method enabled him to "live his character," to awaken real emotions and sustain them over several performances. Stanislavsky saw his method as the definitive solution that could be applied to all parts in all circumstances, chiefly through the medium of three maxims or "exercises": "concentrate on the subject," "stay inside the circle," and "relax your muscles." However, what was so obvious to Stanislavsky often affected his actors in ways that ran counter to what he wanted: their muscles grew tense, and in their desperate efforts to concentrate actors sometimes collapsed from exhaustion. The older actors of the first generation at the Art Theater treated all these "exercises" with a great deal of scepticism, regarding them as eccentricities of the master; the young ones, to whom Stanislavsky was a god, performed them to the letter and with far too much zeal. To verify the usefulness of the method it was therefore necessary to appeal to an intermediary.

In 1911 Stanislavsky rented a small hall in Skobelev Square and set up the first Art Theater Studio. The object was still the same: to train actors according to the "method." The man appointed to head the Studio was the brilliant Leopold Sulerzhitsky, who was a great admirer of Tolstoi. He saw theater as a way of making men better. The Studio was to constitute a family whose members, in their common responsibility to Art, held one another in respect; it was to be a "monastery for followers of the religion of Stanislavsky." The Skobelev Square theater was small (accommodating a maximum of 160 spectators) and austere: footlights–that imaginary frontier between stage and auditorium–were abolished and sets reduced to a minimum. The actors occupied the same space as the spectators, who were therefore aware of the tiniest details and able to follow the slightest movement. Everything mattered; everything was significant. Whereas the Art Theater actor was able to ignore the audience, in the Studio he was constantly exposed to its reactions. In fact the pressure was so great that at times the atmosphere verged on hysteria. The first Studio never presented Dostoevsky, though his spirit filled the air as actors sought to define their creative personalities and set out in search of "man's tormented soul."

Mikhail Chekhov was a great actor (as well as a philosopher) who always played the part of the "idea" represented by the hero. He adopted a highly unconventional acting style, characterized by a wealth of nuances and contrasts. Mikhail Chekhov's enormous talent enabled him to accept every role. Moreover, he loved them all–much to the amazement of his fellow-professionals, who were baffled by the mystery of his immense energy and appetite for work. The first Studio gave the Russian theater not only this actor of genius, Mikhail Chekhov, but also a legendary director in Evgenii Vakhtangov. His first production–of Gerhart Hauptmann's *The Coming of Peace*–in 1913 met with a tremendously enthusiastic response. The critics recognized in the young actor's playing a marked psychological profundity never equalled in the Dostoevsky adaptations at the Art Theater. Vakhtangov had studied "the method," understood its weaknesses, and was looking for the solution. He found it in the joy of the creative process as realized by the whole team. Vakhtangov's finest productions were staged in the early 1920s, but Stanislavsky predicted his success as early as 1915. "You are the first fruit," he wrote to him, "of the renewal of our art. I believe and know that the way you have chosen will lead to the great victory so richly deserved."

In 1914 a St. Petersburg drama critic named Zhulii Eykhenvald gave a lecture in Moscow on the subject of "the death of theater." He argued that theater was not an art, that petty-bourgeois invention could offer no more than a clumsy imitation of life, and that it was better to stay at home, read a book, and imagine what it described. There was nothing fortuitous about Eykhenvald's decision to give his lecture in Moscow: his attacks on theater were directed mainly at the Moscow Art Theater and its supporters. Yet at that very moment a new chapter in the history of theater was being opened in Moscow, a chapter that was to bring theater independent recognition as a wholly autonomous art form.

From the Free Theater to the Kamernyi Theater: The Power of Aestheticism

In 1913 the Free Theater was established in the very premises in which the Art Theater had given its first performance fifteen years earlier. But though the premises were the same, the program was completely different. As far as the Free Theater was concerned, there could be no question of trying to come close to real life or providing a living illustration of literature. The main curtain, made to a design by Konstantin Somov, symbolized the alliance of the Muses. It would perhaps be incorrect to describe the Free Theater as a theater of synthesis, even though the plans of its director, Konstantin Mardzhanov, suggested such a hypothesis. In spite of Mardzhanov's energy and drive and the backing of a wealthy patroness, Madame Sukhodolskaia, the Free Theater survived for no more than a year. Nevertheless, it left theaterlovers with unforgettable memories of such productions as *The Sorochinsky Fair* by Musorgsky, Jacques Offenbach's *La Belle Hélène* (transposed from ancient Greece to Moscow at the time of Napoleon), and above all *Pierrette's Veil*, adapted from Arthur Schnitzler. In the latter, the principal role was played by Alice Koonen, a famous Art Theater actress,

167 **Salomé** by Oscar Wilde, Kamernyi Theater, 1917, directed by Alexander Tairov.
The sets created for the Kamernyi Theater by Alexandra Exter revolutionized theatrical design as well as marking a climax for the new trends in Russian painting. In line with the principles of nonobjectivity in the plastic arts, they were restricted to simple geometrical shapes and pure colors.

and the play was directed by the still virtually unknown Alexander Tairov.

The meeting of these two talents resulted in the emergence of a new theater. Flying in the face of logic, it opened in December, 1914. There was no money, the company was not properly formed, and the political atmosphere was highly unstable. Seven years on, Tairov was to describe the step as "sheer madness." Brushing all difficulties aside, he went from door to door along Tverskoi Boulevard in search of premises. The owners of an old townhouse suc-

168 **Giroflé-Girofla**, operetta by Charles Lecocq, Kamernyi Theater, 1922, directed by Alexander Tairov. Tairov dreamed of a synthetic theater, and his productions made simultaneous use of elements from farce, tragedy, operetta, pantomime, and even circus.

156

169   Alexander Vesnin: costume design for Jean Racine's **Phèdre**, Kamernyi Theater, 1922, directed by Alexander Tairov.
The sets designed by the Constructivist Vesnin brought the concept of architectural discipline to the stage of the Kamernyi Theater. For *Phèdre* he drew freely on classical antiquity to create wholly fresh works.

157

170 **Le Jour et la Nuit** by Charles
Lecocq, Kamernyi Theater, 1926, directed by Alexander Tairov.
Between 1925 and 1930 the Kamernyi
Theater staged a number of musical
comedies, a genre that was extremely
popular with Soviet audiences at the
time. This was also the period of Tairov's collaboration with the Stenberg
brothers, who were among the best of
the Soviet scenographers.

158

cumbed to his persuasive enthusiasm and agreed to eject some bookkeeping classes that were held there to make room for the auditorium of the Kamernyi (Chamber) Theater. The term "Chamber" indicated that the theater was not open to everyone but was reserved for the select few who were drawn by art in its pure, Romantic form. Theater, as Tairov saw it, should above all be "theatrical" rather than psychological or symbolical. There was no longer any question of the actor trying to push his interpretation as close as possible to reality; on the contrary, as an actor-aesthete he must move the spectator by artistic means alone. Even his body became material for theatrical expression, while his words, cleansed of the monotony of the commonplace were now governed by a new system that was both musical and rhythmic. Such an actor could play Harlequin one day and Shylock the next, for he was in control of all human emotions in the pure state. Plot was thus used as a kind of scenario on the basis of which the actor created "an autonomous work." Tairov's approach, aiming to "lead theater back to theater," was admittedly not unique. Yet he stood out in consequence of his perseverance, his originality, his talent, and his highly innovative approach to the materials of art. He received encouragement and support from painters, in particular from Alexandra Exter, who became not only his ally but also his guide.

As they moved toward abstraction, the members of the avant-garde in the fine arts were discovering new means of artistic expression that put them well in advance of their colleagues in the theater. The first performance of *Famira Kafirel*, based on the play by Innokentii Annensky (November 2, 1916), was a crucial moment in the history of world theater. Exter's scenography, conceived as a rhythmic sequence of three- and two-dimensional forms—cubes, reliefs, cones, and flat planes—placed the actor "inside" the set. His moving silhouette became a module of a severe abstract composition. Actor and space lived to the same rhythm of words and move-ments. Like painting, theater now sought to construct its own environment by appealing to a new kind of imagination on the part of spectators and inviting them to discover the autonomy of pure forms.

The Post-Revolutionary Theater as an Instrument of Propaganda

The revolution temporarily brought all these experiments to a halt. The decree "on the unification of theaters" signed by Lenin in August, 1919, put a stop to a whole series of initiatives embarked upon since November, 1917. The age of the great patrons such as Savva Mamontov or Savva Morozov and of private theaters and private entrepreneurs was at an end. Before the revolution Moscow had had only two state theaters: the Bolshoi (Great) and the Malyi (Little). After the revolution all theaters were nationalized. The state promised subsidies, certainly, but while allowing "creative collectives" their freedom it reserved the right "to supervise the repertoire in order to bring theater closer to the laboring masses and the ideals of socialism."

Given these conditions, the creation of an Association of Academic Theaters, founded by Alexander Iuzhin of the Malyi Theater, Stanislavsky, Nemirovich-Danchenko, and Tairov, represented a major success. Soon it included the Bolshoi as well as the Children's Theater and the Jewish Chamber Theater for which Marc Chagall painted his famous sets. Its heterogeneous character sometimes made the Association look a little strange. However, its founders were convinced that membership of it would guarantee state subsidies and official recognition. Those hopes were soon to be dashed. Yet despite enormous material difficulties during the Civil War years, the actors continued to perform and the theaters stayed open. Tairov produced Wilde's *Salome* at the Kamernyi Theater with sets by Exter; and Fedor Kommisarzhevsky improvised a series of complicated shows blending opera, drama, and ballet in a bid to help performers of

171, 172   Sergei Eisenstein: set designs for **The Mexican**, adapted from Jack London, Proletkult Theater, 1921, directed by Smyshlaev.
The famous Soviet cinematographer Sergei Eisenstein began his career in the theater. Between 1921 and 1924 he worked with Vsevolod Meierhold as a set designer.

173   Alexandra Exter: costume design for Wilde's **Salomé**, Kamernyi Theater, 1917, directed by Alexander Tairov.
For Exter, designing theater costumes was a kind of dynamic sculpture using color.

174 Isaak Rabinovich: set design for Chekhov's **The Fiancée**, Vakhtangov Studio, 1920, directed by Evgenii Vakhtangov.
Vakhtangov believed that the set must participate in the action just as much as the playing of the actors. He succeeded in making maximum use of all aspects to create a harmonious whole.

all kinds. According to contemporary accounts, the best patronized theaters were the ones with the most efficient heating. "I have become a proletarian," Stanislavsky wrote. "I am not destitute. But money is becoming scarce, and my pay is wretched. I make do with a smoked herring and a scrap of bread made of God knows what."

Theater henceforth was an instrument of education and propaganda. There was a great deal of it–and in all sorts of places, including factories, workingmen's clubs, and barracks. Audiences expected to find their favorite theaters corroborating their own feelings and impressions and offering a commentary on current affairs.

In 1918 the Kamernyi Theater produced *The Posadnik*, a drama set in ancient Russia that was promptly acclaimed as a protest against dictatorship. Byron's *Cain*, produced at the Art Theater in 1920, was seen as a parable of the fratricidal Civil War. Several theaters were closed by the authorities. The "Palace of the Revolution," which opened in the Hermitage in 1919, mounted only one production: *The Carmagnole*; however, problems facing victims of the French Revolution were just too topical. Even the Bolshoi, which

175 Boris Erdman: costume designs for **La Cagnotte (The Kitty)** by Eugène Labiche, Art Theater Studios, 1922, directed by B. Ferdinandov. The actor and director Ferdinandov, one of the founders of the Experimental Studio, was also the inventor of "heroic realism," a new theatrical genre imbued with revolutionary pathos.

Lenin saw as "a place of entertainment for lords," was threatened with closure —as was the Moscow Art Theater, which was accused of "putting on too much Chekhov."

But for the cold and hungry Muscovites the theater sometimes offered the only distraction from their daily cares. While the city waited for the National Theater projected by the authorities to become a reality, a number of little theatres opened in all sorts of places such as factories, parks (depending on the season), and neighborhood clubs. The idea of a National Theater was well received by the profession. Vakhtangov thought in terms of a great cultural center embracing all trends and all

schools; the poet Viacheslav Ivanov dreamed of a mass theater of high artistic quality. The organizers of Proletkult naturally saw it as a great proletarian theater that would exclude all individualism and give expression to the collective consciousness of the masses. Vakhtangov and Ivanov were both leading figures in the Theater department of the People's Commissariat of Education. The department's head, appointed in 1920, inclined towards the ideas of Proletkult. In his speeches he insisted on the need to create a revolutionary theater—the only valid kind in a revolutionary period—and condemned the idea of "apolitical" theater. This old "Dr. Daperturto" (as he had once signed his articles

in *The Love of Three Oranges*, St. Petersburg's avant-garde theatrical review) was none other than Vsevolod Meierhold, who had joined the Bolshevik party in 1918.

Meierhold and the Experimental Theater

Meierhold's party membership was to earn him some sharp criticism from his colleagues: "He simply traded his top hat for a cap and his coat for a peasant's blouse," said Tairov. And on Meierhold's zeal he commented: "Making revolutionary propaganda after the victory of the revolution is like turning up after the show is over." For his part, Tairov remained true to his ideas and continued to create pure scenic compositions, his skill and talent reaching their peak in a production of *Princess Brabilla*, based on the Hoffmann story. The play was a kind of harlequinade, and its quality of joyful fantasy enabled audiences to forget the horrors of the Civil War. Meierhold, on the other hand, endeavored to make reality the subject matter of his art. Under his direction the Bolshoi Theater —which, incidentally, he renamed the Theater of the Russian Soviet Federated Socialist Republic—staged *Les Aubes* by Emile Verhaeren. The set suggested the platforms of revolutionary orators (dark cubes with counter-reliefs floating above them, probably inspired by the works of Vladimir Tatlin). Meierhold introduced a number of topical effects into the text: military communiqués about the Red Army offensive in the Crimea, leaflets bearing the slogan "Proletarians of all countries, unite!," red flags, military marches, and the singing of the *Internationale* as a finale. Conceived as a political rally, the production created a new form of epic theater. The audience, though unaccustomed to this kind of thing, was nevertheless seduced. The day after the first performance *Pravda* was severely critical: "Difficult to describe the set: an incongruous arrangement of planes, cubes, and cylinders.... The presentation of the Russian proletariat as a Shakespearean rabble

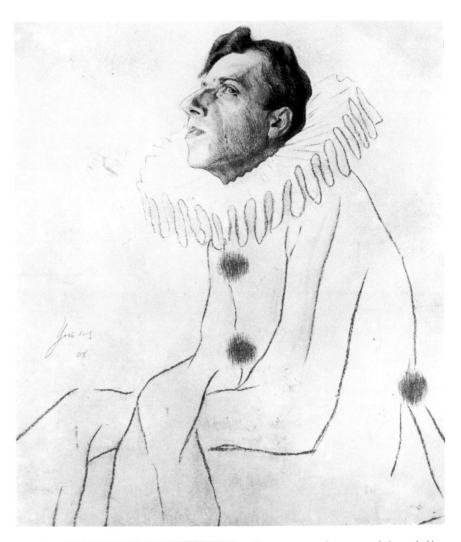

177   N. Ulianov, Vsevolod Meierhold in Pierrot costume, 1908.
Of all the great figures of the Russian and Soviet theater, Meierhold is the one whose work has remained most relevant.

178   Vsevolod Meierhold in 1923.
A former director of the Imperial Theaters, Meierhold embraced the revolution with genuine enthusiasm. His activities were legion, but his aim was always the same: to create a truly revolutionary theater, both politically and aesthetically.

165

179 V. Dmitriev: set design for Emile Verhaeren's **Les Aubes (The Dawn)**, Theater of the Russian Soviet Federated Socialist Republic (Bolshoi Theater), 1922, directed by Vsevolod Meierhold. "As far as we are concerned, the word set means nothing any more. It is all right for the Secession group and the restaurants of Munich or Vienna.... Above all we want none of that rococo spawned in museum attics! If we turn to the disciples of Pablo Picasso and Vladimir Tatlin, it is because we are traveling the same route. We are building and so are they" (Meierhold on the subject of the scenography for *Les Aubes*).

180 **Le Cocu magnifique (The Magnificent/Munificent Cuckold)** by Fernand Crommelynck, Higher State Studios for Directing (G. V. Y. R. M.), 1922, directed by Vsevolod Meierhold with sets by Liubov Popova. "The production was to form the basis of a new acting technique in a fresh scenic context that broke with the usual surroundings made up of flats and the stage framework of the acting area. Justifying the new principle, it was to expose completely all the lines of construction and take that technique to the extremes of schematization.... It may now be taken as read that the entire 'theater of the left' still bears the stamp of that production" (Meierhold, writing in 1926).

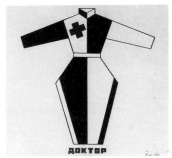

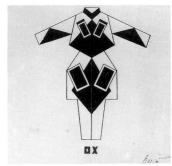

that any self-opinionated fool can lead by the nose is an affront. The portrayal of woman as a servant is an insult to revolutionary activities. The whole thing is offensive."

The article was written by Lenin's wife, Nadezhda Krupskaia, who as a leading figure in the People's Commissariat of Education also concerned herself with theater. Following this attack Meierhold had to step down as head of the Theater department in February 1921. The Theater of the RSFSR, after having staging 75 performances of Maiakovsky's *Mystery Bouffe*, was closed down in the same year. Expelled from his theater, Meierhold opened a series of "production studios" called successively GVRM, GVTM, and Gitis. Eventually he took premises at 32 Novinsky Boulevard and began rehearsing *Le Cocu magnifique* by Fernand Crommelynck, which received its first performance at the State Theater of Communist Dramaturgy in April, 1922.

The condition of the building, which had become completely delapidated during the Civil War, forced Meierhold to study the problem of producing plays without a stage. The result was a new kind of acting technique in a fresh scenic context that departed from the usual framework of wings, stage, and proscenium arch. Justifying this principle, he laid bare all the lines of construction and took the reduction-to-essentials technique to a logical extreme. Meierhold called his new method "bio-mechanics." The actor had to learn how to be in complete control of his "raw material" by "making correct use of his body's means of expression." (Like many of his contemporaries, Meierhold drew inspiration from the kind of quasi-industrial terminology so frequently used by the Constructivists.)

To achieve Meierhold's goal all the actor had to do was to develop his sense of co-ordination and precision and place himself well in the space around him. He had to be able to "look at himself from all sides." Creation was simply a happy, straightforward act of cognition and of strong, healthy volition. The acting might be accompanied by music,

181-184 **Tarelkin's Death** by Alexander Sukhovo-Kobylin, GITIS Theater (National Institute of Theatrical Art), 1922, directed by Vsevolod Meierhold with sets by Varvara Stepanova. With this production Meierhold's studios continued to battle against traditional theater: "The scenic machine tool – a single piece of apparatus in *Le Cocu magnifique*– was here broken down into a series of different pieces of apparatus, theatrical appliances capable of backing up the exceptionally taut playing of the actor."

185　**The Earth Rises Up** by Sergei Tretiakov, adapted from Marcel Martinet, Meierhold Theater, 1923, directed by Vsevolod Meierhold with sets by Liubov Popova.

"In the apparatus of the production," Meierhold explained in his characteristic manner, "the Constructivist [Popova] has set out to force the audience to pay attention mainly to the production's agitatorial intention.... Rather than try to perform an aesthetic function, she strives to affect the spectator in such a way that he sees no difference from what life itself offers him...." *The Earth Rises Up* was indeed an elaborate piece of revolutionary propaganda conceived as a montage of real facts and events.

which was a useful way of sustaining the required rhythm. Everything had to be precisely *constructed*. This idea of construction was brought to the theater by Liubov Popova, designer of the set and costumes for *Le Cocu magnifique*. The success of their collaboration prompted Meierhold to extend his experiments to the acting and the sets. For his next production—*The Death of Tarelkin* by Alexander Sukhovo-Kobylin—he asked Varvara Stepanova to develop "the specific tools of the theatrical undertaking." Success was complete and marked an epoch. From then onward nearly every theater in Moscow began to look upon the stage as a real space filled with real objects of everyday use. There were to be no tricks and no embellishments. "Let us leave elegance to the hairdressers and shoemakers," Meierhold declared. Construction thus became an object in itself.

This concern for truth and documentary quality reached a peak in *The Rearing Earth*, a play by Marcel Martinet that Meierhold and Popova adapted in 1923, reducing it to two acts. The production was constructed as a montage of episodes, the titles of which were projected—with comments—on a screen. Real motorcycles were used, and the auditorium was filled with the smells of exhaust fumes, hot metal, and war. Dedicated to the commander-in-chief of the Red Army, Leon Trotsky, *The Rearing Earth* was also produced outside the theater—notably in Sparrow Hills Park on the occasion of the Third Congress of the Communist International. In this way Meierhold's desire to "bring theater out into the street" found successful fulfillment.

Another Meierhold production dating from 1924 exerted a lasting influence on the amateur and workers' theaters with names such as "Blue Overalls" and "Living Newspapers" that had sprung up in the wake of the October Revolution. The ballet *D.E.* ("Objective: Europe") represented the unrelenting struggle between capitalism (them) and socialism (us). This kind of dichotomy, ubiquitous in Russia, was very typical of the period (one thinks of Maiakovsky's "Pure" and "Impure"). Dynamic and impulsive, the production was enthusiastically received by the critics. The discovery of the dynamism of scenic composition became a bone of contention in the theatrical world. In 1923 the theatrical press got involved in a full-scale battle to decide who had been the first to introduce moving stage sets (in

this instance lifts and pavements): the Kamernyi Theater with *The Man Who Was Thursday* or the Theater of the Revolution with *Lake Lull.*

Lake Lull was staged with the backing of Meierhold, who regarded his theater as experimental and was looking for a place that could take a large audience. A romantic melodrama set "somewhere in the West, or possibly in the Far East," and filled with "fatal" passions, it was one of the achievements of the revolutionary theater as far as the stage adaptation of a contemporary play was concerned. Many later productions were to employ the same techniques of "cinemontage" and using the building itself as an independent set. *The Man Who Was Thurs-*

186 **The Man Who Was Thursday**, adapted from G.K. Chesterton, Kamernyi Theater, 1923, directed by Alexander Tairov with sets and costumes by Alexander Vesnin.
"The pathos of the modern age lies in simplicity," said Tairov when he staged this play. For it Vesnin designed a complete Constructivist "architecture": the stage, divided into three spaces, was filled with tubes and metal cages linked by moving staircases. "The engineer has taken the place of the artist," one contemporary critic noted.

187 **The Forest** by Alexander Ostrovsky, Meierhold Theater, directed by Vsevolod Meierhold.
Meierhold's response to the "back to Ostrovsky" watchword issued by Anatolii Lunacharsky was to present *The Forest*, rewritten and restaged in 36 episodes. The use of a variety of techniques, both theatrical and cinematographic, together with new music resulted in a wholly unexpected interpretation of this stock item from the classic repertoire.

188 **The Government Inspector** by Nikolai Gogol, Meierhold Theater, 1926, directed by Vsevolod Meierhold with sets by V. Kiselev.
No play earned Meierhold so much critism as his version of *The Government Inspector*. Charged with mysticism, eroticism, and asocial tendencies, he replied: "... because there is no waving of red flags on stage and no one sings the 'Internationale' and because the production is not accompanied by slogans, they conclude that *The Government Inspector* is not revolutionary. Afflicted by a sort of color blindness, they are incapable, in the absence of flags, of seeing the revolutionary density of this production."

189-191 Ignatii Nivinsky: costume design for **Princess Turandot** by Carlo Gozzi, Third Studio of the Art Theater, 1922, directed by Evgenii Vakhtangov.

"Our theatergoer sees nothing around him but the fighting and destruction caused by the Civil War," Vakhtangov said. "But he would like to see the future as well... and dreams about it. With Princess Turandot let us dream of the victory of Good over Evil, let us dream of our future." Nivinsky's set–a "Chinese baroque" architectural fantasy– added a certain decorative lightness to the stock-in-trade of the avant-garde theater.

day was the splended outcome of collaboration between Tairov and Alexander Vesnin (who had already worked together on Racine's *Phèdre* the year before, in 1922). The G.K. Chesterton play allowed Vesnin to work out "a vast, universal space" in the form of an ideal project of functional, contemporary stage architecture. It was in fact a theater set design that ushered in the era of Russian architectural constructivism.

"Americanism," the technology of modern city life so characteristic of the early years of the NEP, fascinated both Meierhold and Tairov—as it perhaps fascinated all the inhabitants of Moscow, still a city of wooden buildings and patriarchal ways. It became possible to blend the novel with the traditional, and Meierhold drew on the repertoire of the past to make some revolutionary adaptations. *The Forest* written by Alexander Ostrovsky, a classic of Russian theater, when staged in 1924, was "developed to meet the demands of the new age." As Meierhold put it: "Leaving the deep roots of the work untouched, we have made it more expressive." In fact he had completely rewritten the play and given the characters a quite different interpretation, usually according to which class they belonged to.

Other directors soon followed Meierhold's example in reworking classic plays. One of Meierhold's best pupils, Sergei Eisenstein, also drew on Ostrovsky when he staged *It's All in the Family* at the Proletkult Theater. The adaptation verged upon circus, with soliloquies being delivered from trapezes and high wires. Meierhold did not demand such a multiplicity of talents from his actors and was severely critical of Eisenstein's work. On the other hand he admired Stanislavsky's adaptation of another Ostrovsky play, *Burning Heart*, which was presented at the Art Theater in the same year. He did so in spite of the attacks on academicism launched by the "left-wing" press at the time. Indeed, the Constructivists were not slow to extend their empire to the theater. Among the finest achievements one thinks of the sets that Isaak Rabinovich (a disciple of Alexandra Exter) designed for the Jewish Theater and the scenography for Aristophanes' *Lysistrata* in the production by Vladimir Nemirovich-Danchenko. It was on seeing these that Stanislavsky, just back from an extended tour of Europe and the United States, cried: "Now the Cherry Orchard's burning!" However, not even Stanislavsky's "method" escaped the attentions of the Constructivist artists: *Princess Turandot*, which Evgenii Vakhtangov produced in 1922, was a huge success thanks largely to the sets by Ignatii Nivinsky. Vakhtangov had just finished collaborating with another Constructivist, Nathan Altman, from whom he had accepted an arrangement of wholly abstract monumental planes as the setting for *Gadi-*

buk. Even the Bolshoi Theater, that "paupers' grave of dancers," momentarily found its Constructivist in the person of Boris Erdman.

New Political and Ideological Pressures

Although the NEP era placed emphasis on the number of theatergoers "voting by ticket purchase" (i.e. according to their ability to pay), it also improved the general level of productions. Moreover, the authorities' policy remained very open during this period: the party knew how to turn even *Le Cocu magnifique*, *Phèdre*, and *Princess Turandot* to its advantage by providing an ideological interpretation for the occasion.

Toward the end of the NEP era, however, ideological pressures increased. New slogans and watchwords such as "Demonstrating the unity of party and people" and "The guiding role of the party in building up the state" were followed by threats: "Anyone who cannot adapt will disappear." New plays emerged which dealt with the new subjects now in demand. They were not all bad: *Armored Train 14-69* by Vsevolod Ivanov is probably one of the finest theatrical creations based on the events of 1917, as is *The Days of the Turbins* by Mikhail Bulgakov, which before Stalin's intervention was the object of fierce attacks. "We have no more avowed counter-revolutionary than Bulgakov," said the indignant Lunacharsky. "The only thing left for him to do is to bury his face in Stanislavsky's waistcoat and weep for himself."

The party slogan, "Closer to life," finally forced Soviet theater into the straitjacket of life as the party would have liked it to be, and it became very difficult to break out. Tairov sought to avoid having to deal with Soviet everyday life by taking refuge in the dramas of Eugene O'Neill. He produced *The Emperor Jones*, for example, with its emphasis on both the social and the psychological. Yet he did have the courage to produce *The Red Island* by Bulgakov in 1928—a play that was quite rightly

192   K. Velov: costume design for **Stenka Razin** by Vasilii Kamensky, Theater of the Revolution, 1923-24, directed by V. Bebutov.
Stepan Razin, a seventeenth-century Cossack leader of a peasant revolt was one of the historical characters who were "retrieved" by the revolution when artists made them the subjects of paintings, plays, or films. Velov's designs won the silver medal at the 1925 Exposition des Arts Décoratifs in Paris.

193 V. Shestakov: set design for **A Profitable Job** by Alexander Ostrovsky, Theater of the Revolution, 1923, directed by Vsevolod Meierhold and A. Velizhev.
"Ostrovsky's harmless and politically right-wing play is elevated, in Meierhold's interpretation, to the status of an ominous symbol of the past age" (from a contemporary Soviet press notice).

194 **Lohengrin** by Richard Wagner, Bolshoi Theater, 1923, directed by V. Lossky with sets by F. Fedorovsky. In the aftermath of the revolution, the Bolshoi Theater was seen as a symbol of aristocratic and bourgeois culture and was several times threatened with closure. Lenin himself had to intervene to safeguard the "classic" repertoire in the face of repeated attacks from "leftist" artists.

195   Boris Erdman: costume designs
for **Joseph the Handsome** by Sergei
Vasilenko, Bolshoi Theater, choreographed by K. Goleizovsky.
In the late 1920s ballet, like opera, also
recovered its place in Soviet culture.

regarded as an attack on the sovietization of the theater and the profanation of art for false ideological ends. During the same period Meierhold produced two plays that have become milestones in the history of Soviet theater: *The Mandate* by Nikolai Erdman in 1925 and *The Government Inspector* by Gogol in 1926.

The Mandate, a grotesque and bizarre comedy, satirized a new class of rulers greedy for material goods and power. One character in it boasts of having the authority, thanks to the mandate of the party, to arrest "almost the whole of Russia!" The new production of *The Government Inspector* was conceived as a musical score (Meierhold described it as "musical realism") with separate episodes linked together to form a unique

whole. The "three deadly sins" (Meierhold's phrase) that the critics found in this production were mysticism, eroticism, and an asocial character. Meierhold's reply to these charges of "profanation" was as follows: "Our theater is full every night, despite what the critics think.... Just because no one on stage waves red flags or sings the *Internationale* and the production is not accompanied by slogans, *The Government Inspector* is thought to be counterrevolutionary! Such color-blind people cannot discern revolutionary content unless they see flags waving."

However intelligent and genuine Meierhold's defense, it was offered in vain. In 1928, like many figures in the arts, he went abroad, though unlike the others he had no intention of joining

197   **The Blue Shirt**, a revolutionary propaganda production, 1927. Encouraging nonprofessionals to participate in all fields of artistic endeavor was a key policy of the Soviet regime. The Blue Shirt, one of a number of amateur theater companies, was composed principally of Young Communists. Its "revolutionary agitation" productions were inspired by the formal experiments of the avant-garde.

the emigré community. Yet his theater was threatened and its subsidies cut. The press, with *Pravda* in the lead, attacked him: "The directors thought they could do what they liked because they had the advantage of a supposed talent...." Meierhold then returned to Moscow "out of courtesy to his theater." Ten years later he and his theater were both "liquidated."

The plays performed in Moscow in 1930 were all alike—"as if they had been written by the same author," was how Tairov put it. The era of the "disturbing creativity of the days of *Le Cocu magnifique*" was over. It was already being replaced by the simplifications of a "Socialist realism."

Elena Rakitina

6 Town Planning and Architecture

Architecture at the End of the Nineteenth Century

Any investigation into modern architecture in Moscow has, first of all, to distinguish between the architecture that evolved between the end of the nineteenth century and the outbreak of World War I, on one hand, and the projects and visions of the avant-garde on the other. Conceived in the 1920s, only to falter in the 1930s, the avant-garde projects gave way to so-called Stalinist architecture, which remained dominant until the 1950s.

What was the image of Moscow at the end of the nineteenth century? How can one explain the abrupt upsurge of building activity? What determined the character of the architecture of this period?

During the second half of the nineteenth century, Russia underwent major political and economic changes. Tsar Alexander II (1855–81) promulgated an agrarian reform that, among other things, resulted in an influx of peasants into the cities. The abolition of serfdom in 1861 was the heart of the "Great Reforms" of the 1860s and early 1870s, which affected local self-government, the judicial system, and the army—and also defined a new system of municipal organization. The law of 1870 introduced urban self-government based on a limited suffrage (see Chapter 1).

Although Russia lagged behind the West in the late nineteenth century, it experienced a period of capitalist expansion, marked by a dynamic development of Russian industry and urbanization, which lasted until the outbreak of World War I. In this respect the years following the Russo-Japanese War of 1904–5 were particularly productive. From the abolition of serfdom to the end of the nineteenth century industrial output rose by nearly 300 percent. In the ensuing period prior to World War I heavy industry alone grew by another 80 percent. The population of Moscow, which exceeded 300,000 in the middle of the nineteenth century, numbered over one million by 1900 and reached two million by 1914. Little wonder, then, that architecture in Moscow underwent a dynamic transformation.

Different architectural styles flourished, especially in industrial buildings: workshops and factories, warehouses, railroad stations, workers' settlements set up by certain industrial firms, banks and commercial office buildings. The economic might of the bourgeoisie stimulated the construction of private residences, too. The advances in the development of the urban infrastructure (paved streets, lighting, and sewers) paralleled initiatives of a commercial and civic character, such as the construction of municipal museums.

198 **Apartment building** on Podzenskii Passage, 1903. Detail of the facade. Architect: G. Makaev.

179

199 The main shopping center (today the **department store GUM**) in Red Square, 1889–93. Architect: Dmitrii Chichagov.
GUM was constructed in the International style as requested by Moscow's leading merchants. The store remains the most frequented building in the entire city and continues to offer the widest choice of products in Moscow.

200 **GUM department store**: interior galleries.

St. Petersburg and Moscow took on increasingly different characters. While the former city remained the nation's capital until the revolution, and was the seat of the monarch and the hub of the central administration, Moscow rose to prominence in the late nineteenth century as the country's chief industrial, commercial, and financial center. Against this background, it is easy to understand the growing importance of the bourgeoisie as the principal source of artistic patronage, which also covered the commissioning of buildings.

Art Nouveau

During the late nineteenth and early twentieth centuries, different attitudes came to the fore in discussions about architecture. Technical progress enabled architects to make use of new materials, especially iron. This was an age when engineers became architects and built factories, bridges across waterways or rail lines, and so forth, in which the structure was left very much in evidence. In most cases, however, the new materials and techniques made it easier for architects to employ a variety of decorative forms on buildings that had a metal framework. The mannered historicist style came into fashion, while Art Nouveau brought in stylized forms. Questions concerning the social, ethical, political, and national functions of architecture now acquired a major new significance.

In the latter half of the nineteenth century, historicist architecture was predominant. Architectural theory and practice both looked back to the national style of architecture reminiscent of neoromantic historicism. In Moscow such architecture was visibly tinged with elements of stylized folklore. In time, however, Russian architects came to emulate the classicism of St. Petersburg, and this tendency became preeminent in Moscow, too, after 1900. The turn of the century also witnessed the emergence of Art Nouveau; in opposition to the other two movements, it offered a fresh and universal "modern" style. All these currents turned the new techniques to their advantage, even though each of them puritanically concealed the structural framework of the buildings. Until the second decade of

180

201 The **State Pushkin Museum of Fine Arts**, Volkhonka Street. Architect: Roman Klein.
Roman Klein constructed in Moscow more than sixty buildings of the most diverse styles. Journalists of the day commented that "grouped together these buildings would make up a small city." The Pushkin Museum, one of Klein's rare Neoclassical designs, earned him, among other honors, the title of academician. Its construction was keenly followed, stage after stage, by the press.

202 Bird's-eye view of the **Volkhonka quarter**, with the Pushkin Museum of Fine Arts at the left.

182

the twentieth century, Constructivist architecture–typical of industrial buildings–remained outside the mainstream of architectural concerns. The department store today known as GUM *(Glavnyi universalnyi magazin)*, designed in 1885 by Alexander Pomerantsev, is an exception. This was the first time that iron and glass were employed on such a vast scale in a non-industrial building. The manner in which the volumes and the interior were organized contrasted with the heavily decorated exterior.

The most interesting specimen in Moscow of historicist architecture, carried out according to the canons of the national style, is the State Historical Museum in Red Square, built from 1875 to 1883 according to plans by Vladimir Shervud and A. Semenov. The building consists of superimposed volumes, arranged symmetrically around a central section surmounted by two towers and embellished with an imposing portico. The regular rhythm of the arches and the decorative triangular shapes on the

203　The **State Historical Museum**, 1875-83. Architect: Vladimir Shervud, according to plans by A. Semenova. The red-brick Historical Museum, in "Neorussian" style, facing St. Basil's Cathedral in Red Square, was supposed to match the ancient walls of the Kremlin.

204 **Apartment building** on Mias-nitskaia Street (today Kirov Street) about 1890. Architect: Roman Klein. Klein's eclectic architectural tastes sometimes incited him to include the most varied elements from around the world.

205 The residence of the Igumnov family (today the French Embassy), Dimitrov Street, ca. 1896. Architect: N.I. Pozdeev.
Rooted deeply in national tradition, the Neorussian style matched perfectly the tastes of Moscow's wealthy bourgeoisie.

facade and towers were intended to match the decor of St. Basil's Cathedral, which is across the square; this dates from the sixteenth century and was considered at the time as the formal and spiritual prototype of Neorussian architectural design.

The same principles inspired the construction in 1896 of the residence of the Igumnov family, designed by N.I. Pozdeev. In contrast to the overall order characterizing the State Historical Museum, the choice of decors and the richly ornamented facade of the Igumnov residence seem to be conceived more freely. The irregularly arranged volumes are accentuated by the variety of the multiple roofs and the tumult of the wall surfaces, in which windows, galleries, friezes, columns, pilasters, balconies, and porticoes are set at random.

A relatively late example of Neorussian architecture is the Kazan Railroad

206 The **Kazan Railroad Station**, 1913–26. Architect: Alexei Shchusev. Creator of the famous Tretiakov Gallery and much later of the Lenin Mausoleum, Shchusev applied elements of the ancient architecture of Novgorod and Pskov in building the Kazan Railroad Station. This enormous building seems to be an assemblage of independent parts which differ in volume as well as in decor.

207 **Komsomolskaia Square**: the Leningrad, Iaroslavl, and Kazan Railroad Stations.

185

Station, begun in 1912 according to plans by the academic architect Alexei Shchusev. Here too the construction eschews homogeneous volumes in favor of very diversified parts. The decor draws on the historicist repertoire.

It must be borne in mind that the impact of historicist architecture in Russia went well beyond these illustrative examples. Neorussian architecture was a version of the historicist style that interests us here on account of its ideological motivations. Contemporary with it were other dynamically developing forms of architecture that drew their inspiration from universally acknowledged stylistic models. During the late nineteenth and early twentieth centuries, the most frequently emulated architectural styles in Russia were Byzantine, Romanesque, and Classical, as well as Italian Renaissance and Oriental. In 1912 Oskar Munts was commissioned to build the

main Moscow Post Office. He first adopted the Byzantine style, only to change course during construction in favor of Romanesque. Roman Klein, on the other hand, drew inspiration from the Chinese style in his design for the offices of a firm that imported tea from China.

At the beginning of the century there was also a revival of interest in neoclassicism, which played a singular role in the evolution of a national Russian form of architectural expression. The model for this current, which aspired to be both modern and national, was the architecture of St. Petersburg in the early nineteenth century. There is no doubt that, by adopting this model, the Neoclassicists were trying to recover the spiritual climate of that period in Russian history.

It is important to note that the elevation of the architecture of St. Petersburg to the rank of national architecture

occurred in a context rife with nationalist sentiment. Yet another manifestation of the same phenomenon was the very solemn commemoration of the centenary of the victory over Napoleon, as well as that of the tricentenary of the Romanov dynasty. It is hardly surprising, therefore, that in the architecture of the period the Neoclassical style was regarded as a symbol of patriotic feeling.

This explains the popularity of this style after the revolution and its rebirth in the doctrine of "Socialist realism" in the 1930s; yet it is not easy to find examples of such Neoclassical architecture in the period immediately prior to World War I. Apart from the Alexander III Museum (today the Pushkin Museum), the building of the present Lenin Pedagogical Institute, or the residence of Prince S. S. Shcherbatov (built in 1911–13 according to plans by Alexander Tamanian), early examples are a villa in Ostrovsky Passage (constructed by N. Lazarev in 1906), the residence of V. N. Gribov (built in 1909 by A. N. Miliukov), as well as a house by the architect Fedor Shekhtel constructed in 1909–10. All these edifices display the same type of construction: the austere volumes are dominated by a monumental Doric portico.

The decorative elements of neoclassicism also made their way into housing

209   The **Metropole Hotel**: detail of the facade. The mosaics are by Mikhail Vrubel.

187

210 The **Iaroslavl Railroad Station**. 1902-5. Detail of the main facade. Architect: Fedor Shekhtel.

211 The **Iaroslavl Railroad Station**, 1902-3. Detail of the lateral facade.
Shekhtel found magnificent solutions for combining the principles of the modern style with elements of traditional northern Russian architecture.

design and commercial architecture in Moscow. The most interesting examples combine the monumental columns and the friezes of Classical architecture with modernist functionalism. One of the best examples is the residence of I.E. Kuznetsov, built by Boris Velikovsky and A.N. Miliukov, with a facade erected in 1910 according to plans by Alexander Vesnin.

The turn of the century also saw the emergence, alongside the eclectic historicist style, of Art Nouveau. Its modern decor quickly took root in Moscow's architecture, finding numerous adherents among the bourgeoisie.

Art Nouveau architecture in Moscow was supple, almost mannered, in form, and although it was occasionally pictori-

al, it favored an essentially sculptural decor. This is evident in the Metropole Hotel, erected by V.F. Valkot (William Walcot) between 1899 and 1903; the hotel's iron frame construction was the work of the engineer A.E. Erikhson. The facade of the edifice was richly decorated with turrets and balconies and girded with a stucco relief bearing numerous stylized sculptures. The gently curved gables were decorated with panels of shell mosaic after paintings by Mikhail Vrubel. This monumental, decorative, and constructionally well-integrated edifice is a typical example of modernism in Moscow.

Among the Art Nouveau architects in Moscow pride of place falls to Fedor Shekhtel. Universal in scope, he was

212   The **residence of S.P. Riabu-shinsky**, Malaia Nikitskaia Street (today Kachalov Street), 1900–2. Staircase. Architect: Fedor Shekhtel.
The main staircase of the Riabushinksy residence is widely esteemed as a masterpiece of Russian Art Nouveau, which is noted for breaking down the boundaries between beauty and utility, function and decoration.

known especially for his Neorussian, Neogothic, and Neoclassical edifices. Rich though the tastes of other eclectic architects of the period were, Shekhtel's projects, in any of these styles, manifested an altogether special artistic feeling. Two of Shekhtel's buildings are of particular interest: the house he erected between 1901 and 1902 for Stepan Riabushinsky, and the Iaroslavl Railroad Station in Moscow. The former is composed of asymmetrical volumes covered by a flat roof. The windows, doors, terraces, and balconies—all varied in shape and dimensions—were freely arranged in the respective facades. The curves in the gratings and railings provide a characteristic and distinctive decorative accent. Although the edifice is girded by a mosaic frieze with a plant motif, the dominant motif of the interior decor is aquatic. It appears in the curves of the facade, in the designs in the mosaic and the stained glass windows, and on the marble balustrade of the staircase, a masterpiece of Art Nouveau.

190

213   Fedor Shekhtel: **Entrance** to the residence of A. Morozov.

214   Fedor Shekhtel: The **study** in A. Morozov's private residence.

215   The **residence of A. Morozov**, 1890–93. Today the House of Friendship with Foreign Peoples. Architect: Fedor Shekhtel.
Shekhtel conceived several projects for the homes of the ultra-wealthy Morozov family. He designed the least of details, even the most ordinary everyday things.

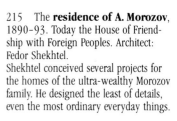

216 The **Moscow Art Theater**, 1902. Lanterns on the facade. Architect: Fedor Shekhtel.
In 1900 Shekhtel agreed to refurbish the facade and hall of the Moscow Art Theater, considered as one of his greatest achievements.

217 **Apartment building** of A. T. Filatova, Arbat Street, 1913-14. Architect: Vladimir Dubovsky.
The Filatov family built several apartment buildings in the center of Moscow, combining in a unique style Art Nouveau features and Neoclassical decors.

218 **Apartment building** of E. Filatov, 1906-7. Detail of the facade. Architect: Vladimir Dubovsky.

The Iaroslavl Railroad Station conceived by Shekhtel was the first modern construction of this type in Russia. It consists of a spacious hall with ticket windows, waiting rooms that open out directly onto the platforms, and a variety of rooms adapted to the specific needs of the station. The facades are fitted with turrets to make up a set of volumes of various shapes. The main entrance is emphasized by a large semicircular glass skylight. The muted shades of the station's walls contrast with the encircling green ceramic frieze, punctuated by bits of multicolored majolica. Shekhtel did not hesitate to combine the stylistic motifs of Art Nouveau with various Neorussian motifs.

While the roof is trapezoidal in shape and the tower roofs tentlike, the entrance niche is topped by a characteristic arch-shaped molding.

Toward the end of the first decade of the twentieth century, interest in Art Nouveau gave way to a penchant for Neoclassical architecture. During the relatively short period immediately prior to the outbreak of World War I, therefore, architecture in Moscow was marked by a return to Classical forms and decoration, especially evident in the monumental dimensions of the buildings, which at the time were not antithetical to functionalism.

Whereas the search for new, unconventional forms of expression in Rus-

219 **Apartment building** at Kozi-khinsky Street (today Ostouzhev Street), ca. 1900.

220 Detail of **facade** decorated with bas-reliefs of an apartment building on Kozikhinsky Street, ca. 1900.
Art Nouveau brought about a sweeping transformation in urban design in Moscow. While the individual home remained the usual solution, certain streets underwent a radical change in appearance due to the construction of apartment blocks. Henceforth multi-storied houses, decorated lavishly and set side by side, became an integral part of the city's landscape.

221 The residence of the **Belaev family**, Spiridonovka Street (today Tolstoi Street), 1904. Architect: I. Boni.
At the beginning of the century Spiridonovka was the fashionable street of a residential quarter. The historian P. Bartenev wrote that "Here, far from noisy shops, in an idyllic calm, live people of the educated and most respectable classes of our society": plutocrats, industrial magnates, and bankers such as the Morozovs, the Tarasovs, and the Riabushinskys.

change. As a result, the overall harmony of rationalist constructions is offset by internal tensions that endow this architecture with a very dynamic aspect.

Konstantin Melnikov, one of the better known collaborators of ASNOVA, deserves mention. Not given to theoretical musings, Melnikov designed and built some of the most interesting projects in postrevolutionary Russia. Melnikov's works defined the specific features of rationalist architecture and went beyond its doctrines. With respect to artistic form, Melnikov is as important to the development of modern architecture as Alexander Vesnin, who was a close collaborator of the Constructivists. It is important to keep this broader perspective in mind when analyzing Melnikov's work.

Melnikov's personality came to the fore in his earliest projects for competitions dating from 1922 and 1923. His design for a workers' settlement on Serpukhovskaia Street in Moscow, to be called Atom, employs repetition of standard elements and so anticipates later standardized housing. Equally interesting is the plan he submitted for the competition of 1923 to build a Palace of Labor in Moscow. The structure is much in evidence here. Nevertheless, the most famous of Melnikov's edifices is the Makhorka Pavilion constructed for the Moscow Agricultural Exhibition of 1923. The somewhat irregular character of the building derives from the supporting pillars, which are complemented by glass surfaces and by the angles of the volumes that give a sense of openness. Similar features occur in Melnikov's design for the offices of *Leningradskaia Pravda* in Moscow, but especially in his design for the Soviet pavilion at the Exposition Universelle in Paris in 1925.

Art Deco

After 1925 C. Melnikov's work also comprised projects for workers' clubs that were typical of his creative style. Some of these were built in Moscow and its environs. In a way these designs represent a rationalist's answer to the principles of the Constructivists and Functionalists, for whom the new architecture was closely connected to new needs. Workers' clubs were supposed to reinforce social relations while simultaneously performing an ideological function. Melnikov took over the principal thesis of the rationalists—that spatial divisions play a fundamental role in the formation of the new consciousness. He foresaw changes of spatial configuration and utilized "mechanized interior forms." The plan for the Rusakov Club in Moscow, for example, provided for balconies in the playhouse that could be added or removed at will. Similar ideas crop up in other projects.

Melnikov's own house, conceived and constructed in Moscow in 1927, counts among his better-known works. Its very original spatial organization is due to the interpenetration of cylinders with hexagonal windows on their surfaces. The entrance is highlighted by means of simple geometric forms, and the interior of the building is ordered around its skeleton, in which the elevator shaft occupies the central position. The structured arrangement and the use of volumes and interpenetrating spaces make this house a representative work of rationalist architecture.

Productivism and Functionalism

Architecture, especially as the rationalists conceived it, made up but one wing of avant-garde research. The other wing comprised artists who defined themselves as Constructivists, and were later called Productivists or Functionalists. This movement grew directly out of research by younger artists—mostly painters and sculptors—for whom experimentation in architecture was a way of transcending the formal and, as they saw it, shut-in concept of an artistic structure. Toward the middle of 1921, a group of Constructivists established themselves in Inkhuk alongside the rationalist architects. This former group consisted mainly of painters and sculptors who, after abandoning their earlier

research into "surface composition," had given themselves over to projecting "useful works in space." Among them were the painters Rodchenko and Stepanova, the architects Alexander Vesnin and Alexei Gan, as well as the sculptors Konstantin Medunitsky and the Stenberg brothers Georgii and Vladimir. As time passed, their inimical relationship to the rationalists became exacerbated—especially when constructivism evolved into productivism and artistic issues gave way to ideological concerns.

Constructivism in architecture began its most active period of development when its proponents encountered architects who shared their point of view and did not interfere in their attempts to resolve typically architectural problems. The process began within Vkhutemas but developed in the context of the Union of Contemporary Architects (OSA), which, as we know, was founded in 1925 and headed by Vesnin,

Gan, and Ginzburg. The Constructivists considered themselves as heirs to Tatlin's architectural ideas, which they felt were symbolized by his monument to the Third International. Their conception of contemporary architecture was based on a belief in the direct connection between new techniques and revolutionary ideology. By transforming human existence, architecture should contribute to the creation of the New Man, they declared. The architect was called upon to be a builder of the new society. Thus the Constructivists began with technological concerns but ended up with a vision of a social utopia.

The Functionalist and Productivist conceptions worked out in Constructivist circles placed form in a secondary role to function (that is, to the useful qualities of the work-as-product). For Constructivists the new revolutionary society was identified almost automatically with the new technical form, the

231 **The residence of Konstantin Melnikov**, Krivoarbatskaia Street, 1927.
During the Stalinist period the Melnikov house was cited as the worst example of "formalist and bourgeois" architecture. Today it is regarded as a synthesis of all kinds of experiments by the international avant-garde of the 1920s.

232 Konstantin Melnikov: **detail of the artist's house**, Moscow, 1927.
In planning his house, in which he set up his workshop, Melnikov implemented several models of natural lighting: the showcase window of the wall facing the street, the numerous small openings from the ceiling to the floor in the cylindrical form on the courtyard, the overlapping circular areas and rectilinear planes.

modern form, which explains why during the 1920s theoretical discussion centered increasingly on society to the neglect of artistic problems. Solutions to artistic problems were virtually dictated by the belief that collectivism was to be the future form of communist society.

With this all-encompassing social goal before them, the architects affiliated with the Constructivist movement concentrated more and more on urban architecture. The "new city" was a popular theme at the outset of the 1930s, for it corresponded to their vision of the New Man, who would have all his needs satisfied by the collective in its basic form—the communal house. In this way, the city and the communal house became the focal points of Constructivist collectivism—its macrocosm and microcosm, so to speak.

In the development of constructivism an important part was played by the meetings held in Inkhuk in the latter half of 1921, devoted to discussing pedagogic ideas, by the teaching program for the industrial departments at Vkhutemas, and eventually by the architects' collaboration with OSA. A significant stage in the development of constructivism came in the autumn of 1921, with the announcement by a number of artists that, encouraged by Osip Brik, they were giving up pure artistic creation in order to devote themselves to work in and for industry. It was at this time that Vesnin and Rodchenko executed their "last paintings" and took up "useful" research in the applied arts and in architecture.

The architect Anton Lavinsky, a close collaborator of the Constructivists, presented a paper entitled "neo-engineerism" and exhibited his project for a "new city on springs," a fantastic circular city: a single multistory building running along the axis of a spring. The city would be made of aluminum and glass. The roads, free of noise and vibration, would enable direct access to the different sectors of the city, each with its precisely defined functions.

In his paper, Lavinsky argued that "hardly a step separates non-objective art from engineering." An engineer-architect who has at his disposal a variety of technical means need not bother with natural laws; he can impute novel functions to architecture. Lavinsky's paper led the artists in Inkhuk to criticize the "constructions" that the Stenberg brothers and Medunitsky had exhibited shortly before and to charge them with failing to provide precise social definitions for their edifices.

In 1923, in its turn, Vkhutemas became the center of polemics. At the time proponents of productivism dominated the school's industrial departments (metal and woodworking); they tried hard to transform the program of the Architecture department. Productivist and Functionalist Constructivists alike selected the journal *Lef*, edited by Maiakovsky, to publish their views. Articles appeared in *Lef*'s pages directed against the rationalists' experiments and favoring socially defined architectural projects. The outcome was the formation at the beginning of 1923 of the Group of Architects of *Lef*-Inkhuk, made up in part of some militant students from Ladovsky's workshop. Their leaders were Rodchenko, Brik, and Vesnin. This group was established just before the Union of Contemporary Architects (OSA), which Vesnin and Moisei Ginzburg set up in 1925. A year earlier Ginzburg had laid down, in his book *Style and Period*, the principles of functional architecture. Theoretical discussions in the union were published in the journal *Contemporary Architecture*, founded in 1926. Alongside articles about architectural projects, the review provided information on and descriptions of avant-garde architecture throughout the world.

The architects, who belonged to OSA manged to unite the various tendencies within the Constructivist current. Moreover, by opening up a dialogue with the international avant-garde architectural community, they highlighted the common forms and the spiritual kinship of the new functional architecture the world over. To be sure, the Soviet architects were keenly aware of the specific sociopolitical situation of revolutionary Russia, and thought that Russian architecture would play a special role in the world movement. Ginzburg wrote in *Contemporary Architecture*: "The general platform of constructivism is based on three points: goal, means, and form. Every architect, even the most estranged formalist, works with a definite goal in view. This is doubtless true, but the root of the problem is that the Constructivists ascribe another meaning to the concept of goal. Whereas for the traditional architect the goal is defined by a commission from an individual, for the functionalist it is defined by obtaining a commission that engages him by reason of its social importance. For the Constructivist the goal is the radical transformation of the old concepts...." He continues, "Hence our goal is labor in common with the proletariat, participation in the task of edifying a new life, a new way of life."

From Vesnin to Utopia

Alexander Vesnin was one of the most consistent representatives of Constructivist architecture. His functional works are of interest on account of their plasticity. In his works Vesnin managed to unite a certain austerity with the ideals that had animated the engineers in their approach to architecture. Vesnin's entry into the Constructivist movement is marked by two projects: he designed the decor for Meierhold's popular entertainment, *The Struggle and the Victory*,

233   Ilia Golosov: The **Zuev Club**, Moscow, 1926-27.
The Zuev Club was among the buildings erected for the tenth anniversary of the October Revolution. It was one of the few clubs not constructed by Konstantin Melnikov but by Golosov, who belonged to the group OCA.

which was staged for a Congress of the Third International in Moscow; he also provided the stage setting for a play by G.K. Chesterton, *A Man Who Was Thursday*, produced in Alexander Tairov's Kamernyi Theater in 1922 and 1923.

The first project was of gigantic proportions and involved a composition using large masts that were implanted vertically or suspended along diagonal lines on two models. One represented a capitalist city, conceived in the form of a pyramid made of machines piled up chaotically, and the other a socialist city endowed with a structure of clearly ordered geometric volumes. Screens and banners that bore pointedly political slogans were hung between the masts.

The setting for Chesterton's play was similar: a simple rotating scaffolding with podiums, ladders, stairs, turning wheels, and screens formed a construction that was meant to symbolize the new city as an organism, homogeneous in structure, diversified in its details.

Alexander Vesnin worked out his initial architectural designs together with his brothers. Their earliest designs, from the years 1922–25, made use of scaffoldings as the skeletal frame of the edifice. The main parts of the building, which were simple but diversified, with readily discernible vertical divisions, were to serve as the basis for a superimposed construction of masts and antennas. The same principle was put to work in the plans for the Palace of Labor (1922–23), the Telegraph Office (1925), as well as, in 1924, for the branch offices in Moscow of *Leningradskaia Pravda* and the Arcos company. All these designs highlighted the skeletal frame of the construction. The work of the Vesnin brothers in the 1920s, just prior to the establishment of OSA, wholly determined the specific features of avantgarde architecture in Russia. After 1925 the influence of the international avantgarde movement became increasingly pronounced and widespread.

There is no doubt that among Alexander Vesnin's projects of the later 1920s—which bring Le Corbusier's architecture to mind—the most interesting are those for the Lenin Library. Two versions dating from 1928 employ the principle of a building planned with a horizontal emphasis and composed of several volumes that are simple and geometrical, yet varied according to the functions they fulfill; the whole building would be dominated by a central unit. The main element of the facade consisted of large glass panels. The second version used inclined windows to ensure optimal interior lighting and bestow a rhythm on the edifice that would serve to differentiate the very austere cubic structure. The simplicity of the spatial arrangement and the highlighted structure of the building are typical traits of other projects by Vesnin, which were executed until the early 1930s, for the most part outside Moscow.

Similar problems exercised other architects in OSA, among whom the brothers Panteleimon and Ilia Golosov stand apart. The younger brother, Ilia, made an original artistic contribution which was designated in Constructivist circles as "romantic symbolism." Ilia Golosov was convinced that there was a symbolic tie uniting form and society. He maintained that the dynamic form of an ascending spiral best represented the idea of the revolutionary proletariat, whereas the simplicity of geometric volumes represented the universality of the working-class movement. On the basis of these principles, Golosov drew up a plan in 1923 for the Palace of Labor in Moscow which prefigured his later work. The palace, as an "enormous machine," is supposed to incarnate the organized force of the proletariat. Another early, but perfectly mature, project for a club in Moscow on Lesnaia Street was carried out in 1927. The plan for its exterior is reminiscent of the blueprint for a machine. The whole building is meant to symbolize the link between the new way of life and the new techniques. Similar elements crop up in other designs by Golosov in the later 1920s, most notably in those for the House of Textiles, the Central Telegraph Agency, and the Electro-Bank, in which symbolism of form plays a role.

234   Alexander and Viktor Vesnin:
**Design for the offices of the Len-
ingradskaia Pravda newspaper**,
Moscow, 1924.
The Constructivists' initial projects were
characterized by an aesthetics glorifying
the machine, which they held to be the
only medium for overcoming Russian
technical backwardness and constructing a genuinely Socialist world.

211

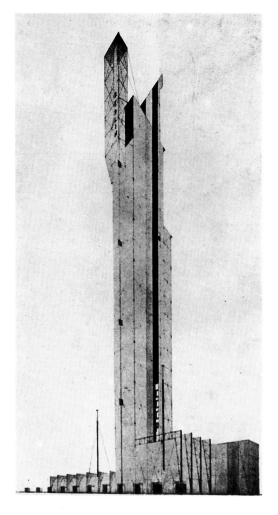

Moisei Ginzburg, cofounder of OSA, was the theoretician of functional architecture. His interest in theoretical and formal issues dates back to the 1920s. In his first book, *Rhythm in Architecture*, Ginzburg demonstrated that there is a connection between the rhythm of architectural form and the "rhythmic beat of our day." Ginzburg's most interesting and typical works included dwellings dating from 1925–30, in which he attempted to homogenize the houses' structures while varying their facades. He used mainly horizontal divisions, with long rows of windows and passageways leading to the interior. The facades are embellished by a regular arrangement of balconies and overhangs. Along with a building erected in 1926–27 on Malaia Bronnaia Street, two other typical buildings of the later 1920s deserve notice: a house on Novinsky Boulevard (1928), designed with Ignatii Milinis, and a house in Rostokino, planned in collaboration with Solomon Lisagor. The first project, especially its execution, became an example for other designs of functional houses. Pillars supported the tall building, which had the characteristic two levels of apartments. The city's roads run underneath the construction, in the space between the pillars. The flat roof has been transformed into a garden forming a kind of terrace that enhances the appearance of the upper story.

It should be evident from the foregoing that the architects in OSA were associated with several artistic currents that were not mutually exclusive. So-called pure constructivism, which championed the link between architecture and new technologies, as well as functionalism, which stressed the links between architecture and the new society, were the twin poles of orientation in the association's development. Interest in all architectural forms that "organize life," in the widest sense of the term, grew throughout the 1920s.

At the start of the 1930s the tasks set for new architecture drew attention increasingly to communal houses and urban construction. "Communal life" was the basic principle of the new city that architects were striving to render in a structural form. L. Sobsovich, an economist and early theoretician of town planning, wrote:

the idea of the one-family, isolated house, whose charms may be obvious from the petit-bourgeois, individualist point of view, will no longer have the slightest justification in agglomerations of the socialist type and will consequently no longer be considered a solution. Construction of this kind of small, individual house, will no longer be economically feasible; it will be uncomfortable and consequently of little attraction. Most likely the typical habitation (to be sure, exceptions are always possible) will be an immense

212

apartment building equipped with all the amenities, electrified and heated by a central thermo-electric plant, fitted out with elevators, mechanical equipment for maintenance and cleaning, baths and showers, perhaps even exercize facilities, and so on.

At this time, the architects in OSA, and Ginzburg in particular, originated the idea of a reconstruction of Moscow on socialist principles. Ginzburg, who periodically worked on the "multifunctional" communal house, was an advocate of "deurbanization," by which he meant the disappearance of a distinct urban organism in the future. In his view, although the process of transforming the city would be slow, its inception was already visible. Thanks to decentralization and the construction of new dis-

tricts, the urban structure would burst its boundaries and spread out into nature.

In 1930 Ginzburg and Mikhail Barshch published in *Contemporary Architecture* a project for a "garden city" that conformed to their ideas for a new, "deurbanized" Moscow:

Moscow should be turned into a vast green park for leisure and culture toward which the new zone lines will converage. This does not involve immediate demolition but rather waiting patiently for buildings to deteriorate naturally. In this way Moscow will progressively become an immense park, in which only indispensable cultural and administrative installations will survive, as well as a kind of "museum city" with the most characteristic monuments and city quarters.

236 Ivan Leonidov: Design for the **Palace of Culture**, Moscow, 1930. The Sport Pavilion.
Leonidov wrote that the Palace of Culture "is the basis of the workers' cultural activity... it helps in organizing the entire system of political and cultural education in the urban sector where it is situated." This style, in another form, to be sure, found favor later in the Stalin era, whereas none of Leonidov's grandiose designs was ever carried out.

The Palace of Soviets

The competition for the Palace of Soviets was a crucial turning point in the development of modern architecture in Moscow. In effect, the competition marked the end of progress in architecture. In 1930–31, during the first phase of the competition, which attracted the best-known European architects as well as Russian innovators, none of the projects submitted satisfied the political authorities. The same fate befell the 160 plans submitted in the second phase. Anatolii Lunacharsky formulated the specific criteria for the contestants eligible to enter the third phase of the competition. This time participation was restricted to Russian architects, and designers affiliated with the avant-garde were excluded. Lunacharsky wrote:

The palace must give expression to the grandeur—that is, the power, simplicity, and joyful attitude toward life–so—of the proletariat. The spirit of the masses must be incarnated in the building: it must be its organic component as well as its ornamentation. The edifice must not only bear witness to the highest degree of technological expertise, but also exhibit an emotional force and speak directly to the new man.... The architect in a position to satisfy all [these] demands would produce an edifice with a nearly classical allure, much as in Greece, displaying grandeur, stability, harmony of proportion, light, and extensive use of sculpture.

The competition was closed in 1933, and the winning project, by Boris Iofan, was to become the paradigm for other "creative solutions" put forward throughout the 1930s. So it was that the struggle for a new architecture, waged in avant-garde circles in the 1920s, was lost. The new socialist-realist classicism came to define the character of architecture in Moscow until mid-century. Academic architects like Ivan Zholtovsky, Alexei Shchusev, and Ivan Fomin rose to prominence once again, followed by a group of young artists who launched violent broadsides against the representatives of rationalism, constructivism, productivism, and functionalism.

To be sure, the new situation in architecture was affected by political changes. Stalin himself promoted the idea of constructing the Palace of Soviets. By soliciting plans on a monumental scale, he took a decisive step toward creating a

237 Le Corbusier in Moscow in 1928.
In 1927 Le Corbusier was entrusted with the construction of Tsentrosoiuz, the office of the central committee of cooperatives, in Moscow. At the time Le Corbusier gave several lectures in the capital's architectural institutes, and his theories gained great popularity.

238 Iakov Chernikhov: **Composition** with different architectural forms, 1930.
Aware of the great technical and material difficulties in which the Soviet Union found itself at the end of 1920s, Chernikov considered his series of "architectural fantasies" as a game, a never-to-be-realized dream.

214

239 **Pushkin Square** (formerly Strastnaia Square) with the editorial offices and printing establishment of *Izvestiia*. According to the project by Grigorii Barkhin, 1926–27. Barkhin's original project for a tower was not carried out, since the law forbade tall buildings in the center of Moscow.

symbolic center of power in architectural form: "the spiritual center of a socialist country." Andrei Zhdanov ascribed considerable importance to architecture in formulating the doctrine of socialist realism. Architecture alone, he wrote, "is able to reflect the grandeur of the period in an objective way." He concluded, "In a society constructing socialism an architect is not only a building engineer and street engineer, but also an engineer of human souls."

Andrzej Turowski

215

7 Musical Life

Moscow and St. Petersburg

The history of Russian music forms a whole in which the parts contributed by Moscow and St. Petersburg are not easily distinguished. The specific musical character of each city did not hinder continual exchanges between them. Many great musicians played in St. Petersburg and in Moscow; many works were performed in each of the two cities in close succession. It may seem natural that in music, as in other areas of cultural life, the capital attracts the best forces and thus offers the widest range of productions. This was indeed the case in regard to certain aspects of musical life, as we shall see, but in ballet, for example, St. Petersburg and Moscow took turns as the leading centers from one decade to another.

There was fairly keen rivalry between the two cities before as well as after the revolution. Although the seat of government was transferred to Moscow in 1918, the city did not automatically assume cultural supremacy. However fertile Moscow artists' imagination and readiness to act, it was no mean task for them to match the musical standards of Petrograd (Leningrad, as it became in 1924) during the era of NEP. The dominant position that necessarily accompanies centralization was not finally assured until the 1930s, when the all-pervasive Stalinist ideology had wiped the slate clean of all independent artistic ventures.

The musical panorama in Russia during the second half of the nineteenth century reveals a paradoxical situation when one compares Moscow with St. Petersburg. It was in St. Petersburg, the Western-oriented capital of Peter the Great, that the Group of Five—led by Mili Balakirev and including Caesar Cui, Modest Musorgsky, Alexander Borodin, and Nikolai Rimsky-Korsakov—proclaimed the principles of musical nationalism, the influence of which soon spread to the Conservatory where Rimsky-Korsakov taught composition. Moscow, though seemingly committed to the national tradition, underwent a development that brought it closer to the European, more cosmopolitan musical currents. This trend began with Tchaikovsky and his pupil, the eminent teacher Sergei Taneev and continued with Taneev's disciples, Sergei Rakhmaninov and Alexander Skriabin. On the other hand, a return to the sources of Russian liturgical music took place in Moscow at the Synodal Institute, a development which marked a departure from the Italian and German religious music that had been in style for more than a century in the Imperial Chapel.

The Bolshoi Theater, Russia's most magnificent hall, was located in Mos-

240 **The Bolshoi Theater**. Constructed in 1783, but destroyed by fire in 1853, the Bolshoi Theater we see today dates from the reconstruction of 1856.

241 Léon Bakst: costume design for **Narcisse et Echo** by Nikolai Cherepinn: **the Nymphe**, 1911. Pencil and watercolor on paper, 40 × 27 cm. Musée d'Art moderne, Strasbourg.

242 Léon Bakst: Costume design for **Scheherazade** by Rimsky-Korsakov: **the Eunuch**, 1911. Gouache, 35 × 22 cm. Musée d'Art moderne, Strasbourg.

243 Sergei Prokofiev, 1910. Although Prokofiev (1891–1953) was born in the vicinity of Moscow, he finished his studies at the Conservatory of St. Petersburg, where his exceptional talents were quickly recognized. His earliest works, short pieces and studies for the piano, date from 1907–9.

244 Alexander Skriabin. It is said that Nikolai Rimsky-Korsakov could not contain his excitement when he heard Skriabin (1871–1915) play his *Poème de l'extase* on the piano. As a genuine innovator Skriabin aspired to create a "total art." He exerted considerable influence on the Russian music of his day, in particular on the experiments of the avant-garde. His popularity as a composer is attested by this postage stamp in his honor.

245 Nikolai Rimsky-Korsakov. Rimsky-Korsakov (1844–1908) dominated Russian musical life at the turn of the century as a symphonic and lyric master; some of his pupils, such as Igor Stravinsky, were to become famous musicians in their own right. In 1905 he was excluded for a while from the Conservatory of St. Petersburg for his revolutionary sympathies.

220

246   **Sergei Prokofiev**.
Prokofiev was originally regarded as a
rather iconoclastic composer. When the
Scythian Suite was perfomed in Petrograd in 1916 it provoked quite a scandal, with Alexander Glazunov making a
show of departing the hall. As Prokofiev
was little concerned with the revolution
and its achievements, he took to the
road as a concert pianist, dividing his
time between the United States and
France. He did not return to the USSR
until the beginning of the 1930s.

cow, yet the preeminent Russian operas composed during the last three decades of tsarist rule were first performed in St. Petersburg, at the Mariinsky Theater. Moscow began to make up this distance after 1885, when private opera companies came on the scene, at a time when the imperial companies in both cities were in decline. This rivalry helped to promote the renaissance of the Bolshoi.

Romanticism and Symbolism: Rakhmaninov and Skriabin

Sergei Rakhmaninov and Alexander Skriabin were the most celebrated pupils of the Moscow Conservatory, where they studied until 1882. Apart from intervals due to their somewhat itinerant existence, they both contributed to the city's musical life. Rakhmaninov did so until 1917; while Skriabin, who lived outside Russia from 1904 to 1909, remained active in Moscow until 1915. They were each virtuoso pianists who composed above all for their instrument, but they were also outstanding symphonic composers. Rakhmaninov, the more eclectic of the two, tried his hand at virtually all musical forms: chamber music, songs, cantatas, liturgical music, and opera. Both emulated Frederick Chopin and Franz Liszt; but Rakhmaninov's esteem for Tchaikovsky was matched by Skriabin's scorn for him. Notwithstanding an initial commitment to the same aesthetic principles, their routes soon diverged. Still each in his own way is a perfect example of the disquiet and turbulence that herald a breakdown in civilization.

Rakhmaninov, who soon discovered his proper idiom and scarcely departed from it thereafter, was the last Russian Romantic to give free rein to anguish, suffering, and lyric tenderness, and as such was out of step with his contemporaries. One of the most admired musicians of his generation, Rakhmaninov emigrated in 1917. On March 25, 1917, a few months before his departure, he gave a legendary charity concert at the Bolshoi for the benefit of the victims of World War I. In a single evening he performed his Second Concerto, Tchaikovsky's First Concerto, and Liszt's First Concerto—a show of technique and endurance that few virtuosi would dare to risk even today. It was as if Rakhmaninov, in what was in fact his last public performance in Russia, wanted to leave Muscovites with a memory that would make his departure all the more painful. By this time he had already produced thirty-nine of the forty-five numbers in his opus: virtually all his solo piano works, the Preludes, the *Etudes-Tableaux*, all the songs, the three concertos, two symphonies and what is certainly his orchestral masterpiece, the symphonic poem *Isle of the Dead* (inspired by Arnold Böcklin's painting), with which he paid tribute to Symbolism, the most powerful aesthetic current in prerevolutionary Russia.

There is another paradox here. Symbolism had a more profound effect on the artistic and literary world in St. Petersburg than it did in Moscow. Yet in music a Muscovite, Skriabin, became the most typical representative of symbolism. At first he had imitated the Romantics, but in his passion for mystical philosophy he sought a musical equivalent of his exalted spiritual state and aspirations, becoming imbued with a sense of musical messianism. This is evident in such works as the Third Symphony, or 'Le divin poème' (1904), 'Le poème de l'extase' (1907), *Prometheus* or 'Le poème du feu' (1910), the sonatas (especially nos 5 through 10), as well as the numerous pieces for piano dating from his later years (among them *Toward the Flame*). As Skriabin moved progressively away from traditional harmony and tonality, he elaborated his own sonic world in which musical lines are intertwined and superimposed on one another and chords cluster in bunches. Skriabin, a spiritualist revolutionary, died prematurely two years before the revolution, leaving unfinished the *Acte préalable* that was to have been he prologue to his *Mystère*—the work he hoped would be the musical and spiritual culminating point for all mankind.

222

The Private Theaters

After 1885 the focal point of Moscow opera shifted from the Bolshoi Theater to the private theater of Savva Mamontov. The company that was formed by this wealthy industrialist and patron of the arts put on a total of more than forty works by Russian composers as well as a smaller number of foreign operas: *Carmen, Faust, Samson and Dalilah*, and *Aida*. The company's later years were particularly noteworthy. It was here that, in 1896, the twenty-four year old Fedor Shaliapin burst on the scene in the first performance of the role of Ivan the Terrible in the revised version of the *The Maid of Pskov* by Rimsky-Korsakov. In the same year Sergei Rakhmaninov's hitherto unsuspected talents as a conductor were revealed in Mamontov's theater. Unfortunately, it was at the turn of the century that the private theaters reached their acme. Mamontov's arrest for insolvency in 1899 shows how little artistic quality has to do with financial security. Nevertheless, the theater managed to survive for a few more years thanks to its incorporation into the Prianishnikov company, which had staged productions in Moscow since 1893, when it arrived from Kiev. But in 1904 the Prianishnikov Theater folded once and for all. Its disappearance marked the end of a great artistic venture that had revived the operatic scene in Moscow—even though, in the view of some critics, the productions were sometimes musically flawed, owing to overhasty preparation and Mamontov's own penchant for stage design and acting to the neglect of the music.

But no sooner had one private opera shut its doors than another one stepped in to take its place. From 1904 to 1917 Mamontov's successor was the wealthy businessman Sergei Zimin, no mean rival to the official theater, who opened on October 1, 1904 with a production of Rimsky-Korsakov's *May Night*. Soon thereafter Petr Olenin, a singer and set designer, took over artistic direction of Zimin's company. While continuing Mamontov's support for native Russian works up to a point, Olenin did not hesitate to pursue a different, more eclectic direction in his choice of operatic works to be performed. An admirer of French opera, he took considerable risks on more than one occasion in presenting "experimental" productions that were hardly likely to captivate Russian audiences; thus Camille Saint-Saens *Henry VIII* and Gustave Charpentier's *Louise* were complete failures. On the other hand, Giacomo Puccini's *La Bohême*, Edouard Lalo's *Le Roi d'Ys*, and Richard Wagner's *Meistersinger* met with enthusiastic critical acclaim.

The most singular success, the veritable exploit, of Zimin's opera company was the first night of Nikolai Rimsky-Korsakov's *The Golden Cockerel* in 1909. Written in the wake of the events of 1905, this was the composer's last opera. It is a fable combining the enchantment of the Orient with a pitiless satire of tsarism, and it naturally ran up against the barrier of official censorship. Thanks to more or less extensive revisions of the libretto, *The Golden Cockerel* enjoyed a critically acclaimed first night (just ahead of the Bolshoi production) under the baton of the talented conductor, Emil Cooper. Unfortunately, however, Rimsky-Korsakov, grand master of Russian music since Tchaikovsky's death, had passed away more than a year earlier, in June 1908.

After some of the most notable musical events of the era had taken place on its stage, Zimin's theater came to a tragic end. On the night of April 18, 1917 fire destroyed the sets and costumes for all the extant productions.

The Bolshoi Theater

What was happening in the Bolshoi Theater during this period? Having expended its energies during the summer of 1894 in a noteworthy if labored production of *Siegfried*, at the turn of the century, the Bolshoi barely hung on with a repertoire totaling only about ten operas. Though it lacked neither great voices nor means, the company had become sclerotic. The music critic Kash-

247 **Fedor Shaliapin** as Ivan the
Terrible in Nikolai Rimsky-Korsakov's
Maid of Pskov.
Shaliapin's greatest roles were those of
Ivan the Terrible in this opera by
Rimsky-Korsakov and in particular Bo-
ris Godunov in Modest Musorgsky's
opera of that name.

248 **Fedor Shaliapin**.
Shaliapin (1873–1938) gained prominence as one of the most original stage
personalities of his day, in particular by
popularizing Russian opera. His true-to-
life interpretations were entirely in the
modern spirit of lyric drama.

kin wrote that the Bolshoi differed in no essential respect from a typical provincial *theater*:

Dargomyzhsky's *Rusalka* is canceled for lack of a new stage design; Glinka's two operas, *A Life for the Tsar* and *Ruslan and Liudmila*, are interpreted despicably; Tchaikovsky is represented only by *Eugene Onegin* and *The Queen of Spades*; Rimsky-Korsakov's *Snow Maiden*, part of the regular repertoire, is rarely performed.

This criticism was all the more justified in light of the fact that in the same period Mamontov's opera was able to stage some forty works. Nevertheless, this competition, later enlivened still more by Zimin, was salutary in helping the Bolshoi to pull itself out of its administrative lethargy. The arrival of Shaliapin in 1899 did much to promote this reawakening. Other singers whose names are tied to the Bolshoi in the first quarter of the century were the baritones Gryzunov and Georgii Baklanov, but especially the soprano Antonina Nezhdanova, doubtless one of the leading Russian singers of her time, whose regular partner was the illustrious tenor Leonid Sobinov.

In 1901 (five years after Mamontov), the Bolshoi staged Rimsky-Korsakov's *Maid of Pskov*, and in the course of that decade it produced the other monuments of Russian opera *(Boris Godunov, Prince Igor, Khovanshchina)*. Moreover, Shaliapin was active in bringing variety to the repertoire by promulgating and participating in certain less renowned operas, such as Caesar Cui's *Angelo*, Alexander Serov's *Judith* and *The Force of Evil*, and Alexander Grechaninov's *Drobrynia Nikitich*. The appointment of Rakhmaninov as conductor, from 1904 to 1906, was an event of considerable significance. His first undertaking, on the occasion of the centenary of Glinka's death, was to revive *A Life for the Tsar*, which he was careful to restore to its original version, reinserting passages ordinarily ommitted and cutting out the Italianate ornamentation that had been foisted on the work by a dubious interpretative tradition. "How much fresh-

ness and force Rakhmaninov shows," wrote the critic Iulii Engel. "His conducting is remarkable by dint of this ability to capture the vital nerve of each distinct tempo."

Rakhmaninov also originated a principle of conducting that, while not new in itself, had languished in Russian theater, namely to conduct facing the stage (in the manner long since familiar to us). This replaced the usual practice, inconvenient for singers and conductor alike, whereby the podium was placed below the footlights facing the orchestra and the public. Rakhmaninov's engagement

249 **Sergei Rakhmaninov**. Rakhmaninov (1873-1943) was a typical representative of the great romantic tradition of pianist-composers. His best works for piano (the sonatas, preludes, and *études-tableaux*) were composed prior to the revolution. After emigrating he traveled widely as a virtuoso concert pianist.

of the same title) and *Francesca da Rimini* (based on Dante's *Divine Comedy*). The venture was hardly successful. Shaliapin had been chosen to sing the title role in *The Miserly Knight*, but he refused, declaring that "Pushkin's play is more forceful than what you have written." The role fell to the baritone Baklanov who, according to the critics, was "a good artist to all comers." Rakhmaninov's disappointment over this was compounded by the replacement of Nezhdanova in the role of Francesca by Salina, a singer of mediocre quality.

In 1906 Rakhmaninov gave up his post as conductor in order to devote himself entirely to composition. He was succeeded by Viacheslav Suk who remained in this post until his death in 1933, by which time he had completed the renaissance of the Bolshoi. Of the other conductors who took the podium over the years one of the most notable was Emil Cooper. Having staged the *The Golden Cockerel* for Zimin, he directed the Bolshoi between 1908 and 1914 in a Wagner cycle; *Lohengrin* (1908), *The Walkyrie* (1910), *The Twilight of the Gods* (1911), *Siegfried* (1912), *Rheingold* (1912), and *Tannhäuser* (1914). In this way the Moscow public got to know the Tetralogy "out of order." It should be mentioned here that in 1889 a German company had staged *The Ring of the Nibelungs* for the first time in Russia, first in St. Petersburg and then in Moscow.

Wagner did not win favor in Russia overnight, all the less so in nationalist Moscow compared with the more European St. Petersburg. Nevertheless, his music did succeed in gaining entry, so that immediately after World War I and the revolution, as if to demonstrate that anti-German sentiments served only the tsarist regime's interests, first *Lohengrin* (1918) and then *Rheingold* (1923) were brought back to the Bolshoi, followed in 1929 by the *Meistersinger*.

As for other foreign operas, there was no dearth of Italian and French productions; from the Italian repertoire Giuseppe Verdi's *Traviata*, Giacomo Puccini's *La Bohème*, Pietro Mascagni's *Cavalleria Rusticana*, Ruggero Leonca-

250 **Sergei Rakhmaninov** (right). Rakhmaninov finished his studies at the Moscow Conservatory under Arensky and Taneev. From the inception of his career, when he received encouragement from Petr Tchaikovsky, Rakhmaninov always had the support of the greatest musicians. He is pictured here with Fedor Shaliapin.

with the Bolshoi enabled him to collaborate with Shaliapin; ever since their encounter in Mamontov's company the two were united by bonds of friendship and mutual esteem. However, their relationship was not without its difficulties. In 1906 Rakhmaninov brought to the Bolshoi his two operas, written during the previous year, *The Miserly Knight* (adapted from Alexander Pushkin's play

vallo's *Paillasse*, while the French works included Jules Massenet's *Manon*, Hector Berlioz' *The Trojans,* and Charles Gounod's *Romeo and Juliet.* Carl Maria von Weber's *Euryanthe* was performed in 1911. Shaliapin staged Massenet's *Don Quixote* in 1911, and on February 10, 1917, on the very eve of the revolution, he brought to life the somber and hard-hearted majesty of Philip II in a memorable single performance of Verdi's *Don Carlos.*

Of the foreign operas staged during the 1920s, Richard Strauss' *Salome* and Puccini's *Madama Butterfly,* both produced in 1925, deserve mention. In the Russian repertoire several works expres-sive of a new aesthetic were performed, such as Alexander Iurasovsky's *Trilby* (1924), or Sergei Vasilenko's *The Son of the Sun* (1928), set in China. The latter work was modeled on the revolutionary romanticism of Reingold Glier's ballet *The Red Poppy,* premiered in 1927. These works were of little importance and are hardly remembered today.

The revival of *Boris Godunov* in 1927, which was only in part due to the Bolshoi, reopened the aggravating issue of the different versions of the opera. In the same year that the musicologist Pavel Lamm restored the original score, which was not performed until the following year in Leningrad, the Bolshoi

251 Kazimir Malevich: **portrait of Mikhail Matiushin**, 1913. Oil on canvas, 106.5 cm × 106.7 cm. Tretiakov Gallery, Moscow.
The gifted and brilliant Matiushin (1861–1934) finished his studies at the Moscow Conservatory. He composed the music for *Victory over the Sun,* a Futurist opera produced together with Kruchenykh and Malevich. Along with his unabating interest in musical research, he founded, with his wife Elena Guro, the Union of Youth, and was an important innovator in the plastic arts.

continued to favor the version by Rimsky-Korsakov. However, in its production the Bolshoi reintroduced a scene which Musorgsky had included in the first version of his opera in 1869 but excised from the second version of 1872. In the scene in question, entitled "Before the St. Basil's Cathedral," the Simpleton and the Tsar come face to face. Because of its dramatic intensity the scene constitutes a crucial moment in the action of the opera. Unfortunately, however, the scene performed was not Musorgsky's original version but a recent orchestration by Mikhail Ippoli-

252 **Fedor Shaliapin** in Modest Musorgsky's *Boris Godunov.* Only Shaliapin's splendid bass could surpass his consummate acting skills. Whether in a comic or tragic operatic role, Shaliapin invariably excelled.

tov-Ivanov who, in his dubious role of "reviser," remained faithful to his master, Rimsky-Korsakov. The credit falls to Stanislavsky for presenting Musorgsky's original version in 1929 in his Opera Studio.

Stanislavsky and the Opera

With the founding of the Moscow Art Theatre, Stanislavsky labored to link the theater and music. He commissioned from Alexander Grechaninov incidental music for productions of Alexei Tolstoi's *Tsar Fedor Ivanovich* and *The Death of Ivan the Terrible*, and later for Alexander Ostrovsky's *Snow Maiden* (a subject on which Tchaikovsky had already written incidental music and Rimsky-Korsakov an opera). Stanislavsky already had to his credit the production of fragments from operas with students of the Moscow Conservatory. But it was not until 1919 that he set up his Opera Studio in the Bolshoi with the intention of applying to musical drama his principles of seeking psychological truth and concentrating on the acting. His musical proclivities ranged across works as different as Domenico Cimarosa's *The Secret Marriage* (1925), Puccini's *La Bohême* (1927), and Vladmimir Dechevov's Socialist-Realist opera, *Ice and Steel* (1930). Nevertheless he accorded priority to the classical Russian repertoire: *Eugene Onegin, May Night, The Tsar's Fiancée, The Queen of Spades, The Golden Cockerel,* and *Boris Godunov.* He produced a composite version of the two versions of Musorgsky's opera based on the texts published by Lamm.

Stanislavsky continued to work in the Opera Studio until his death in 1938. What he did for acting style and diction was to have a lasting influence on future operatic production in the USSR.

The Ballet

Serious though the challenge may have been to the Bolshoi Theater's supremacy in opera, where ballet was concerned it certainly faced no serious competition

in Moscow or elsewhere in Russia. To be sure, until the first years of the century choreography in St. Petersburg enjoyed pride of place thanks to the work of Marius Petipa at the Mariinsky Theater. But it was this French artist's disciple, Alexander Gorsky (1871–1924), who infused new life and a new aesthetic direction into dance at the Bolshoi, first as a soloist from 1901 and then as ballet master until his death. This was the time when the best talents in St. Petersburg were about to depart the country to found in Paris the "Ballets Russes" under

Sergei Diaghilev. Gorsky modernized the choreography of much of the standard repertory, including such evergreens as Ludwig Minkus' *Don Quixote*, Cesare Pugni's *Le petit cheval bossu*, Louis Joseph Ferdinand Hérold's *La Fille mal gardée*, and Adolphe Adam's *Gisèle*. But he also staged more recent ballets–Tchaikovsky's *Sleeping Beauty*, and *Raymonda* by Alexander Glazunov –whose rise to prominence began with Petipa in St. Petersburg. Like Diaghilev he also fell under the spell of Isadora Duncan and turned for a while to free

253   A. Golovin: **stage design for Boris Godunov**.
Modest Musorgsky's opera was first performed during his lifetime in 1874. However, at the turn of the century Nikolai Rimsky-Korsakov's revised version gained widespread popularity. In 1908 Sergei Diaghilev staged a highly acclaimed production in Paris, for which A. Golovin was stage designer.

254 **Igor Stravinsky**.
After hearing *Feux d'artifice* by the young disciple of Nikolai Rimsky-Korsakov, Igor Stravinsky (1882–1971), Sergei Diaghilev was enthusiastic and commissioned *Fire Bird*, with the result that the initial stages of Stravinsky's career were wholly bound up with the "Ballets Russes." After long years spent in Paris Stravinsky settled in the United States.

dance and choreo-drama (e.g. *Salâmbo* in 1910 with music by Max Arend). He also choreographed music that had not been originally composed for the dance; for instance, *Schubertiana* (arranged by Arend) in 1913, but above all in 1918, for the first anniversary of the revolution, he was in charge of a grandiose program that included adaptations of Glazunov's *Stenka Razin*, the scene of the *veche* (medieval popular assembly) drawn from Rimsky-Korsakov's *The Maid of Pskov*, and of Skriabin's *Prometheus*. He returned to classical ballet in 1919 with a production of the *Nutcracker Suite*.

Because most of the dancers at the Bolshoi were closely associated with their theater—unlike their counterparts in St. Petersburg who often performed on Western stages—they were less widely renowned. This did not prevent the Moscow public from bestowing laurels on Vasilii Tikhomirov, Alexei Bulgakov (at the Bolshoi from 1911), and among women dancers Ekaterina Geltser and Margarita Kandaurova. A few, such as Vera Karalli and Alexandra Balakhova, one of Moscow's veritable idols, emigrated after the revolution. In the closing hours of the tsarist regime Balakhova married the wealthy magnate Alexei

Ushkov; but once his fortune was wiped out, the ballerina moved to France (1921), where she danced and taught, dying in her nineties in 1979.

The spirit of innovation and experiment permeating the years of NEP was at least as much in evidence in ballet as it was in opera. At first it may seem surprising that a ballet with a biblical theme, Sergei Vasilenko's *Joseph the Magnificent*, should have been staged in 1925, but its subject was given a humanistic interpretation and it drew praise for the close attention paid to the settings depicting ancient Egypt and the Near East. But no event acquired the kind of artistic and ideological significance as the production of Reingold Glier's *Red Poppy*, mentioned earlier, which ranked as the first ballet imbued with the revolutionary aesthetic.

The Conservatory and Musical Instruction

At the beginning of the twentieth century Rakhmaninov and Skriabin were well established in their careers. Taneev, the much esteemed master, had retired in 1905, a year in which upheavals at the St. Petersburg Conservatory had repercussions on its Moscow counterpart. Vasilii Safonov, who had held the directorship of the Moscow Conservatory since 1889, was replaced by Mikhail Ippolitov-Ivanov, a composer entirely within the generation of epigones much like Vasilenko, the new professor of orchestration and composition. No single inspiring personality came to the fore in musical life in Moscow during the next fifteen years, the period when Sergei Prokofiev was active in St. Petersburg/Petrograd. In 1921 Nikolai Miaskovsky took over the composition class. A personage as prolix as he was academic, and possessed of exemplary devotion and integrity, Miaskovsky trained several generations of composers, paying close attention to technical skills and perpetuating a conservative attitude to musical invention. By contrast, already from the first decade of the century piano instruction was of better quality, for it

was in the hands of virtuosi and pedagogues of the first order like Alexander Goldenweiser and Nikolai Metner, together with Konstantin Igumnov who had taken up his post in 1899.

The revolution did nothing to alter the superlative level of piano instruction attained by personalities like Samuil Feinberg, one of that generation's finest artists and a composer of distinction for his instrument, and Heinrich Neuhaus, who would number Sviatoslav Richter and Emil Gilels among his pupils. The most remarkable voice teachers were Nina Koshits and, in the years 1914–19, Anton Sekar-Rozhansky.

On July 12, 1918 Lenin signed a decree by which the Conservatories in St. Petersburg and Moscow were to come under the People's Commissariat of Education, then headed by Anatolii Lunacharsky.

Another institution for musical instruction established in 1895, the Gnesin Institute, underwent a development that brought it to a position of considerable repute. It was founded by Elena Fabianovna Gnesina and her sisters; their brother Mikhail, a well-known composer, taught there from 1923.

Religious Music

Although religious music was not the most actively pursued domain of cultural life in Moscow, its thirty-year evolution, especially between 1900 and 1917, is of inestimable historical importance—in no way diminished by the fact that political events prevented it reaching its acme. Moscow met the nation's needs in providing liturgical music for the Orthodox Church. Responsibility for this was vested in the Synodal Institute, which promoted not only instruction in religious music (namely in training choir conductors) but also musicological research in collecting old songs (*znamennye*, or neumatics). For over a century first Italian and later German influences were predominant in the Imperial Chapel at St. Petersburg, the spiritual center of Russian religious music, whose vocal style naturally spread to the par-

231

234

255, 256 **The opera of the poor**, at the Kamernyi Theater, Moscow. Alexander Tairov (1885–1950) revolutionized the theater by deliberately turning away from naturalism toward "theater in itself." Acting style underwent noticeable changes, with particular emphasis put on the theatricality of gestures.

235

257 **The opera of the poor**, at the Kamernyi Theater, Moscow.
In the Kamernyi Theater Alexander Tairov sought to give an active dimension to the stage setting and costumes. To this end he collaborated with avantgarde artists such as Alexandra Exter and Alexander Vesnin, who succeeded in instilling a real dynamism into the stage setting by simplifying forms and colors and using a system of symbols (such as geometrical forms, letters, and inscriptions).

centers, to factories and clubs. Boris Asafev, composer and musicologist, authored (under the pseudonym Igor Glebov) program notes for concerts as well as popular texts about music. In 1921 the Institute of Musical Science opened in Moscow for the purpose of disseminating appreciation of the history of music.

The exaltation of collective action was the inspiration for an interesting musical experiment. An orchestra that had no conductor, called the *Persimfans* (The First Symphonic Ensemble), was founded in 1922 on the initiative of the violinist Lev Zeitlin, who performed frequently as a soloist; it existed until 1932. Consisting of the best teachers and stu-

dents from the Moscow Conservatory, as well as of musicians from the Bolshoi Theater orchestra, the *Persimfans* performed programs of classical and contemporary music for concerts in subscription series and on tours to provincial towns and cities. When it rehearsed, individual sections of the orchestra met first and then the orchestra as a whole.

The slogan "art for the masses" implied not only free access to classical music but also an ideologically motivated repertoire that lent itself to easy listening and performance. These were the goals behind RAPM (Russian Association of Proletarian Musicians) set up in 1923. As the musical embodiment of the Proletkult, RAPM extolled songs for the masses as the only appropriate form for the expression of proletarian musical sensibility. But these musicians believed that it was their duty to seek a more elaborate musical language and form than that which sprang spontaneously from the masses. A prolific representative of the movement was the composer Alexander Davidenko, whose innumerable revolutionary songs include the celebrated "They wanted to smash us, to crush us!" The authorities themselves finally judged RAPM to be harmful, and ordered its dissolution in 1932.

In total contrast to RAPM was ASM (the Association for Contemporary Music). The encounter with the music of contemporary western composers–Bela Bartok, Paul Hindemith, Franz Schreker, the French Group of Six, the new Viennese School–encouraged some Russians to seek a new sonic world situated somewhere between Skriabin and Schoenberg. ASM was founded in Moscow in 1929. Its members included Nikolai Roslavets (1881–1944), Alexander Mosolov (1900–73), Samuil Feinberg (1890–1962), and Leopold Polo-

vinkin (1894–1949). None of these men was well known among music-lovers. The association also attracted several musicians such as Boris Asafiev, Nikolai Miaskovsky, and Dimitrii Kabalevsky, who, once their curiosity for the new forms had been sated, soon returned to the security of academicism. ASM published the review *Sovremennaia muzyka* (Contemporary Music) in Moscow from 1924 to 1929. In 1926 a branch sprang up in Leningrad, which counted the young Dmitrii Shostakovich among its adherents. The ASM did not promote a predetermined aesthetic vision, since it was in many respects experimental. One musical current in evidence was Constructivist urbanism, which exalted the power of machines. Arthur Honegger's well-known *Pacific 231* had laid the foundations for this trend; it inspired a 1926 ballet by Alexander Mosolov, *Stal* (Steel), which comprised a well-known symphonic episode, *Zavod* (The Factory).

But before long ASM was in the Soviet authorities' bad graces. It was reproached for emulating decadent and

258   The celebration of **Leo Tolstoi's** birth, Moscow, 1928.
Already widely acclaimed during his lifetime Leo Tolstoi was pronounced after the revolution to be the greatest writer and "progressive" thinker of his day. On the occasion of the centenary of his birth in 1928 a dazzling official ceremony took place at the Bolshoi Theater in Moscow.

artificial Western bourgeois art and branded as "formalist," a term used to cover any art based on a search for "forms," that is, structures or sonorities in and for themselves, at the expense of ideological and emotional content. In the ensuing period this charge was leveled in astonishing and often dramatic ways.

ASM ceased to exist at about the same time as RAPM. Thanks to the work of the West German musicologist Detlef Gojowy nearly a half-century later, these composers and their works have little by little been brought back to life. In 1932 the Central Committee of the CPSU called for a "restructuration of artistic and literary organization." This was the signal for the creation of the Union of Soviet Composers, the sole central agency empowered to be the administrative and ideological watchdog of Soviet musical life, with a mission to guard against real or imagined "deviations" and to suppress them.

André Lischke

259 **Moscow**, ca. 1935.
Today, much as at the beginning of the century, Sverdlov Square is one of the most vibrant spots in Moscow, thanks largely to its places of entertainment. The picture shows, from left to right, the Bolshoi Theater, the Tsum store (built in 1909 in the pseudo-Windsor style), the Malyi Theater, and the well-known Metropole Hotel.

260 **Workers performing a comedy**, ca. 1930.
After the revolution, the theater became a principal means of ideological education of the Soviet masses. Factory committees were exhorted to stage popular entertainments and amusing or edifying plays. Here for instance, in this comic satire, workers are demonstrating the benefits of work in unison and collective method.

8 The Cinema

Birth of the Moscow Cinema

The cinema has offered us various images of Moscow, all seen from outside, even when they did no more than reflect reality. There are the documentary archive pictures of the early years of the century, extravagant in flavor and stamped with the grandeur of the tsardom, the lyrical or painful witnesses to the revolution, the dire, disturbing justification of the Cold War, the serene, tourist-brochure accompaniments to *détente*, the powerful, impressionistic portrayals of military parades in Red Square.

There is no shortage of fictional images, either. We have seen Moscow technicolored by the corruptions of Hollywood, caricatured in an Ernst Lubitsch comedy, distorted by the baroque imagination of Josef von Sternberg, made to look sordid in the interests of anti-Communist propaganda, and softened and romanticized in the memories of White Russian émigrés. Again and again we have seen Moscow in flames, cocking a snook at Napoleon. Let us not forget, however, that Moscow also produced its own images.

It was in 1896 that the pioneers of cinematography first turned their attention to Moscow. In that year Nicholas II decided to hold his coronation in the ancient city of the tsars. The brothers Auguste and Louis Lumière of Lyons, France, thinking there might be money in recording the rite on film, dispatched two cameramen to cover the occasion. Their names were Perrigot and Doublier. They also had orders to organize screenings of Lumière movies while they were there and to assess the potential of the Russian market.

Moscow was delighted. Maxim Gorky declared: "Without any fear of exaggerating we can foresee very extensive use being made of this extraordinarily novel invention." He also sensed that this new type of traveling show was going to evolve more sophisticated forms that would take it a long way from the documentary style.

The French were not the only ones to travel the country with their cameras and projectors; British and American crews competed with them. But it was a Lumière cinematograph that was demonstrated to the tsar at a performance that gave it an immense publicity advantage over the others.

The Grünewald brothers purchased a concession for Russia and placed Doublier in charge of the Head Office of Cinematography that they set up in a store in Moscow's Kuznetsky Most. Felix Mesguich brought them new films, and the tiny company made movies of its own all over Russia, showing them between two circus or music-hall numbers.

261 Georgii and Vladimir Stenberg: poster for **The Trial of the Three Million**, 1926. Colored lithograph, 71 × 106 cm, Kunstgewerbemuseum, Zurich.
Scenario: Oleg Leonidov and Iakov Protazanov; direction: Iakov Protazanov; photography: Petr Ermolov.
Also known as *Three Thieves*, this satirical comedy is a typical example of a genre of which Protazanov became the master and that was virtually nonexistent in the Soviet motion-picture industry at the time. Poorly received by the official critics on its release, *The Trial of the Three Million* was nevertheless a huge commercial and popular success.

241

The Grünewald brothers screened as much as they filmed, but it sometimes happened that events got ahead of the material they had available. When that happened, they resorted to editing to sustain the illusion of reality among their enthusiastic audiences. Such manipulations prompted the thought that the time when cinema had been a mere curiosity was past. The invention itself had ceased to surprise; it was what it showed that excited audiences. A new era had begun.

The major foreign companies shared this new awareness, selling adventure movies, comedies, newsreels, and dramas on the Russian market. The French were bolder, with both Pathé and Gaumont setting up branches in Moscow.

In 1903 I. A. Guzman opened two motion-picture theaters in the city. Four years later there were seventy theaters in Moscow and 150 in St. Petersburg. The Russian craze for movie-going inevitably disturbed the producers of live theater. Bowing to pressure from them, the authorities ordered that cinemas must close at 9 p.m. There was a public outcry, and the official closing time was changed to 11 p.m.

In the early years of the century Muscovites could enjoy motion pictures of all kinds. Pathé monopolized much of the distribution, offering farces, dramas, historical reconstructions, adaptations of works of literature, newsreels, medical movies, and even pornography. Censorship kept an eye on this flood of material. Its severest strictures were reserved for films dealing with the French Revolution. Guillotines were banned, though it was perfectly permissible to screen medical films of amputations, with all the gory details shown. Essentially the censor was there to prevent the distribution of any movie that covered the fall of a monarch. One manager had his theater closed for having shown a film that ended with the execution of Mary Stuart!

The tsar's attitude to cinema was an odd one. He had no great fondness for it, yet he asked his official photographer, the German Hahn-Jagelsky, to get hold of a movie camera in order to film the royal family and document official ceremonies. He even authorized him to sell footage of such films to foreign production companies. Most of the material recorded between 1900 and 1917 was later used by the revolutionaries in edited propaganda movies directed against the tsarist regime.

First Russian Films

It was not until 1907 that the Russians started to make their own motion pictures. The initiative came from a man named Drankov, who was the photographer of the second and third Dumas and a correspondent for the foreign press. After setting up the *First Cine Studio* in St. Petersburg, Drankov decided to turn to fiction, he began by filming *Boris Godunov*, based on a play in verse by Alexander Pushkin. This displeased the top men at Pathé, who opened a production department and invited the Frenchman, Maître, to make a *Boris Godunov* in Moscow. In fact this associate of Ferdinand Zecca made a lively short called *The Don Cossacks*, and Drankov left his own film unfinished.

Undeterred by this failure, he went into production. So, around the same time, did Khanzhonkov, an ex-officer who had established himself as a distributor. Khanzhonkov's earliest productions, based on Slav folklore, were *Drama in a Gypsy Camp*, made by the cameraman Siversen, and *A Russian Wedding in the Sixteenth Century*. Drankov was more ambitious. He made a comedy, *Svabba Kreohinkovo*, and produced a farce, *Userdnyi denshchik*, which Filipov directed, and a historical drama, *Stenka Razin*, written by Goncharov and directed by Romashkov. *Stenka Razin* in particular was an enormous hit and launched the historical genre in Russian cinema.

Faced with this success, Pathé set up its production branch in Moscow and decided to invest in the Russian market. Starting in 1910, a number of foreign companies established themselves in Moscow. Gaumont tried its luck there until 1911. The Italians, the Americans,

and the Danes followed suit and colonized the nascent motion-picture industry, while at the same time distributing their respective national products. An incredible number of private companies flourished in Moscow without seriously challenging the position of Pathé, who enticed away the directors discovered by Drankov and really had only two serious rivals: Khanzhonkov's company, which made more than seventy motion pictures between 1908 and 1913, and a company called Gloria, founded in 1911 by two Germans, Paul Thiemann and Max Reinhardt, who had hitherto represented Denmark's Nord-

isk, Italy's Ambrosio, the American Vitagraph company, and two small French firms, Lux and Le Lion.

Pathé made thirty motion pictures in under three years. Between 1908 and 1913 the Russian cinema's rate of production rose steadily. Six films were made in 1908, 15 in 1909, 20 in 1910, 46 in 1911, 86 in 1912, and 116 in 1913.

As the years passed, particular trends emerged. Historical films were very popular, though they were soon rivaled by works in a black, tragic vein tinged with fantasy. These were directly inspired by the Danish cinema. How-

262 **Father Sergius**, 1918.
Scenario: Alexander Volkov, from a short story by Leo Tolstoi; direction: Iakov Protazanov; decor: Vladimir Baliuzov, A. Loshakov; leading roles played by Ivan Moszhukin, Natalia Lysenko, Vladimir Gardarov.
The last and most important picture Protazanov made before the October Revolution, *Father Sergius* was released only after the fall of the Provisional government.
Tolstoi's story was too delicate a subject for the censor. Moszhukin was never better than in this role, in which he gave deep and complex expression to the slow aging of a man tormented by fleshly desires.

ever, the most highly-prized genre of all was not drama, farce, documentary, or comedy but adapations of masterpieces of Russian literature. Between 1910 and 1913 there were some ten motion pictures based on Alexander Pushkin, seven on Nikolai Gogol (and as many on Mikhail Lermontov and Leo Tolstoi), six on Alexander Ostrovsky, three on Dostoevsky (and the same number on Anton Chekhov and Nikolai Nekrasov), and two on Ivan Turgenev. Other writers were also taken as models. The art film based on literature continued to develop until the advent of the Bolsheviks.

The main filmmaker in this period was Goncharov, the author of *Stenka Razin*. As a director he worked for every company. By 1913 he already had thirty motion pictures to his name, most of which could be classified as epics.

But the most celebrated pioneer of Russian cinema was Iakov Protozanov. This Moscow-born son of a shopkeeper joined Gloria as a translator at the age of twenty-eight. He was by turns assistant director, actor, scriptwriter, and producer. His second film as a director was a hit (*The Prisoner's Song*, 1911). He made a total of forty motion pictures in four years. They were macabre, pessimistic stories tinged with occultism and enhanced by the use of clever sets. His taste for *fin de siècle* decadence did not prevent him from occasionally abandoning extravagance and affectation to try his hand at lyrical naturalism or psychological realism. An eclectic, Protazanov was also noted for his skill at directing actors. And motion-picture actors were not slow to become the idols of the Russian public.

Avant-Garde and Popular Cinema

As in most countries, cinematography caught the interest of the members of the various avant-garde movements. They deplored its repetitive aspect, but they saw in the rhythm of the motion picture a means of asserting the aesthetic revolutions on which they were embarked.

The year 1912 saw the publication of the manifesto *A Slap in the Face of Public Taste*, whose signatories included the poet Vladimir Maiakovsky. In the following year Maiakovsky published *Theater, Cinema, Futurism* and offered the director and producer Persky a filmscript entitled *In Pursuit of Fame*. Viktor Shklovsky recalls it in his *Memoirs*: "A famous futurist has some poems printed by the big merchant Corpsblanc, but he forgot to put his name to them and goes dashing all over the place to sign every copy.... It is a script about fame, looked at humorously.... Back home, the Futurist falls asleep lying on his bicycle.... Such was the broad development of the industrialization of the period."

According to Maiakovsky the script was turned down. "Someone from the company listened to my filmscript with the greatest attention before saying with indignation: 'It's worthless.'... Abashed, I went home and tore up the script. Later a film based on it did the rounds on the banks of the Volga. My script must have been listened to more attentively than I thought."

It was not until January, 1914, that the cinema and futurism actually met, though the artistic movement was used as a pretext rather than providing a theoretical foundation for a film. *Drama at Cabaret 13*, produced by Nikolai Toporkov and Winkler and directed by Vladimir Kasianov, does indeed seem to be not more than a parody of a detective story in which members of the "Donkey's Tail" Futurist society—notably Mikhail Larionov and Natalia Goncharova—agreed to appear. Several more years were to pass before motion pictures ventured into avant-garde territory.

From 1913 onward movie-theater audiences idolized the actor Ivan Moszhukin. Discovered by Petr Chardynin and Goncharov, he made his mark in the works of Evgenii Bauer, portraying heroes who were by turns cynical, passionate, dreamy, and neurotic. Bauer was fond of weird atmospheres and of plots that echoed the phantasmagoria of Gogol, Guy de Maupassant, and Jean Lorrain. Born in Moscow, this cultured, aesthetic, ironic man came to the cinema in 1913 at the age of forty-eight. He explored the possibilities presented by lighting and set design, enjoying a very close working relationship with his cameraman, Boris Zavelev. A skilled exponent of controlled stylization, Bauer was able to tackle a wide variety of genres without once departing from his personal manner. Talking to André S. Labarthe about Bauer *(Cahiers du Cinéma, Nos. 220–221)*, Lev Kuleshov said: "He was one of the finest directors in tsarist Russia. He was also a painter and decorator. That was why, for the period, all his films were very good, very well constructed as regards composition. I remember him very fondly; he was a fine man, a fine friend, and a very wise teacher."

When Russia entered World War I the motion-picture industry set itself the task of mobilizing public opinion. Of the thirty-four films made in 1914, more than half were justifications of Russian patriotism. Moszhukin and the other actors starred as the heroes of a large number of productions marked by bellicose chauvinism. The war was present in all of them, whether they were melodramas, farces, comedies, or detective stories. The reason for this lay in the initial military successes of the tsar's armies. After the reverses of the spring of 1915, however, producers fell back on disembodied romanticism, adaptations of novels, and popular serials. The censor forbade any reference to the shortcomings of the regime. Antisemitism reared its ugly head in a number of productions and led to a ban on works about the Jewish population. German movies were also banned, and German producers such as Thiemann and Reinhardt were harassed, despite the fact that they had made plenty of pro-Russian patriotic films. At the same time a great many strikes testified to the growing influence of the revolutionary movement.

The military conflict did nothing to check the dynamism of the motion-picture industry. Sixty-six films were made in 1915 and eighty-four in 1916. The companies involved (most of them private, with the exception of the Skobelev Committee, which in 1914 was given the job of promoting patriotic films) had a total circulating capital of twelve million gold rubles. Ninety per cent of production was in Moscow, which had eighty-five motion-picture theaters. Seventy per cent of films shown were of Russian origin. Most of them fell within the tradition established by the characters portrayed by Moszhukin—a tradition Lenin was later to define as "Saninism" (after *Sanin* by Mikhail Artsybashev). The actor recalled this period in his autobiography, *When I was Mikhail Strogoff*:

> The productions of that time are hard to describe. The primitive, mystical Slav soul with its sudden, shattering rebellions fills those images with its everlasting song of suffering and hope...; those startling works with their edgy expressiveness. The cruel sincerity of those synthetic dramas, heavy with pent-up passion and mysticism, in which the most naked, direct, stripped-down form idealizes itself with a sensually and sadistically subtle intellectuality.

Apart from Bauer, the makers of such movies included Iakov Protazanov and the Muscovite Alexander Volkov, a former opera-singer, actor, scriptwriter, and studio head who became Moszhukin's regular associate.

In 1915 Vsevolod Meierhold agreed to film Oscar Wilde's *The Picture of Dorian Gray*. Meierhold gave an interview before he began shooting:

> The technical component of cinema is much more important than all the others. My task is in a way to discover that technique, of which no use at all has been made hitherto. I should like to start by studying and fully analyzing the *movement* element in cinema.... The screen calls for a special kind of actor. One often sees excellent stage actors and dancers who turn out to be quite unsuitable for the cinema. Their movements are either too broad or too narrow, their gestures exaggerated.... For me that technique is still *terra incognita*.... We need to distin-

guish two elements in the cinematographic art:

1) motion-picture photography, reproduction of the real, etc.;
2) the artistic direction of events, with the set designer contributing the pictorial element.

I regard it as a serious mistake to transplant to the cinema works such as we see on the stage or at the opera. There being no color in this kind of reproduction, fresh artistic problems arise, and none of the old artistic processes is going to be of the slightest use in solving them. I have my own theoretical approach to the question, and I intend to implement it.... I utterly reject the kind of cinema that exists at the moment. My next job is to explore the means that undoubtedly demand to be utilized but that the cinema is neglecting..., I have written a full filmscript of a particular type in which everything is divided into "domains." In it the actors will find their lines and the producer, the set designer, and the director of photography their instructions. This kind of "score" is indispensable. (Extracts published by B. Eisenschitz in *Cahiers du Cinéna*, Nos. 220–221.)

Meierhold considered his first motion picture a failure (partly because of misunderstandings with his cameraman, Levitsky), though his efforts do appear to have borne fruit in certain respects, namely in the effective use made of Egorov's sets, in the rapid, precise editing, and in the high degree of stylization. Although *The Picture of Dorian Gray* was a flop commercially, the producers asked Meierhold for another movie. He decided on an adaptation of *The Strong Man*, a novel by the Polish author Stanislaw Przybyszewski. Speaking of this project, Meierhold said: "I want to bring to the screen a specific rhythm in the movements that corresponds to the general laws of the lighting effects proper to the events recorded." His film was released in 1917, the year of the revolution.

The Cinema and the Revolution

The day of the tsar's abdication was also that of the annual meeting of theater managers in Moscow. At that meeting a motion was passed unanimously, greeting the political prisoners who had been released in Siberia. A few days later two thousand people who worked in the motion-picture industry gathered in Moscow. The upshot was that the workers organized themselves into a trade union while twenty-four producers and directors formed the executive committee of a "Union for the Cinema."

The abolition of censorship and the difficulty of importing motion pictures from abroad gave a boost to domestic production, which continued along much the same lines as under the tsars. Some ten movies were made about the Rasputin affair. Revolutionary themes became a choice subject for historical drama. Filmmakers from Moszhukin to Bauer mined this new vein, and some of the results were not without quality.

However, another trend emerged in opposition to this neoacademicism. On March 15, 1917, the Petrograd Soviet of Workers' and Soldiers' Deputies set up a cinematographic section to take pictures of Bolshevik demonstrations. At the same time Grigorii Boltiansky, who was in charge of newsreels, gave his cameraman similar orders. Later Alexander Kerensky ordered his men to distribute anti-Bolshevik films showing why it was necessary to continue the war.

In September 1917, what was eventually to become Proletkult met at the instigation of Anatolii Lunacharsky and the Central Council of Factory Committees. A resolution was adopted in favor of making the cinema an instrument of struggle and culture:

We consider that the cinema, one of the great acquisitions of humankind, is currently in the hands of the bourgeoisie, which has turned it into a school of crime, corruption, and moral decadence. It is the vehicle used by the ruling class to foist bourgeois ideas and morality on the proletariat.

246

In conditions of genuine popular government cinema could become an effective and powerful tool for educating the working class and the masses of the people, one of the proletariat's most important weapons in its sacred struggle to free itself from the narrow conceptions of bourgeois art. The cinema will develop class consciousness and international solidarity and elucidate the passionate ideals of the proletarian struggle for socialism.

Following the events of October and the fall of the Kerensky government the Union of Workers of the Cinematographic Art (or Tenth Muse) decided to oppose Soviet power. Its members protested against the nationalization of certain movie theaters and distribution agencies. They called on the industry to boycott these moves by not supplying any more motion pictures. In an attempt to counter this resistance the Bureau of the Moscow Soviet published the following regulations:

1) No requisition attempt will be tolerated, whatever its source;
2) With the object of safeguarding and regularizing the cinematographic industry it has been placed under workers' control.
3) Company owners are required to declare the following material to the cinematographic Commission before March 10, 1918, provided that such material was in their possession on February 14: negative and positive films, Jupiter lamps, cables, cameras and projectors, sets, musical instruments, furniture, accessories, chemicals, raw materials of all kinds, and all instruments and means of production;
4) All transfers to new ownership are forbidden, as are all interruptions of or cuts in production and closures of hiring agencies, cinemas, and laboratories;
5) All workers... laid off on February 14 without the agreement of their trade unions shall be taken back...;
6) A 5% tax shall be levied on cinematographic performances from March 10. Tickets shall be franked by the office of the Cinematographic Commission;
7) Citizens who infringe these regulations shall be liable to penalties ranging from the confiscation of all their assets to imprisonment.

The industry's response was to conceal its stocks of negative and positive film, leading to a dearth of film that lasted throughout the Civil War. On August 27, 1919, Lenin ordered the birth of the Soviet cinema: the motion-picture industry was nationalized. But by that time there was only one movie theater still open in Moscow and one company still capable of operating. The great exodus began with Ivan Moszhukin, Alexander Volkov, Richard Boleslavsky, and Iakov Protazanov leaving the country. Bauer died after a motor accident. Those responsible for the Soviet cinema believed that it could start again on fresh foundations. A College of Cinematographic Art was set up. New directors received their training at the front. Lev Kuleshov actually worked with a sub-machine-gun in one hand as he made films with the cameraman Eduard Tissé (who later worked with the renowned Sergei Eisenstein).

Lev Kuleshov began his career working with Bauer. By the time he was nineteen he had made two films: *Engineer Pright's Project* and *The Unfinished Love Song*. At twenty he was teaching at the college of cinematography that Gardin had founded in Moscow. There he was in charge of editing and the direction of actors. His pupils included Vsevolod Pudovkin, Alexandra Khokhlova, Vladimir Fogel, Pogin, Sergei Komarov, and Boris Barnet. In 1922 he set up an experimental laboratory. Film was in short supply, so experiments were carried out on strips of paper. The most famous one involved a montage of a shot of Moszhukin's face with different scenes, where the juxtaposition determined the feeling expressed by his face. It was an unintentional manifesto of constructivism. Several films emerged from the laboratory, including *Mr. West in the Land of the Bolsheviks* (1923), *The Death Ray* (1925), and *Dura Lex* (1927). These state-financed works were influenced by the narrative technique of American cinema. In them Kuleshov showed a tendency to want to control the construction of every shot while delegating the direction to certain of his actors. *Mr. West in the Land of the Bolsheviks* was a comedy that proved very popular with audiences. *The Death Ray* was a failure, but *Dura Lex* (based on a Jack London story) met with a triumphant reception, despite the views expressed by certain critics who deplored Kuleshov's "formalism."

Among those who championed him was Maiakovsky. *Mr. West* had in fact been written in collaboration with Nikolai Aseev, who was associated with the review *Lef*. Maiakovsky had been working in the motion-picture industry since 1918 as an actor and scriptwriter. In 1926 he published an account of his disappointments in this regard:

> *The Young Lady and the Hooligan* and *Creation Can't Be Bought* are sentimental gibberish made to order, adaptations of *The Workers' Schoolmistress* and *Martin Eden*. Gibberish not because they are any worse than others but because they are no better. They were made by Neptune in 1918. The director, the set designer, the actors, and everyone else involved did all they could to deprive the work of any interest whatsoever.
>
> *The Slave to Film*. Having studied motion-picture technique, I wrote a script that belonged alongside our innovative work in literature. The same Neptune company turned it into a thing so hideous as to cover one with shame.

The poet went on to write about ten filmscripts of which only *Children* and *Octobrine and Decembrine* (Smirnov-Iskander, 1928) were ever filmed. As a Communist Futurist he rejected a whole area of Bolshevik cinema. And in the essay *Help* he set out his ideas:

Question 1: Why are foreign movies better than ours?

Answer: Because the foreign movie finds and utilizes special resources that derive from cinematographic technique and cannot be found in any other mode of expression: the train in *Our Hospitality* (Buster Keaton), Chaplin's metamorphosis into a chicken in *The Gold Rush* (Chaplin), the lights of the moving train in *A Woman of Paris* (Chaplin).

Question 2: Why must newsreels be defended against the acted movie?

Answer: Because newsreels show real things and actual facts.

Question 3: Why is it impossible to sit through an hour-long newsreel?

Answer: Because our newsreels are random juxtapositions of shots and events. Newsreel needs to be organized and to organize itself. A newsreel of that kind one could sit through. Newspapers organize events in that way, and we cannot live without newspapers. It is no more intelligent to reject such organization than to suggest closing *Izvestiia* or *Pravda*.

Question 4: Why is *A Woman of Paris* such a beautiful picture?

Answer: Because it achieves maximum emotional saturation.

Maiakovsky may not have found his theories given tangible form in the motion pictures adapted from those of his scripts that producers did not simply turn down, but the avant-garde did nevertheless infiltrate the motion-picture industry. Most movies, however, continued along the lines of tsarist cinema, simply changing the reactionary content into a Communist statement. Remakes of certain foreign films were produced in this spirit, including Fritz Lang's *Mabuse* by Esther Shub and Eisenstein and Dmitrii Bukhovetsky's *Danton*. The latter, incidentally, contains an amazing piece of editorial manipulation. In the orginal movie Georges Danton spits in Maximilian Robespierre's face, and Robespierre wipes away the spit; in the Russian remake Robespierre wipes away a tear after Danton's insult.

263   Alexander Rodchenko: poster for **Kino-Glaz**, 1924 (reprinted 1969). Colored lithograph, 69 × 49 cm, Kunstgewerbemuseum, Zurich.

248

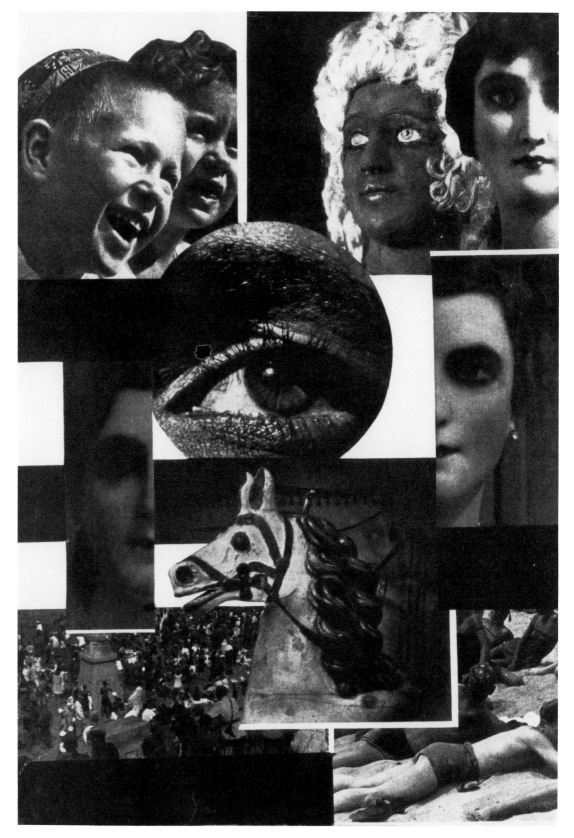

264   "The history of **Cine-Eye**," Dziga Vertov declared in 1929, "is the history of an unremitting fight to change the course of world cinema, to put the emphasis... on nonacted films rather than acted ones, to substitute documentation for direction, to break out of the narrow confines of theater to enter the vast arena in which life itself unfolds." "Showing real events"– to the detriment of an actors' cinema– constituted the very basis of Vertov's program. However, he said, "in order to record reality it is necessary to enlarge– not to copy– the circle that the mind's eye can take in. It is necessary to break out of the narrow field of one's original vision."

265–269 The first number of **Kino-Pravda** came out on May 21, 1921. This famous series of motion pictures was nothing but a newsreel–but a newsreel in an entirely novel and dynamic style. *Kino-Pravda* heralded the genius of Dziga Vertov, which subsequently found expression in more spacious and ambitious works such as *Man with a Movie Camera* and *The Donbas Symphony.*

270   Poster for **Man with a Movie Camera**.

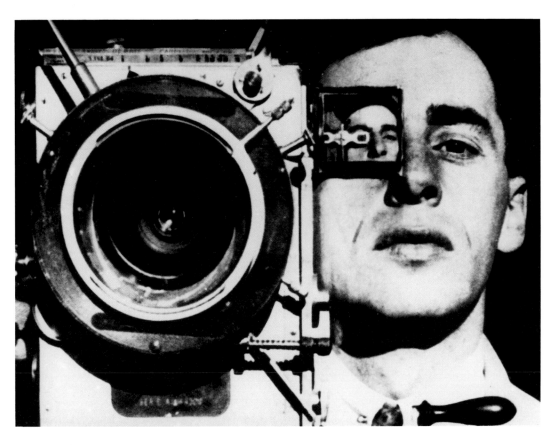

271, 272 **Man with a Movie Camera** is still a major landmark in the history of modern documentary cinema. Thanks to Dziga Vertov, the cameraman becomes the hero of the picture and the camera occupies the foreground.

Two passages symbolize Vertov's method: an image by image sequence at the end, in which the camera takes on a life of its own, without human intervention, whereas at the start we feel that everything is motionless and will be brought to life only by the camera's intervention.

Vertov, Eisenstein, Pudovkin

It was precisely in the realm of editing that the Soviet cinema was to distinguish itself. Alongside Kuleshov's constructivism Dziga Vertov (whose real name was Denis Arkadevich Kaufman) launched his *Kino-Glaz* ("Cine-Eye"). Vertov started the "laboratory of hearing" before directing Soviet newsreels. He made a number of propaganda documentaries and was the creator of *Kino-Pravda* ("Cine-Truth" or "cinéma-vérité"). In 1924 he published the manifesto of *Kino-Glaz* in *Lef*:

Cine-eye as cine-analysis. Cine-eye as "theory of intervals." Cine-eye as

theory of relativity on the screen, etc. I do away with the ordinary 16 frames a second. Ordinary shooting procedures will henceforth include, besides accelerated motion and animation, shooting with a mobile camera, etc. Cine-eye means "what the eye does not see," it means the microscope of time, the possibility of seeing without boundaries or distances, the remote direction of a motion-picture camera; it means tele-eye, ray-eye, "the unexpected glimpse," etc. All these different definitions were mutually complementary, for cine-eye implied: ALL cinematographic means and resources, ALL cinematographic inventions, *ALL* processes and methods, EV-

ERYTHING that might serve to seek out and show forth the TRUTH. Not cine-eye for cine-eye's sake but the truth thanks to the resources and possibilities of cine-eye, that is to say of cine-truth. Not the unexpected shot "for the sake of the unexpected shot" but in order to show people without masks, without makeup, catching them with the eye of the camera when they are not acting, reading their thoughts as the camera lays them bare. Cine-eye: a chance to make the invisible visible, lighten the darkness, lay bare what is hidden, play the game without pretence, turn lies into truth. Cine-eye, a marriage of science and cinematographic realities with the object

of fighting to clear the world for Communism; an attempt to show the truth on the screen through CINE-TRUTH.

Inspite of his revolutionary zeal, Vertov failed to interest the masses in his work. Logically, having condemned cinematographic drama as opium of the people (like Trotsky, who in 1923 wrote *Cinema, Vodka, and the Church* along similar lines), Vertov preferred to invent forms by composing such poems in pictures as *Stride, Soviet!, A Sixth of the World, The Eleventh Year, Man with a Movie Camera,* and *Symphony of the Donbas.* In them he used all the techniques of editing, slow motion, superimposition, dissolves, collage, and even

273, 274 **Strike**, 1924.
Scenario: a Proletkult collective (S. Eisenstein, V. Pletnev, G. Alexandrov); direction: Sergei Eisenstein; photography: Eduard Tissé and Vasilii Khvatov; decor: Vasilii Rakhals.
For this picture, which constituted an introduction to all his other films and marked the beginning of his long association with Tissé, Eisenstein adopted his theatrical principle of "montage of attractions"–a deluge of details, events, and strikingly authentic sets. *Strike* had a profound effect on the whole of Soviet (and subsequently world) cinema. It became a key reference for Eisenstein's theory that cinema is no more and no less than the synthesis of the arts and sciences.

275-277 **Aelita**, 1924.
Scenario: Fedor Otsep and Alexei Faika, from a short story by Alexei Tolstoi; direction: Iakov Protazanov; decor: Sergei Kozlovsky, Alexandra Exter, Isaak Rabinovich; leading roles played by Valentina Konindzhii, Nikolai Tsvetelli, Nikolai Batalov, Konstantin Eggert.
After a brief period of exile (1919-23), Protazanov returned to Moscow, tired of working abroad and no doubt enticed by tempting offers from the producers of the young Soviet motion-picture industry. There he immediately directed a superproduction, *Aelita*, which tells the story of a young Red Army soldier who dreams of taking the revolution to the planet Mars. The vast sets built in the purest Constructivist style, mainly by Alexandra Exter, testify to the ambition of the avant-garde at the time, but the modern viewer will no doubt be equally interested in the scenes of daily life at the beginning of the difficult 1920s.

sound in counterpoint. His very boldness cut him off.

In 1925 Sergei Eisenstein expressed opposition to Vertov's work:

KINO-GLAZ is the symbol not merely of a *vision* but also of a *contemplation*. But we must not *contemplate*: we must *act*. We need not a CINE-EYE but a CINE-FIST. Soviet cinema must crack skulls! And it is not "with the conjoined gaze of millions of eyes that we shall fight the bourgeois world" (Vertov). They will promptly set millions of lanterns before those millions of eyes! It must crack skulls with CINE-FIST, entering and imbuing them until our eventual victory, and now, faced with the threat of the revolution becoming contaminated with "everyday" petty-bourgeois thinking, it must crack them more than ever. "LONG LIVE CINE-FIST!"

Eisenstein's assurance rested on the success of his *Strike*, released in 1924. It was the year of the great renaissance of Soviet cinema, with a total of sixty-seven motion pictures made.

It was also the year of the first movie made by FEKS ("Workshop of the Eccentric Actor"). *The Adventures of Octobrine* by Grigorii Kozintsev and Leonid Trauberg was an agitprop comedy inspired by the style of the great American burlesques. And it was in 1924 that Iakov Protazanov, back in Moscow after several years' exile, made *Aelita*, which was a science-fiction movie enhanced by its use of unusual materials for Alexandra Exter's costumes and set designs.

256

In 1925 the Soviet cinema entered its golden age, the period that saw the first films of Pudovkin, Abram Room, Alexander Dovzhenko, Mark Donskoi, Sergei Iutkevich, and Boris Barnet. Ninety-four motion pictures were made in 1925, 84 in 1926, 121 in 1927, 159 in 1928, 132 in 1929, and 104 in 1930. Moscow was not the only center of production; movies were also made in Georgia and the Ukraine, among other places. Every individual followed his own course while at the same time serving the revolution.

The success of *Strike* made Sergei Eisenstein the outstanding figure in the Soviet cinema. Born in Riga in 1898, he had entered the Moscow military academy in 1918 but subsequently decided to devote himself to the theater. As chief stage designer and manager of the Proletkult art theater, Eisenstein studied under Meierhold and became friendly with Sergei Iutkevich, who was associat-

278 Vladimir Stenberg: poster for **Battleship Potemkin**, 1925 (reprinted 1968), 69 × 49 cm. Kunstgewerbemuseum, Zurich.

257

ed with FEKS. He became a convert to "eccentrism" and directed his own theater company until 1924. In *Strike* he implemented certain dramatic theories while also introducing innovations in editing. With *The Battleship Potemkin* (1925) he imposed his own aesthetics and theoretical thinking.

Eisenstein rejected "American"-style narrative montage and revolutionized the language of cinematography. Yet he never rejected political aims. Before making *October* he began *The General Line* (also known as *Old and New*) on the subject of the collectivization of the countryside. *October* made in 1928,

279   Poster for **Battleship Potemkin**, 1926. Colored lithograph, 93 × 59 cm. Kunstgewerbemuseum, Zurich.

280, 281   **Battleship Potemkin**, 1925.
Scenario: Nina Agadzhanova-Shutko; direction: Sergei Eisenstein; photography: Eduard Tissé; decor: Vasilii Rakhals.
No motion picture in the history of the industry has been so extensively analyzed and reanalyzed as **Battleship Potemkin**. Eisenstein himself considered that "Potemkin could be the report (or newsreel) of an event, but it behaves like a drama." The film has had some curious consequences: since 1925 invented "facts" have taken the place of real ones for everyone– and that includes historians– who has referred to this historical event.

(also known as *Ten Days that Shook the World*) established him as the official filmmaker of the regime. However, at the insistence of Douglas Fairbanks Hollywood claimed him. When United Artists canceled his contract before he reached the States, Eisenstein proceeded to give lectures in most of the capitals of Europe. Eventually Paramount signed him in 1930. After suffering many disappointments in America, he returned to the Soviet Union in 1935. His work had by then impressed intellectuals the world over. Walter Benjamin, for instance, wrote in 1927:

Potemkin is a great motion picture, a rare triumph. It takes the courage of despair to utter one's protest right here. There is more than enough bad slanted art, some of it bad socialist slanted art. Such things are governed by their end effect, count on blunted reflexes, and use ready-made can-

282 **October**, 1928.
Scenario and direction: Sergei Eisenstein and Grigorii Alexandrov; photography: Eduard Tissé; decor: Vasilii Kovrygin.
In *October*, which was made for the tenth anniversary of the revolution, Eisenstein used a very different style from that of his previous films, notably *Battleship Potemkin*. Even his friends were surprised. "Eisenstein is wrong to regard himself as a genius," Osip Brik wrote in the review *Novii Lef*. The film was not appreciated at the time. Audiences expected to see an "epic documentary" and were given a "metaphorical epic."

283 Sergei Kozlovsky: poster for **Mother**, 1927. Colored lithograph, 99 × 67 cm. Kunstgewerbemuseum, Zurich.

284 **Mother**, 1926.
Scenario: Nathan Zarkii, from the novel by Maxim Gorky; direction: Vsevolod Pudovkin; photography: Anatolii Golovnia; decor: Sergei Kozlovsky.
"What emerges from the whole film," said Pudovkin, "is that only my method of editing enables the viewer to perceive smells, tactile sensations, or sounds. One does not photograph a film; one constructs it, using various bits of celluloid, the filmmaker's raw material." Indeed, Anatolii Lunacharsky himself stated that *Mother* was so convincing that one believed one was looking at actual events recorded by an exceptional reporter.

vases. This movie, on the contrary, is ideologically composed and calculated precisely as to every detail, such as the arch of a bridge. The more violently rain blows down on it, the finer the sound it gives. Only the man who shakes it with the tips of his gloved fingers hears nothing and sets nothing in motion. (Reply to O. A. H. Schmitz, *Die Literarische Welt*, nos. 10–11, March, 1927.)

Eisenstein's films were not the only ones to be successful outside the USSR: Vsevolod Pudovkin's *Mother* (1926) met with a similarly enthusiastic reception. The first two motion pictures by this pupil of Lev Kuleshov provided evidence of his eclecticism: *Chess Fever* (1925) was a farcical treatment of a Moscow championship, *Mechanics of the Brain* (1926) a documentary on the subject of Pavlov's theory of conditioned reflexes. *Mother*, made in the same year, astonished audiences with its

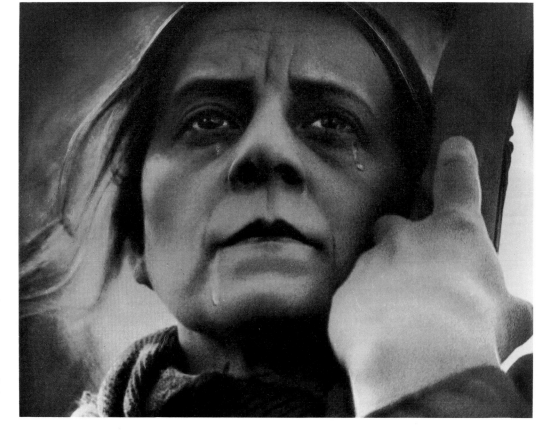

285 Poster for **Storm over Asia**, or **The Heir to Genghis Khan**, 1926. Colored lithograph, 108 × 75 cm. Kunstgewerbemuseum, Zurich.
Scenario: Osip Brik; direction: Vsevolod Pudovkin; photography: Anatolii Golovnia; decor: Sergei Kozlovsky; principal role played by Valerii Inkizhinov.
Storm over Asia assumed a prophetic character after 1931, when the Japanese invented a new kingdom–Manchukuo–and subsequently placed Pu-yi, the last Chinese emperor, on the throne. The film has lost none of its vigor and relevance.

260

ПОТОМОК ЧИНГИСХАНА

РЕЖ. В.ПУДОВКИН

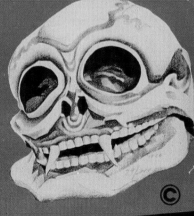

МЕЖРАБПОМ-ФИЛЬМ

В ГЛАВ. РОЛИ
В. И. ИНКИЖИНОВ
ОПЕР. А. ГОЛОВНЯ

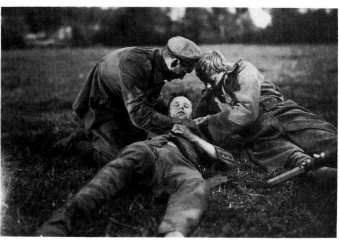

Scenario: Nathan Zarkhi; direction: Vsevolod Pudovkin; photography: Anatolii Golovnia; decor: Sergei Kozlovsky.
Of the many films made to celebrate the tenth anniversary of the revolution, *The End of St. Petersburg* is the most deliberately symbolic, even Symbolist. It is visibly influenced by the poems of Alexander Blok and by Andrei Belyi's novel, *Petersburg.*

seriousness and narrative intention. Pudovkin turned his back on the discoveries of Eisenstein and Kuleshov and accepted the discipline of the classic conception of the story. He worked through lyricism and metaphor to avoid the academic, guided by his poetic inspiration and pictorial sense. *The End of St. Petersburg* (1927) and *Storm over Asia* (1928) followed much the same principle. He was championing sound as early as 1928, seeing it as the answer to the problem of developing montage.

Pudovkin insisted on using professional actors. He took no part in the activities of FEKS; in fact he was often thought of as a commercial filmmaker. Yet the works of Kozintsev and Trauberg, the cofounders of FEKS, were equally sparing in their use of elements bound up with the challenge of con-

structivism. Their associates dealt in every movement possible: futurism, burlesque, the "Ballets Russes," circus, and music hall. Their comic provocativeness disappeared fairly early on. Their movies played in a different register. *The Overcoat* (1926) took liberties with Gogol's text. Kozintsev specified the nihilist resonances written into the movie: "Through the images and events one obvious fact emerged and compelled recognition: social structures partake of nightmare...." *(The Deep Screen).* It was hardly surprising, then, that *The Overcoat* was considered politically unsound! In the following year, however, Kozintsev and Trauberg made *SVD (The Club of the Big Deed)* to commemorate the centenary of the Decembrist revolt in St. Petersburg. Despite its somewhat labored romanticism, the picture

289   A. Zelensky; poster for **The Overcoat**, 1926. Colored lithograph, 108 × 71 cm, Kunstgewerbemuseum, Zurich.

Scenario: Iurii Tynianov, from two short stories by Gogol; direction: Grigorii Kozintsev and Leonid Trauberg; photography: Andrei Moskvin; decor: Evgenii Enei.

For his scenario for *The Overcoat* Iurii Tynianov drew not only on the title story but also on another Gogol story, "The Nevsky Prospect," for a prologue relating a disappointing episode in the wretched civil servant's youth. Kozintsev and Trauberg were among the first Soviet cinematographers to take Gogol as their inspiration in depicting eccentric silhouettes and modes of behavior. The direction here—a romantic variant of expressionism—recalls that of Friedrich Murnau's *Der Letzte Mann (The Last Laugh)*.

263

reveals the generous, utopian quality of its authors. This is confirmed by their masterpiece, *The New Babylon*, a moving evocation of the Paris Commune. Yet once again criticisms were plentiful. This time Kozintsev and Trauberg were taken to task for their fondness for symbols and metaphors–the very elements that made Pudovkin famous.

An associate of theirs, Sergei Iutkevich, was no luckier with the critics. *Lace* and *The Black Veil* were denounced as formalist. In fact Iutkevich based his work on painting. He thought of cinema in terms of animated paintings and found his style in the structuring of the frame and in fluid editing. These enabled him to avoid the naturalism underlying certain products of the period, which clumsily reiterated a dubious realism. Friedrich Ermler also attempted to rethink realism in *Katka's Reinette Apples* (1926) and *The House in the Snow* (1927).

Abram Room was a more complex case. Originally from Lithuania, he started out as a director in an avant-garde children's theater. His earliest cinematographic works were slightly whimsical shorts. These were followed by *The Pursuit of Moonshine* (1924), an amusing propaganda comedy directed against alcohol abuse. He went on to make several pictures in which he succeeded in balancing certain stylistic experiments with a simple lyricism and some penetrating psychological analysis. His most famous work is *Bed and Sofa* (1927), of which Eisenstein had this to say:

This is an interesting picture from the point of view of its subject. We are getting many motion pictures in this genre and we need them badly because they tackle questions of family morality and other questions that are currently preoccupying us. It is a kind of theater of ideas in which various questions are debated.

In 1928 Room used Alexander Shorin's system to make the first Soviet "talkie": *The Plan for Great Works*.

The End of NEP

Until 1927 Soviet cinema conformed to the political line of the New Economic Policy or NEP. A great many comedies were produced, and the master of the genre was Boris Barnet, one of the most attractive personalities of the period. Born in Moscow in 1902, Barnet studied physics and boxed in his spare time. He took lessons from Kuleshov, acted, and did some scriptwriting. He made his first motion picture in 1927, and it was a masterpiece: *The Girl with the Hatbox*. Taking a social reality (the housing crisis) as his starting point, Barnet composed a sunny, affectionate comedy that delivered the occasional challenge to the regime from behind a mask of caricature. He gained immediate acceptance as a director of the caliber of Charles Chaplin and Ernst Lubitsch. His transparent style used montage to give visible expression to the tiniest nuances of feeling. But he also knew how to toe the party line. In 1927 he told the story of the Bolsheviks' battle for control of Moscow in 1917. *Moscow in October* is a busy, almost documentary-style motion picture very different from Eisenstein's stylized poem. His return to comedy (In *The House in Trubnaia Square*, 1928) was marked by an emphasis on satirical details and one unforgettable piece of dialogue. A militant asks the young heroine: "Are you unionized?" Blushing, she replies: "No, I'm a virgin!" Throughout his career Barnet fought hard to bring humor to the screen–together with a certain critical spirit that occasionally landed him in trouble. In 1933 he made the marvellous *Okraina (Suburbs)* and in 1936 *By the Bluest of Seas*, two pictures that established him as one of the most outstanding directors of his day. His own definition of himself was as follows: "I am not an ideas man; I take the material for my movies from life. For good or ill I have always tried to portray the contemporary period, the true man of the Soviet age. But it has not been easy. What I like are the funny things in a drama and the tragic elements in comedy."

290-292 **Arsenal**, 1929.
Scenario and direction: Alexander Dovzhenko; photography: Danylo Demonetsky; decor: Isaak Shpinel and Vladimir Muller.
Arsenal was the first masterpiece of the Ukrainian motion-picture industry. Dovzhenko called it "a 100 percent political picture aiming first to expose Ukrainian nationalism as reactionary and chauvinistic and subsequently to praise the Ukrainian working class." Actually *Arsenal* used enough subjects for five or six films and did not seek unity of tone. It aimed in many directions and even invented fresh ones. A poem-picture, it sustains a constant dramatic tension. Contemporary audiénces, unused to its new cinematographic language, complained of being unable to follow it.

265

293-295 **Earth**, 1930.
Scenario and direction: Alexander Dovzhenko; photography: Danylo Demonetsky; decor: Vasilii Krichevsky.
Earth is undoubtedly one of the
masterpieces of the silent cinema. The
theme– collectivization and its problems– might have made of it a piece of
official propaganda and no more. Yet
Dovzhenko's lyricism, his "biological,
pantheistic" conception of nature as in-
exhaustibly fertile transformed the occasional subject into a meditation on a
universal scale. "... Just as if I had received the physical revelation of the
deaf man who is one day taught what
music is, of the dumb man who is one
day taught what an echo is, the darkness, for me, took on the brightness of
the nights depicted by Dovzhenko. I remember, it was a movie called *Earth*"
(Louis Aragon, recalling in his autobiography *Le Roman inachevé*, his
first impressions on seeing Dovzhenko's
film in 1930).

266

Two Ukrainian film-makers, Alexander Dovzhenko and Mark Donskoi emerged during the 1920s. Donskoi who had studied under Eisenstein at the Moscow Institute of Cinematography, made his first film in 1928. *In the Big City* chronicles the experiences of a peasant poet who moves into the city and observes the behavior of the bourgeois newly resurrected by the NEP. From 1928 Donskoi was associated with the writer Leopold Averbakh. However, his real masterpiece came later: this was the Gorky trilogy, made between 1938 and 1940, *Childhood, My Universities,* and *Earning my Bread.*.

The last outstanding personality of our period was Alexander Dovzhenko. Born in the Ukraine in 1894 into a family of peasant and Cossack origin, Dovzhenko became a schoolteacher before taking part in the Civil War in the Shchors Division (to which he was to devote a motion picture in 1939). He then went into educational administration before transferring to the diplomatic service. In Berlin he studied under the artist Erich Heckel. On his return to Russia he devoted himself to painting and caricature. In 1926, deciding that his art had no future, he approached the VUFKU motion-picture studios in Odessa. He very quickly made his directorial debut with a short comedy entitled *Love's Berries.* Then in 1927, inspired by the adventure movies he had seen in Germany, he made *The Diplomatic Pouch.*

His true œuvre, which was devoted to glorifying the Ukraine, began with *Zvenigora* (1927). Here he found his own epic, metaphorical style. He confirmed his reputation with *Arsenal* (1928), in which his ideological convictions were couched in moving poetry. His use of montage rivaled Eisenstein's, but he rejected the abstraction and stylization of the Constructivists, preferring to retain the full fleshly presence of his characters. An unparalleled masterpiece in this regard was his *Earth* (1930).

After the advent of sound the Soviet cinema did not always retain its lyrical quality. Lecturing at the Sorbonne in Paris on February 17, 1930, Eisenstein gave his opinion of the new process:

To my mind the one hundred per cent talking picture is an absurdity, and I believe everybody shares my view. However, the sound film is something of the very greatest interest, and the future belongs to it. Especially Mickey Mouse films. The interesting thing about these is that they do not use sound as a naturalistic element. They look for the sound equivalent for a movement or for a picture on the screen—not, that is to say, the sound that actually accompanies it but the acoustic equivalent of that optical event. In the Japanese theater hara-kiri scenes are illustrated by sounds that correspond to what you see in terms of the sentimental and emotional reaction they elicit from you. You have the same thing with Mickey Mouse, where the sound track is determined by association and pure equivalence.

Actually it was not so much the introduction of speech that was to lead to a decline in the quality of Soviet cinema as the new ideological climate that sought to harness the motion-picture industry in support of a Socialist realism that was very far removed from any avant-garde concern.

Noël Simsolo

267

Index

The numbers in italics refer to the plate numbers.

Abramtsevo colony 48–54
Agadzhanova-Shutko, Nina *280, 281*
Akhmatova, Anna 17, 19, 62, 132, 134; *111*
AKhRR (Association of Painters of Revolutionary Russia) 103, 106
Alexander II, tsar 179
Alexander III Museum *see* Pushkin Museum of Fine Arts
Alexandrov, Grigorii *273, 274, 282*
Alexeev, Konstantin *see* Stanislavsky
Alexeev, V. A. 233
Altman, Nathan 73, 86, 89, 92, 172; *99, 100, 176*
Ambrosio (motion-picture company) 243
Anarchy 89
Andreev, Leonid 115, 123, 135
Andreev, Vasilii 233
Annekov, Iurii *129, 147, 148, 156*
Annensky, Innokentii 87, 132
Antokolsky, Pavel 134
Apollinaire, Guillaume 68, 70
Apollo 61, 62, 64, 132
Aragon, Louis *293–295*
Arbat Street *217*
     Square 28, 40
Archipenko, Alexander 18, 82
Arcos company 210
Arend, Max 230
Arensky, Anton *250*
Aristophanes 172
Arshipov, Abrams 103
Artsybashev, Mikhail 245
Arvatov, Boris 98
Asafev, Boris 236, 237

ASM (Association for Contemporary Music) 233, 237, 239
ASNOVA (Association of New Architects) 202, 205, 206; *229*
Association of Academic Theaters 159
Association for Contemporary Music *see* ASM
Association for Muscovite Artists 106
Association of New Architects *see* ASNOVA
Association of Painters of Revolutionary Russia *see* AKhRR
Atom (workers' settlement) 206
Averbakh, Leopold 267
Averchenko, Arkadi 123
Azbe, Anton 62

Babel, Isaak 139
Bagritsky, Edward 134, 139
Baklanov, Georgii 225, 226
Baklanov, Gryzunov 225, 226
Bakst, Léon 54, 55, 56, 59, 83; *241, 242*
Balakirev, Mili 56, 217
Balakhova, Alexandra 230
Baliuzov, Vladimir *262*
Balikhin, Viktor 205
Ball, Hugo 64
Balla, Giacomo 65, 78
"Ballet Russes" 19, 56, 229, 262; *254*
Balmont, Konstantin 54, 117, 118, 135; *118, 124*
Baranoff-Rossiné, Vladimir 68, 70, 84
Barnet, Boris 247, 257, 264
Barshch, Mikhail 213
Bartenev, P. *221*
Bartok, Bela 237
Batalov, Nikolai *275–277*
Baudelaire, Charles 54, 56, 116, 117, 119
Bauer, Evgenii 244, 245, 246, 247
Bauman, Nikolai 37

Bebutov, V. *192*
Bednyi, Demian 146; *148*
Bekhteev (von Bechtejef), Vladimir 64
Belaev House *221*
Beloff, Angeline 19
Belyi, Andrei (Boris Bugaev) 117, 118, 119, 121, 135, 144; *127*
Benois, Alexander 49, 52–54, 55, 56, 68, 83
Berdiaev, Nikolai 118
Berlioz, Hector 226
Bilibin, Ivan 54, 55
Blaue Reiter, Der *see* Blue Rider
Blok, Alexander 17, 54, 75, 89, 118, 119, 121, 123, 135, 136; *118, 125, 129, 147*
Blue Rider
     almanac 64
     artists' movement 62
     exhibition 64
"Blue Rose" (exhibition) 59, 61, 62
Blue Shirt (theater company) *197*
Bobrov, Sergei 132
Böcklin, Arnold 56, 222
Bogdanov, Alexander 94, 145
Bogolepov, Nikolai 35
Boleslavsky, Richard 247
Bolshoi
     Opera Studio 228
     Theater 37, 41, 159, 162, 165, 172, 217, 222, 225, 226, 227, 230; *1, 16, 194, 195, 224, 240, 258*
     Theater orchestra 236
Bolotnaia Square *37*
Boltiansky, Grigorii 246
Boni, I. *221*
Bonnard, Pierre 49, 61, 66, 68
Borisov-Musatov, Viktor 56, 59; *64*
Borodin, Alexander 56, 217
Bourdelle, Antoine 61
Bowlt, John E. 9

Braque, Georges   61, 65, 70, 86
Brik, Lilli   *150*
Brik, Osip   98, 139, 140, 208; *150, 282, 285*
British Club (Moscow)   41
Briusov, Valerii   52, 56, 115, 117, 118, 119, 123, 124, 135, 145, 153; *118*
Brodsky, Isaak   103; *117*
Budennyi, Semen   233
Bugaev, Boris   *see* Belyi, Andrei
Bukhovetsky, Dmitrii   248
Bulgakov, Alexei   230
Bulgakov, Mikhail   145, 172; *50, 159*
Bunin, Ivan   115, 123, 135; *26, 123*
Burliuk family   70, 86, 87, 124, 138
Burliuk, David   59, 71, 73, 86, 90, 122, 123, 124, 129, 138; *118, 140, 142, 144*
Burliuk, Ludmilla   68
Burliuk, Nikolai   68, 122
Burliuk, Vladimir   68, 122, 129; *141, 140*
Buster, Keaton   248
Byron, George Gordon, Lord   162

Catherine II, the Great, empress   54, 116
Cavos, C.   *16*
Centrifuge (writers' movement)   131; *152*
Cézanne, Paul   54, 61, 66, 68, 70, 73, 75
Chagall, Bella   *101*
Chagall, Marc   18, 68, 73, 74, 84, 159; *99, 101, 176*
Chapeev, Vasilii   233
Chaplin, Charles   248, 264
Chardynin, Petr   244
Charpentier, Gustave   223
Chashnik, Ilia   97
Cheka   41
Chekhov, Anton   113, 114, 244; *119, 121, 122*
Chekhov House   154
Chekhov, Mikhail   149, 150, 152, 154, 155, 164; *163, 165*
Cherepnin, Nikolai   56; *241*
Chernikhov, Iakov   *238*
Chesnokov, Pavel   232
Chesteron, G.K.   171, 210; *186*
Chichagov, Dmitrii   *199*
Children's Theater   159
Chopin, Frederick   222
Chukovsky, Kornei   124, 131; *129*
Cimarosa, Domenico   228
Cine-Eye   *see Kino-Glaz*
Cine-Truth   *see Kino-Pravda*
City Hall   28, 40
City Soviet   41; 7
Ciurlionis, Mikolajus   18, 52, 62; *126*
Civil War   20–21, 103, 135, 139, 159, 162, 165, 167, 247, 267; *43, 48, 156, 189–191; see also* Revolution
Claudel, Camille   61
College of Cinematographic Art   247
Communal House   200
Continental Hotel   *1*

Cooper, Emil   223, 226
Cormon, Fernand   56
Cosmists, The (writers' movement)   145
Costakis Collection   87
Costakis, George   9
Crommelynck, Fernand   167; *180*
Cross, Henri-Edmond   61, 68
Cui, Caesar   56, 217, 225

Danilin, Nikolai   232
Dante Alighierei   226
Danton, Georges   248
Dargomyzhsky (composer)   225
Davidenko, Alexander   237
Dechevov, Vladimir   228
Degas, Edgas   54, 61, 68
Deineka, Alexander   106; *111, 112, 113*
Delaunay, Robert   65, 71, 78, 132
Delaunay, Sonia   19, 82, 132
Demonetsky, Danylo   *290–292, 293–295*
Denis, Maurice   59, 61, 66; *72*
Deny, Viktor   *42*
Department of Fine Arts   *see* IZO
Derain, André   61, 65, 66, 68; *72*
Diaghilev, Sergei   49, 52, 54, 59, 82, 83, 119, 229; *253, 254*
Dikie, Alexei   *196*
Dmitriev, V.   *179*
Dobuzhinsky, Mstislav   49, 54, 55; *58*
Dokuchaev, Nikolai   202, 203, 205
Dolgorukii, Prince Iurii   *8*
Dombrovsky, Sigismund   200
"Donkey's Tail, The" (exhibition)   74, 244
Donskoi, Mark   257, 267
Dostoevsky, Feodor   111, 114, 154, 155, 244; *119*
Dovzhenko, Alexander   257, 267; *290–292, 293–295*
Drankov (photographer)   242, 243
Dubovsky, Vladimir   *217, 218*
Dukstoi (garden city)   197
Duma (city council)   23, 41, 242; *55*
Duncan, Isadora   229; *154*

Efimov, Alexander   205
Eganbury, Elie   74, 77
Eggert, Konstantin   *275–277*
Egorov *(traktir)*   26
Ehrenburg, Ilia   135, 144; *158*
Eiffel Tower   199
Eisenschitz, B.   246
Eisenstein, Sergei   19, 172, 247, 248, 256–264, 267; *171, 172, 273, 274, 280, 281, 282*
El Lissitzky, Lazar   20, 98, 99, 101, 205; *43, 107*
Ender family   19, 73
Enei, Evgenii   *289*
Engel, Iulii   225
Erdman, Boris   172; *175, 195*
Erdman, Nikolai   176
Ermler, Friedrich   264
Erikhson, A.G.   *188*

Ermolayeva, Vera   19, 49
Ermolov, Petr   241
Esenin, Sergei   140–141, 147; *118, 153, 154*
Experimental Studio   *175*
Exposition Universelle (Paris)   206
Exter, Alexandra   19, 20, 70, 73, 80, 86, 87, 97, 98, 103, 124, 132, 159, 172, 256; *94, 167, 173, 257, 275–277*
Eykhenvald, Zhulii   155

Fadeev, Alexander   145
Fairbanks, Douglas   259
Falk, Robert   49, 61, 70, 106
Favorsky, Vladimir   106
Federative Union of Soviet Artists   106
Fedin, Konstantin   142
Fedorovsky, F.   *194*
Fénéon, Felix   66–68
Feinberg, Samuil   231, 237
FEKS (Workshop of the Eccentric Actor)   256, 258, 262
Ferdinandov, B.   *175*
Fidman, Vladimir   200
Filatova, A.T.   *217*
Filipov (film director)   242
Filonov, Pavel   19, 23, 73, 109, 127; *116*
Filosofov, Dmitrii   52, 54
"5 × 5 = 25" (exhibition)   97
Flaubert, Gustav   132
Fogel, Vladimir   247
Fokine, Michel   56
Fomin, Ivan   56
Forge, The (writers' movement)   145
41° (Lliazd, artists' movement)   138
Free Studios   98
Free Theater   155
French Group of Six (musicians)   237
French Revolution   121, 162, 242
Friesz, Othon   61, 68
Furmanov, Dmitrii   145

Gabo, Naum   98, 99
Gai, Nikolai   48
Gan, Alexei   98, 99, 101, 202, 207
Gardarov, Vladimir   262
Gardin, Vladimir   247
Gauguin, Paul   54, 59, 61, 66, 68; *69, 72*
Gaumont (motion-picture company)   242
Gautier, Théophile   56, 134
Ghil, René   56, 117
Gilels, Emil   231
Ginzburg, Moisei   98, 202, 207, 208, 209, 212, 213
Gitis Theater (National Institute of Theatrical Art)   167; *181–184*
Gladkov, Fedor   145
Glazunov, Alexander   229, 230; *246*
Glebov, Igor   236
Gleizes, Albert   61, 70, 71
Glier, Reingold   227, 231
Glinka, Mikhail   225

Gloria (motion-picture company) 243, 244
Gnesin Institute 231
Gnesina, Elena Fabianovna 231
Gnesina, Mikhail 231
Gogol, Nikolai 154, 176, 244; *188, 289*
Gojowy, Detlef 239
Golden Fleece, The (Zolotoe runo) 59–61, 66, 119
Goldenweiser, Alexander 231
Goldoni, Carl 83
Goleizovsky, K. *195*
Golovanov, Nikolai 233
Golosov, Ilia 210; *233*
Golosov, Panteleimon 210
Golovin, A. *253*
Golovinia, Anatolii *284, 285, 286–288*
Goncharova, Natalia 19, 49, 56, 61, 62, 68, 74–78, 82, 83, 86, 123, 124, 127, 132, 242, 244; *78, 82, 83, 84, 136–138, 140*
Gorky, Maxim (Alexei Maximovich Peshkov) 25, 49, 114–115, 123, 124, 135, 142, 144, 147, 241; *26, 122, 156, 157, 284*
Gorodetsky, Sergei 132, 134
Gounod, Charles 226
Gorsky, Alexander 229
Grand Palace 41
Granovsky, Alexander *176*
Gray, Camilla 47
Grechaninov, Alexander 225, 228, 232
Grekov, Mitrofan 103
Griboedov, Alexander 140, 154
Gribov, V. N. (private residence) 187
Grin, Alexander 144
Group of Five (musicians) 217
Group of Objective Analysis 202
Grünewald brothers 241, 242
Gudiashvili, Lado 18, 138
GUM (Glavnyi universalnyi magazin, department store) 183; *199, 200*
Gumilev, Nikolai 62, 117, 124, 132, 134, 135, 145; *118, 126*
Gurdjieff, Georgii 19
Guro, Elena 71, 73, 122, 124, 129; *130, 251*
Grabar, Igor 49, 68, 70
Guzman, I. A. 242
GVRM studio 167

Hahn-Jagelsky (photographer) 242
Hauptmann, Gerhart 153, 155
Heckel, Erich 267
Heine, Thomas Theodore 56
Hermitage Museum (Leningrad) 42, 66, 162
Hérold, Louis Joseph Ferdinand 229
Hindemith, Paul 237
Hippius, Zinaida 117, 118, 135
Hoffmann, E. T. A. 141, 165
Honegger, Arthur 237
Hotel *see* Continental Metropole

House of Friendship with Foreign Peoples *215*
House of the Soviets 200
Hulten, Pontus 9
Hylaea (artists' movement) 68–71, 123, 124

Iakulov, Georgii 56, 87; *118*
Iaroslavl Railroad Station 40, 190, 192; *207, 210, 211*
Iashvili, Paolo 18
Iastrebtsov (Jastrebzoff), Sergei, known as Férat 70, 82
Igumnov, Konstantin 231
private residence 40, 184; *205*
Ilf, Ilia 44
Imaginists (writers' movement) 140, 141
Inber, Vera 19, 146
Inkizhinov, Valerii *285*
Inkhuk (Institute of Artistic Culture) 98, 201, 202, 208
Institute of Artistic Culture *see* Inkhuk
Institute of Musical Science 236
Iofan, Boris 214
Ioganson, Boris 103
Iliazd *see* 41°
Ippolitov-Ivanov, Mikhail 228, 231
Iukovsky, Stanislav 37
Iuon, Konstantin *103*
Iurasovsky, Alexander 227
Iutkevich, Sergei 257, 264
Iuzhin, Alexander 159
Ivan IV, the Terrible 9, 223; *5*
Ivanov, Viacheslav 117, 118
Ivanov, Vsevolod 142; *156*
Izdebsky, Vladimir 65
IZO (Department of Fine Arts) 89, 92, 98
Izvestiia (newspaper) *235, 239*
Izvestiia Asnova (ASNOVA news) 205

Jack of Diamonds (artists' movement) 65, 70, 71, 87, 106, 123
Jakobson, Roman 127, 140
Jastrebzoff-Férat 82; *see also* Iastrebtsov, Sergei
Jawlensky (Iavlensky), Alexei 62, 64, 65
Jewish Chamber Theater 159, 172, *176*
Joyce, James 120

Kabalevsky, Dimitrii 237
Kachalov Street *212*
Kakabadze, David 18, 138
Kalanchev Square *53*
Kalanchevskaia Street *34*
Kalendo, P. *1*
Kalita, Ivan, tsar 41
Kamernyi Theater 155–162, 169, 210; *167, 168, 169, 170, 173, 186, 255, 256*
Kamensky, Vasilii 73, 80, 122, 124, 138, 139; *118, 145, 192*
Kandaurova, Margarita 230
Kandinsky, Alexander 202

Kandinsky, Vasilii (Wassily) 18, 19, 48, 62–65, 78, 84, 86, 89, 98, 123; *30, 31, 32, 71, 105*
Karalli, Vera 230
Kasatkin, Nikolai 103
Kashkin (music critic) 223
Kasianov Vladimir 244
Kastalsky, Alexander 232
Kataev, Valentin 145, 146
Kaverin, Veniamin 144
Kazakhov, M. *8*
Kazan Railroad Station 184, 186; *206, 207*
Kazmin, Petr 233
Kekushev, Lev *222*
Kerensky, Alexander 40, 246, 247
Khachaturian, Aram 21
Khanzhonkov (film producer) 242, 243
Khitroyka (city district) 25
Khlebnikov, Velimir (Viktor) 18, 20, 21, 56–59, 68, 73, 75, 80, 87, 119, 121–132, 134, 138; *128, 130, 131–135, 136–138*
Khodasevich, Vladislav 134, 135
Khodinsky Field 23
Khokhlova, Alexandra 247
Khvatov, Vasilii *273, 274*
Kino-Glaz (Cine-Eye) 254, 255; *263, 264*
Kino-Pravda (Cine-Truth) 254, 255; *265–269*
Kirchner, Ernst Ludwig 65
Kirov, Sergei *224*
Kirov Street *204*
Krisanov, Semen 139
Kiselev, V. *188*
Kitai Gorod (Chinatown) *13*
Klein, Roman 186; *29, 201, 204*
Kliuev, Nikolai 141; *118*
Kliun (Kliunkov), Ivan 20, 56, 73, 80, 84, 86, 87, 139; *79*
Klutsis, Gustav 101, 102
Knipper, Olga *120*
Kogan, Nina 19
Komarov, Sergei 247
Kommisarzhevsky, Fedor 159
Komsomolskaia Square *34, 207*
Konchalovsky, Petr 68, 70, 106
Konindzhii, Valentina *275–277*
Korovin, Konstantin 48, 49, 68
Kozintsev, Grigorii 256
Koonen, Alice 155
Korolev, Boris 199
Koshits, Nina 231
Kovrygin, Vasilii *282*
Kozikhinsky Street *219, 220*
Kozintsev, Grigorii 262, 264; *289*
Kozlovsky, Sergei *275–277, 283, 284, 285, 286–288*
Kramskoi, Ivan 47, 48
Kremlin 26, 40, 41, 42, *2, 3, 4, 6, 9, 13, 37*
wall *4*
squares *3*
Krinsky, Vladimir 199, 200, 202, 203, 205

270

Krichevsky, Vasilii *293–295*
Krivoarbatskaia Street *231*
Kropotkin, Petr 114
Kruchenykh, Alexei 19, 70, 73, 80, 86, 87, 123–132, 138, 139; *130, 131–135, 139, 143, 251*
Krutikov, Georgii 204
Krupskaia, Nadezhda 167
Kubin, Alfred 65
Kulbin, Nikolai 64, 71, 80, 127
Kuleshov, Lev 245, 247, 248, 254, 260, 262, 264
Kupka, Franz 62
Kupreanov, Nikolai 20, 106
Kuprin, Alexander 68, 70, 106, 115, 123, 135
Kushner, Boris 98
Kustodiev, Boris 49; *28, 40, 96, 196*
Kuzmin, Mikhail 123, 132
Kuznetsky Most 241; *21, 22*
Kuznetsov, I. E. (private residence) 188
Kuznetsov, Pavel 55, 56, 59, 61, 68, 106; *69*

Labarthe, André S. 245
Labas, Alexander 106; *113*
Labiche, Eugène *175*
Ladovsky, Nikolai 98, 199, 200, 202, 203, 204, 205; *229*
Lalo, Edward 223
Lamm, Pavel 227, 228
Lang, Fritz 248
Lansere, Evgenii 54, 55
Larinov, Mikhail 19, 49, 56, 61, 62, 68, 70, 71, 73–86, 123, 124, 127, 244; *24, 56, 65, 66, 78, 85, 86, 136–138, 139*
Lavinsky, Anton 208
Lazarev, N. 187
Lebedev, Vladimir 106; *52*
Lecocq, Charles *168, 170*
Le Corbusier (Charles-Edouard Jeanneret) 210, *237*
Lef (Left Front in Art) 20, 87, 138, 140, 208, 248, 254
Le Fauconnier, Henri 61, 68, 70; *76*
Left Front in Art *see* Lef
Léger, Fernand 65, 71, 77; *79*
Ledentu, Mikhail 74
Ledentu, Paul-Henri 78
Le Lion (motion-picture company) 243
Lenin (Vladimir Ilich Ulyanov) 20, 41, 42, 44, 94, 95, 113, 145, 159, 196, 245, 247; *117, 150, 194*
  Club *48*
  Library 210; *224*
  Mausoleum *3, 53, 206*
  Pedagogical Institute 187
Leningrad (since 1924) 13, 17, 96, 97, 108, 217, 227, 231; *207*
  Institute of Art and Culture 108; *109*
Leningradskaia Pravda (newspaper) 210; *234*
Lentulov, Aristarkh 25, 68, 70, 106; *44*
Leoncavallo, Ruggero 226

Leonidov, Ivan *235, 236, 261*
Leonov, Leonid 145
Lermontov, Mikhail 244
Leskov, N. *196*
Levitan, Isaak 48, 59, 68
Levitsky (cameraman) 246
"Link, The" (exhibition) 70
Lipchitz, Jacques 18, 82
Lisagor, Solomon 212
Liszt, Franz 48, 222, 233
Little Theater 150; *see also* Malyi Theater
Liubimov, Grigorii 233
Livshits, Benedikt 68, 80, 123, 132; *127, 129, 157*
London, Jack 248; *171, 172*
Lorrain, Jean 244
Loshakov, A. *262*
Lossky, V. *194*
Louis XIV, king of France 54
Lourié, Arthur 18, 21
Lubianka (Cheka headquarters) 41
Lubitsch, Ernst 241, 264
Lumière, Auguste 241
Lumière, Louis 241
Lunacharsky, Anatolii 89, 95, 138, 145, 172, 199, 214, 231, 246; *149, 187*
Lux (motion-picture company) 243
Lysenko, Natalia 262

Macke, Auguste 65
Mackintosh, Charles Rennie 54
Maeterlinck, Maurice 54, 56, 117, 152, 157
MAF (Moscow Association of Futurists) 87, 139
Maiakovsky, Vladimir 19, 20, 21, 44, 68, 87, 89, 91, 92, 123–132, 136, 138–139, 141, 146, 147, 152, 169, 208, 244, 248; *39, 40, 44, 106, 118, 128, 144, 150, 151*
Maillo, Aristide 61, 68
Maître (film producer) 242
Makaev, G. *198*
Makhno, Nestor 90
Makhorka, Pavilion 206
Makovsky, Sergei 62
Malaia Bronnaia Street 212
Malaia Nikitskaia Street 212
Malevich, Kazimir 19, 20, 62, 68, 71, 73, 76, 78–87, 89, 92, 96, 97, 106, 123, 124; *44, 77, 79, 87, 88, 89, 90, 95, 102, 104, 109, 115, 130, 136–138, 143, 145, 251*
Maliavin, Phillip 68
Maliutin, N. 103
Malyi Theater *1, 259*; see also Little Theater
Mamontov, Elizabeth 48
Mamontov, Savva 48, 159, 223, 225; *39, 54*
Manezhnaia Square *38*
Mandelshtram, Osip 18, 62, 132, 134, 135, 144; *118, 129*
Marc, Franz 64, 65

Marcade, Valentine 47
Mardzhanov, Konstantin 155
Mariengof, Anatolli 141
Marinetti, Filippo 75, 80, 124, 132
Markovnikov, Nikolai 197
Marquet, Albert 61, 68
Martinet, Marcel 168; *185*
Marx-Engels Institute 41; *19, 47*
Marx, Karl 20
Mascagni, Pietro 226
Mashkov, Ilia 49, 61, 68, 70
Massenet, Jules 227
Matisse, Henri 59, 61, 65, 66, 68; *72, 74, 75*
Matiushin, Mikhail 71, 73, 78, 108, 119, 122, 251; *109, 130*
Matveev, Alexander 106
Maupassant, Guy de 244
Maurer, Alfred 68
Maxim Gorky Theater 154
Medunitsky Konstantin 207
Meierhold, Vsevolod 19, 89, 150, 153, 165, 167, 168, 171, 172, 209, 245, 246, 257; *125, 171, 172, 177, 178, 179, 180, 181–184, 185, 193*
Meierhold Theater *187*
Melnikov, Konstantin 21, 199, 205, 206; *227, 230, 232, 233*
  (private residence) *231*
Mercereau, Alexandre 59
Merezhkovsky, Dmitrii 54, 117, 118, 135
Merrileas, Muir *29*
Metner (Medtner), Nikolai 21, 231
Mesguich, Felix 241
Metropole Hotel 188; *1, 208, 209, 259*
Metzinger, Jean 61, 70, 73
Miaskovsky, Nikolai 231, 237
Miasnitskaia Street 28; *204*
Milinis, Ignatii 212
Milioti brothers 55
Milioti, Vasilli 56, 61
Miliukov, A. N. 187, 188
Minkus, Ludwig 229
Mir iskusstva see World of Art
Mitrokhin, Dmitrii 155
Mocholav, Pavel 150
Modigliani, Amedeo 118, 144
Mokhovaia Street *38*
Monet, Claude 54, 62, 65, 66
Moravov, Alexander 103; *214, 215, 221*
Moreau, Gustave 56
Moreau, I. A. 70
Morice, Charles 59
Morozov, Ivan 66–68
Morozov, Mikhail 66
Morozov, Savva 42, 49, 59, 159; *75*
Morozova, Z. G. *213*
Moscow Academy 103
  "Agricultural and Craft Exhibition" 197, 206
  Artists' Association 64
  Art Theater (MKhAT) 39, 49, 149–55, 164, 172, 228, 233; *35, 162, 163, 216*

Art Theater Studio 154, 155; *175*
Association of Futurists *see* MAF
Conservatory 217, 222, 228, 231; *21, 22, 243, 250, 251*
Linguistic Circle 140
School of Applied Arts 98
University 32; *8, 38*
Moscow News 37
Moskvin, Andrei 289
Mosolov, Alexander 21, 237
Mostrog (department store) *29*
Moszhukin, Ivan 39, 244, 245, 246, 247; *262*
Muller, Vladimir *290–292*
Munts, Oskar 186
Murnau, Friedrich *289*
Mukhina, Vera 106
Münter, Gabriele 65
Museum of the Revolution 41
Musorgsky, Modest 56, 155, 217; *247, 252*

Nabokov, Vladimir 18
Narkompros (People's Commissariat of Education) 89, 145, 164, 167, 198, 231
Napoleon Bonaparte 155, 187, 241
National Art College 49
National Theater 164
Nekrasov, Nikolai 244
Nemirovich-Danchenko, Vladimir 149, 150, 159, 172; *35*
NEP (New Economic Policy) 21, 44, 45, 95, 103, 171, 172, 217, 231, 233, 264, 267
Neuhaus, Heinrich 231
New Lef (Novii Lef) 146, 147; *282*
Nezhdanova, Antonia 225, 226
Nezlobin Theater 167; *1*
Nicholas I, tsar 41
Nicholas II, tsar 23, 241; *14, 44*
Nietzsche, Friedrich 117
Nijinsky, Vaslav 83
Nikitin, Nikolai 144
Nikitsky Boulevard 149
Nikolskaia Street *35*
Nirensee House 154
Nivinsky, Ignatii 172; *189–191*
"Non-Objective Art and Suprematism" (exhibition) 95
Nordisk (motion-picture company) 243
Novii Lef see New Left
Novsinky Boulevard 167, 212
Nosov (private residence) *222*

OBMAS (United Architectural Studios) 202, 203
Obukov, Nikolai 21
Oettinger, Baroness 70
Offenbach, Jacques 155
Okhotnyi Riad 26; *10*
Olesha, Iurii 145
O'Neill, Eugene 172

Opoiaz (Society for the Study of Poetic Language) 140
OSA (Union of Contemporary Architects) 202, 207, 208, 210, 212, 213; *233*
OST (Society of Easel Painters) 106; *111, 113*
Ostouzhev Street *219*
Ostrovsky, Alexander 172, 228, 244; *187, 193*
Ostrovsky Passage 187
Otsep, Fedor 275–277

Palace of Culture *236*
Palace of Labor 197, 206, 210; *224, 225*
Palace of the Assembly of the Nobility 41
Palace of the Revolution 162
Palace of Soviets 214
Parkin, V. 74
Pasternak, Boris 132, 139, 140; *152*
Pathé (motion-picture company) 242, 243
Pavlov, Ivan 260
Pechstein, Max 65
People's Commissariat of Education *see* Narkompros
Perrigot (motion-picture company) 241
Persimfans (First Symphonic Ensemble) 236
Persky (film director and producer) 244
Pestal, Vera 19
Peter I, the Great 9, 23, 217; *23*
Petripa, Marius 229
Petrograd (1914–24) 13, 40, 41, 42, 75, 86, 92, 96, 141, 145
Petrov, Evgenii 44
Petrovka Street *29*
Petrov-Vodkin, Kuzma 61, 62, 106; *70, 114*
Pevesner, Anton 98, 99
Philipp II, king of Spain 227
Piatnisky, Mitrofan 233
Picasso, Pablo 65, 66, 68, 70, 71, 75, 86; *179*
Pilniak, Boris 120, 144, 146, 147; *127, 157, 159*
Pimenov, Iurii 106
Pirosmanishvili, Niko 18, 74
Pisarro, Camille 61, 66, 68
Pletnev, V. *273, 274*
Plevitskaia, Nadezhda 39, 232
Podzenski Passage *198*
Poe, Edgar Allan 117
Plenov, Vasilii 48, 49
Polovinkin, Leopold 237
Pomerantsev, Alexander 183
Popova, Liubov 19, 70, 80, 84, 86, 91, 98, 101, 103, 139, 166, 168; *76, 102, 185*
Pougny, Jean *see* Ivan Puni
Pound, Ezra 132, 134
Pozdeev, N.I. 164; *205*
Pozner, Vladimir 141

Presnia Square 25, 36; *25*
Prianishnikov Theater 223
Prishvin, Mikail 144
Prokofiev, Sergei 18, 21, 75, 231; *243, 246*
Proletkult (Proletarian Organization for Culture and Education) 92–95, 98, 145, 233, 246
Theater 164, 172; *171, 172*
Proofreaders' House *35*
Protazanov, Iakov 244, 245, 247, 256; *261, 262, 275–277*
Przybyszweski, Stanislaw 246
Puccini Giacomo 226, 227, 228
Pudovkin, Vsevolod 247, 257, 260, 262, 264; *284, 285, 286–288*
Pugni, Cesare 229
Puni, Ivan (Jean Pougny) 68, 73, 80, 84, 86, 89, 98, 97; *80, 93*
Punin, Nikolai 89, 90, 91, 95, 97
Pushkin, Alexander 87, 114, 122, 226, 242, 244
Pushkin Museum of Fine Arts 42, 66, 187; *201, 202*
Pushkin Square *7, 239*
Puvis de Chavannes, Pierre 54, 56

Rabelais, François 134
Rabinovich, Isaak 172; *174, 275–277*
Racine, Jean 171; *169*
Radakov, Alexei *41*
Raikh, Iakov 200
Rakhals, Vasilii *280, 281*
Rakhmaninov, Sergei 21, 217, 222–226, 231, 232; *249, 250*
RAPM (Russian Association of Proletarian Musicians) 142, 146, 236, 239
RAPP (Russian Association of Proletarian Writers) 146
Razin, Stepan *192*
Red Square 28, 241; *2, 5, 32, 54, 199, 203*
Red Stadium *228*
Redon, Odilon 56
Reinecke, Carl 62
Reinhardt, Max 243, 244
Remizov, Alexei 120, 212, 123, 144; *127, 146*
Renoir, Auguste 61, 66, 68
Repin, Ilia 48, 49, 52
Resurrection Square *55*
Revolution
Bolshevik 40, 66, 87, 89, 114, 138, 246, 264
February 89
1905 20, 36, 135; *25*
October 40, 44, 89, 92, 136, 169; *32, 92, 95, 112, 149, 233, 262*
see also Civil War, French Revolution
Revolution Square
Riabushinsky, Nikolai 59
Riabushinsky, Stepan P. (collection) 42; *75*
(private residence) 18, 190; *212, 221*

272

Richter, Sviatoslav 231
Rimbaud, Arthur 19, 56
Rimsky-Korsakov, Nikolai 18, 49, 83, 217, 223–233; *242, 244, 245, 247, 253, 254*
Rivera, Diego 118; *158*
Robespierre, Maximilian 248
Rockline, Vera 19
Rodchenko, Alexander 20, 80, 86, 87, 97–102, 139, 200, 202, 207, 208; *106, 108, 263*
Rodin, Auguste 61
Roerich, Nikolai 49, 54, 59, 83; *9, 57*
Romanov, imperial family 9, 37; *14*
Romashkov (film director) 242
Room, Abram 257, 264; *150*
Roslavets, Nikolai 21, 237
Rosso, Medardo 61
Rosta (Russian Telegraph Agency) 92, 138, 210
Rostokino (city district) 212
Rouault, Georges 61
Rousseau, Henri (le Douanier) 65
Rozanova, Olga 19, 73, 78–97, 124; *88, 131–135, 136–138*
Rubinstein, Ida 49
Rudnev, V.V. 40
Rukhliadov, Alexei 200, 205
Russian Association of Proletarian Writers
    see RAPP
Rumiantsev, Count Nikolai *12*
Rusakov Club 206, *227*
Russian Popular Choir 233
Russian Revolution *see* Revolution
Russian Telegraph Agency *see* Rosta
Russkoe slovo (Russian Word) 37; *223*
Russo-Japanese War 20, 135, 179

Sadovaia Boulevard 149
Safonov, Vasilii 231
St. Basil's Cathedral 184, 228; *5, 203*
St. Petersburg (until 1914) 9, 12, 17, 18, 23, 40, 52, 54, 55, 56, 61, 62, 64, 65, 71, 80, 84, 86, 117, 155, 165, 180, 186, 217, 226, 230, 231, 233, 262; *3, 163*
    Academy of Arts 47
    Conservatory 217; *243, 245*
    Mariinsky Theater 222, 229
Saint-Saens, Camille 223
Saltykov-Shchedrin, M.E. 154
Sapunov, Nikolai 55, 68, 153
Sarabianov, Dimitrii 47
Sarian, Martiros 49, 59, 61, 106; *67, 68*
Scales, The (Vesy) 56, 70, 119
Schmitz, O.A.H. 260
Schnitzler, Authur 155
Schoenberg, Arnold 236
Schreker, Franz 237
Seifullina, Lidiia 19
Sekar-Rozhansky, Anton 231
Selvinsky, Ilia 139
Semenko, Mikhilo 18
Semenov, A. 183; *203*

Serafimovich, Alexander 144
Serapion Brothers (writers' movement) 140, 141, 144
Sergeev-Tsensky, Sergei 144
Serov, Valentin 37, 48, 49, 59, 68
Serpukhovskaia Street 206
Severianin, Igor 124, 131
Shakespeare, William 134
Shaliapin, Fedor 225, 226; *247, 248, 252*
Shcherbatov, Prince S.S. 187
Shchukin, Sergei 42, 59, 65–66; *72, 73, 74, 75*
Shchusev, Alexei 186, 214; *206*
Shekhtel, Fedor 18, 187, 190, 192; *162, 210, 211, 212, 213, 214, 215, 216*
Shengelaia, Nikolai 18
Shershenevich, Vadim 80, 124, 141
Shervud, Vladimir 183; *203*
Shestakov, V. *193*
Shestov, Lev 118
Shevchenko, Alexander 73, 74, 75, 200
Shklovsky, Viktor 119, 120, 139, 140, 199, 244
Sholokhov, Mikhail 145
Shorin, Alexander 264
Shostakovich, Dmitrii 21, 237
Shpinel, Isaak *290–292*
Shterenberg, David 74, 89, 92, 106; *99*
Shub, Esther 19, 248
Signac, Paul 61
Simov, V. *165*
Sinskulptarkh (Synthesis of Sculpture and Architecture) 199
Sisley, Alfred 61, 66
Skobelev Committee 245
Skobelev Square 154
Skriabin, Alexander 54, 59, 222, 230–231, 237; *244*
Slaviansky, Bazar 149; *35*
Smirnov, Alexander 132
Smirnov-Iskander (film producer) 248
Smolensk Boulevard *31*
Smolensky, Stepan 232
Smyshlaev (film director) *171, 172*
Sobinov, Leonid 225
Sobsovich, L. 212
Society of Art and Literature 149
Society of Easel Painters *see* OST
Society for the Study of Poetic Language *see* Opoiaz
Soffici, Ardengo 70
Sokol (garden city) 197
Sologub, Fedor 54, 117, 123, 135; *118, 127*
Soloviev, Vladimir 118
Somov, Konstantin 54, 55, 56, 68, 132, 155
Sovremennaia muzyka (contemporary music) 237
Spiridonovka Street *221*
Sport Pavilion 213
Stalin, Joseph V. 21, 45, 135, 214; *127, 157*

Stanislavsky (Alexeev), Konstantin 39, 49, 114, 115, 149–154, 159, 162, 172, 228; *35, 164, 165*
State Historical Museum 183, 184; *203*
State Theater Board 21, 22
State Theater of Communist Dramaturgy 167
Steiner, Rudolf 62, 118
Stenberg, Georgii 102, 170, 202, 207; *261*
Stenberg, Vladimir 102, 170, 202, 207; *261, 278*
Stepanova, Varvara 19, 20, 86, 98, 103, 139, 168, 207; *181–184*
Sternberg, Josef von 241
Strastnaia Square 7
Strauss, Richard 226
Stravinsky, Igor 18, 21, 82; *245*
Stuart, Mary, queen of Scotland 242
Sudeikin, Sergei 153
Suetin, Nikolai 97
Suk, Viacheslav 226
Sukhovo-Kobylin, Alexander 168; 181–184
Sulerzhitsky, Leopold 154
Surikov, Vasilii 48
Survage (Stürzwage), Leopold 18, 68, 70, 82
Sverdlov Square *1, 259*
Svetlov, Mikhail 140, 146
Synodal Institute 217, 231
    Choir 232
Sytin, Ivan 223

Tabidze (poet) 18
Taganskaia Metro Station 21
Tairov, Alexander 83, 156, 159, 165, 171, 172, 210; *166, 167, 168, 169, 170, 173, 186, 255, 256*
Tairov Theater 87
Tamanian, Alexander 187
Taneev, Sergei 217, 231; *250*
Tarasov (industrialist) *221*
Tarabukin, Nikolai 98, 101
"Target, The" (exhibition) 74
Tatlin, Vladimir 20, 21, 49, 68, 73, 74, 84–87, 89, 95–98, 109, 124, 127, 131, 165, 198; *46, 56, 77, 92, 179, 226*
Tchaikovsky, Petr 217, 222, 225, 229, 233; *250*
Technical Studios (Vkhutemas) 201, 202, 203, 204, 207, 208; *229, 235*
Temple of Nations 200
Tenisheva, Maria, princess 54
Terentiev, Igor 86, 138
Terpsikhorov, Nikolai 103
Theater of the Revolution *192, 193*
Theater of the Russian Soviet Federated Socialist Republic 165, 167; *179*
Theater Square *1, 10*
Thiemann, Paul 243, 244
Third (Communist) International (Comintern) 44; *46*
    Congress 168

Monument 96, 109, 198, 199, 200, 207; *46, 226*
Tikhomirov, Vasilii 230
Tissé, Eduard 247; *273, 274, 280, 281, 282*
Tiflis (artists' movement) 86
Tikhonov, Nikolai 134, 144
Toborkov, Nikolai 244
Tolstoi, Alexei 135, 144, 145, 154, 228; *26, 127, 160, 258, 275–277*
Tolstoi, Count Leo 47, 111–115, 123, 244; *119, 121, 122, 262*
Tolstoi Street *221*
Toulot, Paul-Jean 132
traktirs (café-inn) 26
"Tramway V: Futurist Exhibition" 86
Trauberg, Leonid 256, 262, 264; *289*
Traveling Exhibition Society 47, 103; *see also* Wanderers
Tretiakov Gallery *206*
Tretiakov, Pavel 47
Tretiakov, Sergei 42, 139, 146; *185*
Trotsky, Leon 41, 45, 145, 168
Trubetskoi (private residence) 241; *19, 47*
Tsum (department store) *259*
Tsvetaeva, Marina 17, 19, 134, 135; *118*
Tsvetelli, Nikolai *275–277*
Tsvetkov (art collector) 42
Turgenev, Ivan 154, 244
Tverskaia Street 28, 149, 154; *10*
25th October Street *35*
Tynianov, Iurii 140; *289*
Tyshler, Alexander 106

Udaltsove, Nadezhda 19, 70, 80, 86, 89, 98
Ulianov, N. *177*
Union for the Cinema 246
Union of Contemporary Architects *see* OSA
Union of Painters, Sculptors, and Graphic Artists 106
Union of Russian Artists 103
Union of Soviet Composers 239
Union of the Four Arts 106
Union of Urban Architects (ARU) 205
Union of Workers of the Cinematographic Art (Tenth Muse) 247

Union of Youth 71–73, 251
United Architectural Studios *see* OBMAS
Ushkov, Alexei 230
Utkin, Alexei 61
Uspensky, Petr 118

Vakhtangov, Evgenii 155, 164, 172; *174, 189–191*
Vakhtangov Studio *174*
Valkot, F. (William Walcot) 188; *208*
Valseva, Anastasia 39
van der Velde, Henry 54
Van Dongen, Kees 61, 65
Van Gogh, Vincent 54, 61, 68
Vasilenko, Sergei 227, 231, 233; *195*
Vasnetsov, Apollinarius 48, 49
Vasnetsov, Viktor 48, 49
Vassilieff, Marie 19, 82
Velikovsky, Boris 188
Velizhev, A. *193*
Velov, K. *192*
Verdi, Guiseppe 226
Verhaeren, Emile 117, 118; *179*
Verlaine, Paul 54, 117
Vertinsky, Alexander 39
Vertov, Dziga (Denis Arkadevich Kaufman) 254, 255, 256; *264, 265–269, 271, 272*
Vesnin, Alexander 97–98, 171, 188, 199, 206–210; *169, 186, 224, 225, 234, 257*
Vesnin family 98; *235*
Vesnin, Viktor 199; *224, 225, 234*
Viacheslav, Ivanov 164
Viennese School 237
Villiams (Williams), Petr 106
Villon, François 134
Vinogradov, Sergei 68
Vitagraph (motion-picture company) 243
Vkhutein (Higher Artistic Technical Institute) 98
Vkhutemas (Higher State Workshops for Art and Technology) 98, 103, 106; *102, 111; see also* Technical Studios
Vlaminck, Maurice de 68
Volkhonka Street *201* quarter *202*
Volkov, Alexander 245, 247; *262*

Voloshin, Maximilian 56, 118, 135; *158*
Vrubel, Mikhail 48, 52, 55–62, 68, 188; *59, 60, 61, 62, 63, 209*
Vsevolod, Ivanov 172
VUFKU (motion-picture studio) 267
Vuillard, Edouard 66, 68
Vultat, Louis 68
Vvedensky Square *222*
Vyshegradsky, Ivan 21

Wagner, Richard 223, 226; *194*
Wanderers 47–48, 62; *see also* Traveling Exhibition Society
Weber, Carl Maria von 226
Wells, H.G. 145
Werefkin (Verevkin), Marianna 62, 64
Whitman, Walt 117
Wilde, Oscar 87, 117, 124, 245; *167*
World of Art *(Mir iskusstava)* artists' movement 19, 49, 52
   journal 54–59, 119
Winkler (film producer) 244
World War I 18, 28, 37, 40, 66, 83, 132, 135, 141, 179, 187, 192, 222, 226, 245
"Wreath" (exhibition) 68–70
Writers' Union 147

Zadkine, Ossip 18, 82
Zakharov, Vladimir 233
Zamiatin, Evgenii 120, 142, 145, 147; *155, 159, 196*
Zarhii, Nathan *284, 286–288*
Zavelev, Boris 245
Zdanevich, Ilia 74, 86, 138
Zdanevich, Kiril 74, 86
Zecco, Ferdinand 242
Zeitlin, Lev 236
Zelensky, A. *289*
Zelinsky, Kornelii 139, 146
Zhdanov, Andrei 113, 215
Zhivskulptarkh (Synthesis of painting, sculpture, and architecture) 200, 202
Zholtovsky, Ivan 214
Zimin, Sergei 39, 223, 225, 226
Zoltovsky, Ivan 198
Zoshchenko, Mikhail 142–144, 145, 146
Zubovskaia Square *31*
Zubovsky Boulevard *31*
Zuev Club *233*

Photo Credits

The photo research for this book was done by Stanislas Zadora in collaboration with Ingrid de Kalbermatten. The illustrations not listed below were kindly put at our disposal by the authors. The numbers refer to the plates.

Abramtsevo Museum 61, 62

Busch-Reisinger Museum, Cambridge Massachusetts 107

Central Museum of the Armed Forces, Moscow 112

Cinémathèque Suisse, Lausanne 265, 266, 267, 268, 269, 272, 275, 276, 277, 286, 287, 288, 290, 291, 292, 293, 294, 295

Cosmos Paris 273, 274, 280, 281, 282, 284

Hermitage Museum, Leningrad 71, 74, 75

Kunstgewerbemuseum, Zurich 261, 263, 270, 278, 279, 285, 289

Los Angeles County Museum of Art 110

Ludwig Collection, Cologne 83, 106 (photos Rheinisches Bildarchiv, Cologne)

Musée d'Art moderne, Strasbourg 241, 242

Musée des Beaux-Arts, Lyons 140

Musée national d'Art moderne, Georges Pompidou Center, Paris 24, 56, 65, 80, 86, 93, 105

Museum of Architecture, Moscow 13, 21, 22, 25, 29, 34, 212, 214, 216, 217, 223

The Museum of Modern Art, New York 89

National Art Gallery of Armenia, Erevan 68

Igor Palmine (illustrations taken from *Art Nouveau russe* and reproduced by courtesy of Editions du Regard, Paris) 198, 208, 209, 210, 211, 213, 218, 219, 220, 221, 222

Puskin Museum of Fine Art, Moscow 60

Roger-Viollet, Paris 7, 14, 27, 33, 35, 54, 123, 199, 201, 203, 205, 206, 215, 246, 252

© Boyer-Viollet 202

© Collection Viollet 1, 3, 4, 5, 56, 8, 11, 12, 19, 26, 36, 39, 47, 48, 50, 51, 53, 120, 122, 144, 146, 149, 157, 159, 160, 207, 239, 243, 244, 245, 247, 248, 254, 255, 256, 257, 258, 259

© Harlingue-Viollet 2, 15, 16, 49, 119, 154, 240, 249, 260

© Lipnitzk-Viollet 124

© San-Viollet 17, 18, 200, 232

Solomon R. Guggenheim Museum, New York 84

State Gallery of Painting of the USSR, Moscou 97, 98

State Museum of Oriental Art, Moscow 9

State Russian Museum, Leningrad 20, 40, 66, 76, 77, 78, 79, 88, 90, 95, 99, 100, 109, 111, 113, 114, 115, 116, 128, 145

Stedelijk Museum, Amsterdam 81, 143

Svenska Filminstitutet Stockholm 262, 271

Tretiakov Gallery, Moscow 23, 28, 30, 31, 32, 58, 59, 63, 64, 67, 70, 91, 92, 96, 101, 103, 117, 251

Victoria and Albert Museum, Londres 57

Yale University Art Gallery, New Haven 87